Making Connections

Engaging Students in Language, Literacy, and Global Issues

Teacher's Guide

Facing THE Future™

Making Connections
Engaging Students in Language, Literacy, and Global Issues
Teacher's Guide

Copyright © 2010 *Facing the Future*

This product was funded through a grant from Washington State Department of Ecology. While these materials were reviewed for grant consistency, this does not necessarily constitute endorsement by the Department.

ISBN 978-0-9815577-4-8

Printed on recycled paper.

Facing the Future is a nonprofit organization dedicated to educating and motivating today's students to be responsible stewards of tomorrow's world. We develop and deliver standards-based hands-on lessons, student textbooks, curriculum units, and professional development opportunities for educators that promote critical thinking on global issues, sustainability, and positive solutions. *Facing the Future* curriculum is in use in all fifty U.S. states and over 100 countries by teachers and students in grades K-12, in undergraduate and graduate classes, and across multiple subject areas.

For more information, visit www.facingthefuture.org.

FACING THE FUTURE
811 First Avenue, Suite 454
Seattle, WA 98104
(206) 264-1503
www.facingthefuture.org

We dedicate this book to Evelyne Rozner for her incredible support of *Facing the Future's* mission and her relentless pursuit of an excellent education for all.

We also want to express our utmost gratitude to David White-Espin for his inspirational work as a teacher and his continued dedication to *Facing the Future*.

Contributions and Thanks

This book was developed in alignment with national education standards, and with the input of a number of experts and educators. The standards addressed are indicated for all chapters in the Teacher's Guide, and all references are listed at the end of the text.

The following literacy and language experts provided advice and feedback on this text:

Kristina Anstrom, EdD
Assistant Director
The George Washington University Center for Equity and Excellence in Education

Letitia Basford, PhD
Assistant Professor
Hamline University School of Education

Margarita Calderón, PhD
Author, Teaching Reading to English Language Learners Grades 6-12: A Framework for Improving Achievement in the Content Areas
Margarita Calderón and Associates, Inc.

Dr. Magda Costantino
Former Director of the Master in Education Program
The Evergreen State College

Gloria Delany-Barmann, EdD
Professor of Bilingual Education
Western Illinois University

Joey Hawkins
Writing Consultant and Author,
Writing for Understanding
Vermont Writing Collaborative

Dr. Gina Mikel Petrie
Assistant Professor of English as a Second Language/ELL Endorsement Program
Eastern Washington University

Cecilia Minden-Cupp, PhD
Literacy Consultant and Children's Book Author

Dr. Katherine L. Schlick Noe
Professor and Director of Literacy
Seattle University College of Education

Lorrie S. Verplaetse, PhD
Professor and Coordinator of Bilingual Education and TESOL
Southern Connecticut State University

Dr. Sherry Walton
Director of Teacher Education Programs
The Evergreen State College

Primary Curriculum Developers
Sheeba Jacob, MEd
Laura Skelton, MS

Layout and Graphic Design
DECODE, Inc.

Copy Editing
SEED EDIT

The following individuals reviewed, edited, and otherwise contributed to this text:

Suzanne Bardasz
English Professor
Korea Advanced Institute of Science and Technology,
South Korea

Matthew John Brewer
Science Teacher
Eckstein Middle School,
Washington

Ayora Berry
Social Studies Teacher
India

Klaus W. Bethke
Founder and Admissions Director
Colegio Internacional Tlalpan,
Mexico

Wendy Church, PhD
Facing the Future

Emma Graves, MEd
Literacy Consultant
Oregon

Jon Gunther

Beth Hintz, MS
Facing the Future

Barbara Ishida
ELD/English Teacher
Thomas Downey High School,
California

Alicia Keefe, MEd
Facing the Future

Jessica C. Levine
Science Teacher
Eckstein Middle School,
Washington

Cecilia Lund, MS
Facing the Future

Allison Mangin
ESL Teacher
R.J. Reynolds High School,
North Carolina

Marie Marrs
Retired Educator
Washington

Anne Metcalfe
Retired Educator
Washington

Sandi Phinney, MPA
Applied Linguistics Student
University of Massachusetts Boston

Jeri Pollock
Independent Scholar
California

Kim Rakow Bernier, MPA
Facing the Future

Achariya Rezak
Doctoral Student
University of Georgia School of Education

Chris Summerville
Lecturer/Academic Coordinator
Global College Japan Center,
Japan

Barbara Suter
ESL Teacher
Bowling Green Elementary School,
New York

David White-Espin
ELL Teacher
Secondary Bilingual Orientation Center,
Washington

Dave Wilton, MEd
Facing the Future

Diego Xavier Roman
Doctoral Student
Stanford University School of Education

Field Testing

Thank you to the following teachers and their students for field testing these materials:

Keino Baird
Social Studies Teacher
Explore Charter School,
New York

Jill Berge
Literacy Teacher
Rose Hill Junior High School,
Washington

Leila Boodhoo
ESL Teacher
Queensborough Community College,
New York

Alison Cochrane
ESL Teacher
Queensborough Community College,
New York

Kristin Day
ELL Teacher
Bay View School,
Washington

Kayti Denham
Language Support Teacher
Bali International School,
Indonesia

Kari Gjerde
English Teacher
Cap Cana Heritage School,
Dominican Republic

Inna Hanson
ELD Teacher
Spokane Garry Middle School,
Washington

Mary Healy
ELL Teacher and Department Chair
Ingraham High School,
Washington

Carey Hodges
ELL Teacher
Hillside Middle School,
New Hampshire

Janet Jenkins
ELD Teacher
Glover Middle School,
Washington

Kevin Johnson
Teacher
Osaka YMCA International School,
Japan

Noel Jost-Coq
ESOL Teacher
Newmarket Jr/Sr High School,
New Hampshire

Naeem Khowja
ESL Literature Teacher
Alief Middle School,
Texas

Solomon Kilburn
Science Teacher
Prestonsburg High School,
Kentucky

Mary Leming
ESL Teacher
Smithtown High School East,
New York

Shannon Lowrie
Language Arts/History Teacher
Chimacum Middle School,
Washington

Anne Marsac
ESL Teacher
Eisenhower Middle School,
New Jersey

Dasha Marshall
ESL Teacher
Buffalo Public Adult Education
Department,
New York

Keleigh Muzaffar
ELL Teacher
Mariner High School,
Washington

Victoria Payne
ELL Teacher
Nashua High School North,
New Hampshire

Andrea Pokrzywinski
Science Teacher
Lower Kuskokwim School District,
Alaska

Shannon Potter
ESL Instructor/Adjunct Faculty
Olympic College,
Washington

Judy Predmore
ESL Teacher
Rush Henrietta Senior High School,
New York

Mary Quinton-Barry
ELL Teacher
Lebanon High School,
New Hampshire

Carla Reynolds
Science and Writing ELL Teacher
Arts and Academics Academy,
Washington

Jodi Ritter
ELL Teacher
Woodinville High School,
Washington

Soojin Stickney
ELL Teacher
Gilbert H. Hood Middle School,
New Hampshire

Kathryn Turnbull
ESL Teacher
Glashan Intermediate School,
Canada

John Peter Watts
English Teacher
Mabelvale Middle School,
Arkansas

Jacquelyn Walz
ELL and Reading Teacher
Poudre High School,
Colorado

David White-Espin
ELL Teacher
Secondary Bilingual Orientation Center,
Washington

Facing the Future Advisory Council

Char Alkire
Retired Science Educator and Teacher Supervisor

Jamie Bender
Outreach Coordinator, Center for International Studies, University of Chicago

John de Graaf
PBS Producer and Author, Affluenza

Dee Dickinson
Founder, New Horizons for Learning

Wendy Ewbank
Teacher, Seattle Girls' School

Scott Jamieson
Teacher, Lakeside School

Marie Marrs
Retired Global Sustainability and Language Arts Teacher

Kate McPherson
Director, Project Service Leadership

Abby Ruskey
Executive Director, Environmental Education Association of Washington

Bill Stewart
Administrator, Gladstone School District

Dr. Debra Sullivan
Dean, Praxis Institute for Early Childhood Education

Dr. Anand Yang
Director, Jackson School of International Studies, University of Washington

Introduction for Educators

How to Use This Book

Making Connections can be used in a number of ways with students to support:

- Language acquisition for intermediate English language learners

- Language acquisition for striving readers

- Reading comprehension of nonfiction materials in an English language arts class

- Increased knowledge of global issues in a social studies or science class

- Student engagement in the classroom around current, relevant issues

Why Use This Book?

According to the Alliance for Excellent Education, 8 million of the 32.5 million students in grades 4 through 12 read below grade level. By the time students reach middle and high school, they need sophisticated vocabulary and reading skills in order to read complex texts. If a student is a newcomer to the United States or has had significant gaps in his or her education, these skills may not be fully developed. A lack of vocabulary, reading strategies, and prior knowledge can significantly impact a student's education and leave him or her ill-prepared for the literacy demands of the 21st century. [1]

Research has shown that a variety of teaching methods help students acquire higher-level language skills. Several best practices critical to academic literacy development in different content areas can support student success in the classroom.

Making Connections was developed with the following best practices in mind:

- Engaging language and literacy activities

- Explicit reading comprehension instruction

- Explicit vocabulary instruction

- Differentiated instruction

- Real-world content and themes

- Multiple reading, writing, speaking, and listening opportunities [2]

Making Connections targets students in middle school, high school, and beyond. Through nine chapters, students gain the skills and knowledge necessary to excel academically while becoming informed about important issues and ways they can contribute positively to their communities. Language learning is purposeful as students learn language skills and directly apply these skills to current, relevant topics. Students learn about a wide range of interconnected topics, including building community, current environmental issues, population growth, and quality of life. This type of content-based learning can be a great motivating factor in and out of the classroom. [3]

Each chapter has a specific structure that allows students to build knowledge through a series of lessons and activities. The Teacher's Guide includes explicit instructions on how to guide students in learning the content.

---

1. Alliance for Excellent Education, "Adolescent Literacy Fact Sheet," February 2009, http://www.all4ed.org/files/AdolescentLiteracyFactSheet.pdf.

2. Deborah J. Short and Shannon Fitzsimmons, "Double the Work: Challenges and Solutions to Acquiring Language and Academic Literacy for Adolescent English Language Learners," Alliance for Excellent Education, http://www.all4ed.org/files/DoubleWork.pdf.

3. A. U. Chamot and J. M. O'Malley, *The CALLA Handbook: Implementing the cognitive academic language learning approach* (New York: Longman, 1994).

Introduction for Educators, *continued*

Service learning-based action projects and additional resource ideas are included to allow for learning beyond the classroom.

Components of This Book

Each chapter includes the following components:

1. Activating Knowledge

ELL readers and striving readers should have exposure to multiple experiences with topics before, during, and after reading. [4] *Making Connections* begins by activating students' prior knowledge. Students brainstorm and write to initiate comprehension of the chapter topic. The first part of each chapter also gives students a chance to make connections between the chapter topic and the knowledge they already have.

2. Vocabulary Development

By the time students reach middle school, there is a large amount of vocabulary they need in order to comprehend what they read. *Making Connections* introduces students to key vocabulary that is both rigorous and relevant to each chapter topic. Through explicit instruction by the teacher and multiple vocabulary activities, students have the opportunity to continuously practice using these words in context. When students reach the chapter reading, they have become familiar with the meaning of these words. These words are also incorporated into chapter writing activities.

3. Dialogue

Listening and speaking opportunities are an important part of improving language. Dialogue activities are included in each chapter. Students can first listen to the dialogue and then practice the dialogue with a peer. Many additional activities require students to speak and collaborate with each other. Consistent practice with speaking and listening can help to expand ideas and build upon background knowledge. [5]

4. Reading

In order for students to truly engage in a chapter or lesson, they need to be active learners. Since expository and informational texts have specific features, providing students with the tools to understand these types of texts makes the readings accessible. When students are given explicit strategies to use while reading, they can actively work to improve their reading abilities. [6] *Making Connections* takes this into consideration, as students are given opportunities to see their teacher model the use of comprehension strategies while reading and to practice these strategies with the support of graphic organizers.

5. Writing

Throughout the text, students have opportunities to write in multiple genres. Each chapter includes both writing warm-ups and structured writing activities. Before writing in a particular genre, students analyze a writing sample. With the additional support of rubrics, graphic organizers, and peer editing checklists, students are equipped with the

---

4. Julie Meltzer and Edmund T. Hamann, "Meeting the Literacy Development Needs of Adolescent English Language Learners through Content-Area Learning, Part Two: Focus on Classroom Teaching and Learning Strategies," The Education Alliance at Brown University, http://www.alliance.brown.edu/pubs/adlit/adell_litdv2.pdf.

5. Ibid.
6. Ibid.

---

tools necessary to create their own pieces of writing. Each writing assignment is directly connected with a chapter topic. Grammar suggestions are included in the Teacher's Guide to support each writing genre.

6. Culminating Activity

The culminating activity is an opportunity for students to show what they have learned through communication and collaboration. These hands-on activities at the end of each chapter give students the opportunity to talk with each other and grapple with critical questions around global issues and sustainable solutions in fun, engaging ways. Culminating activities require students to use both communication skills and content knowledge authentically. [7]

7. Assessments

Making Connections includes both formative and summative assessments. The various types of assessments provide a clear picture of where teachers can meet students' needs. Ongoing formative assessments throughout the chapter can give teachers insight into their students' literacy skills and content knowledge. [8] At the end of each chapter in the Teacher's Guide, there is a writing rubric, a summative assessment, and a personal beliefs assessment. The summative assessment can be used as both a pre- and post-test to measure student improvement of vocabulary, content, and reading comprehension. The personal beliefs assessment can be used to gauge changes in students' beliefs about their ability to make an impact on global issues.

8. Engaging Content-Based Themes

The themes included throughout *Making Connections* give students multiple opportunities to engage in real-world investigations of current issues and to think critically about solutions. Skills developed through these activities, such as collaboration and taking a global perspective, will help prepare students for the future and engage them in problem-solving activities similar to ones they will encounter as active, engaged citizens in the 21st century. Students can build on knowledge as they move from one chapter to the next, make relevant connections between learning and their own lives, and learn how to take part in sustainable solutions to current challenges.

Conclusion

Making Connections has been designed to support students by giving them the knowledge and skills they need to learn both content and language. Best practices inform each chapter, providing students a meaningful and fun context for learning. Here is a text that can engage students in the classroom, help them to excel academically, and provide them an opportunity to develop as empowered global citizens who can make a real difference in both local and global communities.

---

7. Lorrie Verplaetse, "How content area teachers allocate turns to limited English proficient students." *Journal of Education* 182, no. 3, (2000): 19-36.
8. Julie Meltzer and Edmund T. Hamann.

Table of Contents

I. Introductory Materials

II. Chapters

1. Envisioning Our Future

Reading Skill: Main Idea

Writing Genre: Poetry

2. The Natural World

Reading Skill: Textual Details

Writing Genre: Five-sentence Paragraph

3. Environmental Issues and Solutions

Reading Skill: Cause and Effect

Writing Genre: Persuasive Essay

4. Thinking about Consumption

Reading Skill: Sequencing

Writing Genre: How-to Guide

5. Population around the World

Reading Skill: Making Predictions

Writing Genre: Community Plan

© FACING THE FUTURE www.facingthefuture.org

6. Improving Our Quality of Life

Reading Skill: Drawing Conclusions
Writing Genre: Realistic Fiction

7. Peace and Conflict

Reading Skill: Theme
Writing Genre: Advice Column

8. Community Development

Reading Skill: Context Clues
Writing Genre: Speech

9. Creating Our Future

Reading Skill: Character Traits
Writing Genre: Letter

III. Appendix

IV. Endnotes

V. Photo Credits

Chapter 1

Envisioning Our Future

Through brainstorm, dialogue, and writing activities, students reflect on issues affecting the world today and what can be done to create a sustainable future. After learning vocabulary relevant to sustainability, students read about three young people who are working to improve their lives and communities. Students work to identify the main idea of the reading passage and answer a variety of comprehension questions. After the reading activity they will write a poem about their vision of the world. The chapter culminates with a kinesthetic activity that illustrates how global issues are connected.

Possible Scope and Sequence
(based on one-hour class periods)

Day 1	Day 2	Day 3	Day 4	Day 5	Day 6	Day 7
Activating Knowledge Writing Warm-up Expanding Vocabulary	Using Words in Context: *Completing a Paragraph* Breaking Down the Meaning	Dialogue: *What in the World?* Reading Skill Focus: *Main Idea* Pre-reading: *Anticipation Guide*	Chapter Reading: *Been Around the World* Reading Skill Follow-up: *Main Idea*	Compre-hension Questions	Writing about Sustainability: *Poetry*	Culminating Activity: *Making Global Connections*

Time
Approximately seven one-hour class periods

Essential Questions
- What are the biggest issues affecting the world today?
- How do society, economy, and the environment relate to global sustainability?
- How can young people work toward creating a sustainable world?

Integrated Subject Areas
- Social Studies
- English Language Arts
- Science

Content Objectives
Students will:
- Identify different issues affecting the world today
- Identify different ways young people can help to create a sustainable world
- Explain interconnections among global issues

Language Objectives
Students will:
- Analyze photographs depicting various global issues
- Write an opinion about the biggest issues affecting the world today
- Define and use new vocabulary words
- Discuss global issues with a classmate
- Read about sustainable solutions to global problems

- Identify the main idea of a reading
- Write, evaluate, and edit poems

Key Concepts
- Global issues
- Interconnections

Vocabulary
- Sustainability
- Economy
- Environment
- Society

Standards Addressed
- TESOL standards
- NCTE standards
- NCSS standards
- NSES standards

* Please see Appendix A for a list of national standards addressed.

Assessment Option
Use the Chapter 1 assessments of student knowledge and outlook/personal beliefs as pretests for the chapter. Follow up with the same assessments at the end of the chapter to assess changes in knowledge and outlook/personal beliefs.

Instructions

1. Read the introduction with students.

2. Have students team up with a partner to discuss their answer to the question: *"Do you ever think about how you want the world to be in the future?"*

3. Ask if they think the future should look different than the present.

4. Have the pair share their answers with the class.

5. Explain to students that in Chapter 1 they are going to talk about problems they see in the world as well as possible solutions to these problems.

Chapter

1 Envisoning Our Future

Did you ever think about how you want the world to be in the future? Do you wonder what you can do to help create a better world?

This chapter will introduce you to thinking about the future and help to prepare you to create the kind of world you want. First, you will **speak** to your classmates about problems you see in the world and possible solutions to these problems. You will **listen to** and then practice a dialogue between two students who realize that global issues are connected to their own lives. Then, you will **read** about three young people and the choices they are making in their lives to prepare for the future. Finally, you will **write** a poem about what you want the world to be like.

Students in China started a recycling program at their school.

In this activity, you will brainstorm ideas about global issues. When you **brainstorm**, you come up with as many possible answers to a question or idea as you can. The word "brainstorm" is a compound word:

BRAIN + STORM = brainstorm.

Example: Look at the photo below. What do you think is happening in this photo?

Phrases you can use to talk with your partner:

• In this photograph, I see...

people outside. The people look like they do not live in the United States. There are several plastic containers around them. Some people have cups in their hands. The young child in the center of the photo looks sad. Some of the women have cloth wrapped around them like a skirt.

• A problem the people in this photograph might have is...

they may have to share food and water. They may be poor.

• I wonder why...

the young child in the middle of the photo looks so sad. I wonder where these people are from. I also wonder if they have their own homes or if they have to live together.

Instructions

1. Have students examine the photo.
2. Ask students what they notice about the photo. What words or feelings come to mind?
3. Read aloud the answers given in the example.

Instructions

1. Have students work with a partner to choose one of the four photos and determine what is happening in the photo. The suggested phrases are discussion prompts.

2. Give students the following information:

   • The first photo is of two people fighting at a peace rally in the United States.

   • The second photo is of deforestation, or removal of trees from an area.

   • The third photo is of a slum in India.

   • The fourth is of two young children swimming in polluted water in India.

3. Ask students if they have ever seen anything similar to the problems depicted in these photos. Also, how do these problems compare to ones they see where they live?

4. Ask students if they believe there are solutions to these problems.

Directions: With a partner, choose one photo from this page. Brainstorm what you think the problem in the photo might be. Use the sentence starters below the photos to discuss the problem with your partner.

Phrases you can use to talk with your partner:

• In this photograph, I see…

• The problem in this photograph might be…

• I wonder why…

Directions: Respond to the following questions. Write continuously and include every idea you can think of until you are told to stop. Be ready to share your ideas with a partner.

What is the biggest problem in the world today?

Why does this problem exist?

What do you think is a solution to this problem?

Writing prompt: The biggest problem in the world today is…

Instructions

1. To prepare students for the writing warm-up, ask the following question: *What are some of the biggest issues affecting the world today?*

2. As students share their answers, write them in a place everyone can see.

3. For the writing exercise, have students write independently about the global issue they think is most important—the one they think affects many people and has a significant impact on the world.

   • **Differentiated Instruction:** If beginner students are more comfortable writing in their native language, allow them to do so.

   • **Differentiated Instruction:** If beginner students are comfortable drawing diagrams or pictures to support their writing, allow them to do so.

4. Have students share their response with a partner or with the class.

5. **Option:** In a place all students can see, record the issues students think are most important. This information could be useful when thinking about service learning ideas after this unit is completed.

6. Explain that their writing will be discussed again during the last activity.

Instructions

1. Have students study the four photos on their own.

2. Have students share what they think each word means either with a partner or the class.

3. Discuss possible definitions with them.

4. **Option:** Copy this page on an overhead or display it with a document camera. As students are brainstorming ideas for each vocabulary word, list these in the box with the photo.

5. **Option:** Review the following derivatives and root words:

   • *society (n) – societies, social, sociology*

   • *environment (n) – environmental, environs*

   • *economy (n) – economic, economical, economics*

   • *sustainability (n) – sustainable, sustain, unsustainable*

6. **Option:** Review the following root words:

   • *sustain – to maintain*

   • *society – from the Latin root* societas *meaning "friendly association with others"*

7. Have students share a sentence using each vocabulary word with either a partner or the class.

8. **Differentiated Instruction:** Have beginner students create picture dictionaries to go with the new vocabulary words.

Directions: Look at the following images and vocabulary words. Guess what each word means based on the given image.

A

society

B

environment

C

economy

D

sustainability

Using Words in Context: Completing a Paragraph

Directions: Read the paragraphs below. Use the words from the box to fill in the blank spaces.

society	environment	economy	sustainability

It's the first day of school. You walk into class and the teacher gives you a text-book you will use this year. You open the book and notice someone has written on pages throughout the entire book and several pages have been ripped out. Do you think the person who did this thought about the person who would use this book next? If you were to receive a brand-new book, how would you treat it to make sure that the next person was able to get as much use out of it as you did?

In a way, our world is like this textbook. Just as we use Earth's resources like water and trees, other people will use those same resources in the future. What are some ways you can take care of your needs *and* the world so that people can enjoy life in the future? _____ is the idea that we can take care of our own needs and resources without limiting the ability of future generations—our children and grandchildren—to meet their needs.

Asking certain questions can help you begin working toward a sustainable future. Are the people who live in your _____ healthy and happy? If not, what is preventing them from being healthy and happy? Do the people around you try to take care of the _____ by using land, oceans, and rivers carefully instead of damaging them? Do your country's leaders make decisions about how to spend money in ways that help the _____ ? Simply put, working toward sustainability means developing a thriving society, a healthy environment, and a strong economy.

Using Words in Context

Instructions

1. Read the activity aloud to students.

2. As students listen, they can determine the appropriate placement of the vocabulary terms.

3. Have students review their answers with a partner.

4. Ask a volunteer to read the completed paragraphs aloud to the class.

Answers

1. Sustainability
2. society
3. environment
4. economy

Instructions

1. Explain the directions. After reviewing the definitions, explain to students they will (1) answer the question, (2) create a sentence using the vocabulary word, and (3) choose the one word that does not relate to the vocabulary word.

   • **Differentiated Instruction:** Demonstrate how the activity works by filling in one of the boxes.

   • **Differentiated Instruction:** Enlarge the four boxes to poster size and fill in one of the boxes. Work as a class to fill in answers for each box and write them on the poster. The poster can remain hanging in the room throughout this unit of study.

2. This activity could be done independently, in pairs or small groups, or as an entire class.

3. **Option:** Have students search for and cut out magazine pictures that relate to each vocabulary word.

4. **Option:** As a homework assignment, have students write a single paragraph using the four vocabulary words.

Directions: Each box below includes one of the four vocabulary words from the previous page as well as its definition. Below each definition:

1. Answer the question.

2. Write a sentence using the vocabulary word.

3. Choose the one word in the group that does not relate to the vocabulary word.

society

Definition: *a group of people that share common interests or common culture (example: American society)*

1. What is the best thing about the society you live in?
2. Use *society* in a sentence.
3. Which word does not belong?

   people   culture   community   shopping

environment

Definition: *everything that surrounds us and supports our ability to live and grow*

1. What type of outside environment do you enjoy spending time in most: the ocean, forest, mountains, or desert? Why?
2. Use *environment* in a sentence.
3. Which word does not belong?

   trees   rocks   computer   river

economy

Definition: *the way a community, region, or country makes and uses money, goods, and services*

1. What country seems to have a strong economy?
2. Use *economy* in a sentence.
3. Which word does not belong?

   money   polar bear   bank   credit card

sustainability

Definition: *the ability to meet the needs of people now and in the future*

1. What is an example of sustainability in your school or neighborhood?
2. Use *sustainability* in a sentence.
3. Which word does not belong?

   future   basic needs
   taking care   fighting

Answers

society

1. Answers will vary.
2. In some Spanish-speaking societies, young girls celebrate their Quinceañera when they turn fifteen.
3. shopping

environment

1. Answers will vary.
2. The environment and climate in Southern California is much different than the environment and climate in Alaska.

3. computer

economy

1. Answers will vary.
2. Many people lost their jobs when the economy was weak.
3. polar bear

sustainability

1. Answers will vary.
2. Veronica thinks sustainability in her community is important so that her neighbors have good health, good jobs, and a clean environment.
3. fighting

Dialogue: What in the World?

Directions: Read the following sample dialogue with a partner to learn about Talib and Reena's thoughts about global issues. As you read, write down every word you think is a global issue—that is, an issue that affects many people all over the world.

Talib: Hi, Reena!

Reena: Hi, Talib! Can you believe what we learned in class today?

Talib: I know, I never realized there were so many problems in the world.

Reena: Seriously! I also never realized that people from different places around the world can have really similar stories about their lives.

Talib: What do you mean?

Reena: My family had to leave my country when I was three years old because there was a war. My dad didn't want us to be around conflict and violence, so he thought we should move. When Mr. Thomas was talking to us in class, I realized that many people have had to leave their countries in search of more peaceful places, just like my family did.

Talib: Wow, you make a really good point. It seems like people share more experiences than they might think.

Reena: How about you, Talib? What did you think about class today?

Talib: I was really surprised to hear what Mr. Thomas said about education.

Reena: What surprised you?

Talib: I didn't realize that over 75 million children around the world do not go to school.[1] It seems like every child around the world should be able to learn. It's difficult to think about so many children growing up without an education.

Reena: You're right; it is hard to think about.

Talib: Did you find anything else in class interesting?

Reena: Yes, I was surprised to find out that air pollution from cars and trucks can lead to health problems like asthma. I had not really thought about the causes of asthma and other health problems before.

Talib: I'm really glad we're learning about these different world issues.

Reena: Me too. After learning more about pollution, education, and conflict, I feel like I know more about the world.

Dialogue

Instructions

1. Have students listen as you read the dialogue aloud so they can hear proper pronunciation.

2. Ask students if they are unfamiliar with any words, and assist them in understanding the words if they are unclear.

3. Have students pair up with a partner to read the dialogue. Have pairs read the dialogue twice, switching roles the second time.

4. Ask students to share any words they think are connected to global issues. What global issues are found within the dialogue? Encourage students to connect these global issues with society, environment, or economy.

Instructions

1. Explain to students that the reading skill for this chapter is identifying the main idea. Ask students what they think the main idea of a reading is, based on their understanding of the words *main* and *idea*.

   • **Differentiated Instruction:** For visual learners, have students analyze a painting, photograph, or cartoon to identify the main idea. For auditory learners, have them listen to a song and identify the main idea or message the song is trying to convey.

2. Have students read the definition of main idea provided in the box.

3. Read the short paragraph about the Global Youth Action Network to the class.

4. Review the completed graphic organizer with students to guide them through identifying the main idea.

   • **Differentiated Instruction:** Have students find the details within the paragraph and underline them.

What exactly is the main idea? To understand **main idea**, think about your favorite song. What do you think is the point of the song? What is its message? What details in the song help to support this message? The **main idea** is the most important idea in a passage or text. It is what the author wants you to know. Details throughout the passage or text can provide information that supports the main idea.

Example: When you read the paragraph below, think about the most important idea and find three details to support this idea. Then, review the graphic organizer to see how to identify and organize this information.

There are many problems in the world these days, but are there enough solutions? Millions of young people think there are! The Global Youth Action Network (GYAN) is a youth-led group that started in 1999. GYAN believes young people have the power to make a difference in the world, and that by taking positive action now, they can reduce the number of problems in the future. Through programs like Global Youth Service Day, GYAN helps young people in more than 125 countries work on service projects in their communities. For example, teenagers in Bolivia taught their community about the dangers of drinking unclean water. In the United States, youth educated people about the importance of voting. In Thailand, students taught leadership and life skills to children who were orphaned when their parents died of AIDS. Global Youth Action Network is one group of young people who truly believes they can change the world![2]

Main Idea
The Global Youth Action Network believes young people have the power to make a difference on global issues.

The Global Youth Action Network started in 1999 and believes positive action now can help prevent problems in the future.

GYAN helps to organize Global Youth Service Day, where young people from over 125 countries create service projects that help their communities.

Youth from Thailand, Bolivia, and the United States worked on service day projects supporting their communities.

Reading Skill Focus: Main Idea

Directions: Read the paragraph below and complete the graphic organizer with the main idea of the paragraph and three supporting details.

Have you ever heard of teenagers being teachers? At Cleveland High School in Seattle, teenage students had the opportunity to become teachers while they were still in school. These students were refugees who had left their home countries in order to find safety. Their teacher, David White-Espin, realized that his students' experience as refugees could be shared with other students. This was a way that non-refugee students could learn about issues they had never experienced. Most of the Cleveland students came from countries in Southeast Asia and East Africa. They had many stories about conflict and migration to share. They had seen people fight with weapons and they had escaped from dangerous places. The Cleveland students created a video to tell their stories about living as refugees. The students visited local middle and high schools to present their video and talk to students. Their audiences were amazed by all the different languages they could speak and how they were able to survive such difficult times. By sharing their experiences with other students, this group of refugees helped other students to understand the effects of conflict and migration.

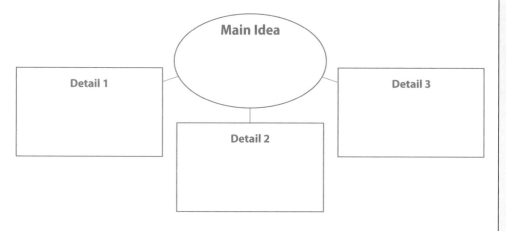

Instructions

1. After reviewing the previous example, have students read the paragraph about Cleveland High School students and complete the graphic organizer.

   • **Differentiated Instruction:** Have students think-pair-share with a partner about the main idea of the paragraph.

2. **Additional Resource:** If students need more practice with main idea, additional nonfiction articles can be found on the *New York Times'* Learning Network: http://learning.blogs.nytimes.com.

Answers

Main Idea

Students from Cleveland High School educated other students about what life was like as a refugee.

Detail 1

David White-Espin realized that his students were very knowledgeable about conflict and refugee issues and decided it was time for them to educate others.

Detail 2

Students spoke to local middle and high school students about their personal experiences as refugees.

Detail 3

Students made a video that told about their personal experiences as refugees.

Instructions

1. Ask students if they are familiar with the prefix *anti*. Explain that it means "before."

2. Ask students what they think an *anticipation guide* is.

3. Have students work through the anticipation guide. Explain that they should rate the statements on the guide as honestly as they can because there are no right or wrong answers.

4. **Option:** Partition the room into five sections and label the sections 1 through 5. Read the first statement and have students move to the section that corresponds with the answer (number) they chose. Ask volunteers to explain their answers. Repeat with the remaining statements.

Directions: Read the four statements below, one at a time. On a scale of 1-5, 1 meaning you **completely disagree** with the statement and 5 meaning you **completely agree**, circle the number that reflects how you feel about each statement. The answer is based on your opinion so there are no right or wrong answers.

If there are problems occurring where I live, I should spend time trying to solve them.

| 1 | 2 | 3 | 4 | 5 |

Young people can make a difference in the world.

| 1 | 2 | 3 | 4 | 5 |

The choices I make in my own life have an effect on my community and the world.

| 1 | 2 | 3 | 4 | 5 |

Fifty years from now, I want the world to be a better place.

| 1 | 2 | 3 | 4 | 5 |

Now, add together the numbers you circled.

Read the statement that matches your total:

4-8: You are not convinced that you can or should help solve world problems.

9-15: You know there are problems that people face around the world. You think you might be able to help solve these problems, but you're not sure.

16-20: You believe that even though there are many problems in the world, you can help to find some solutions.

Been Around the World

Maninho lives in South Africa, Raul lives in Peru, and Maria lives in the United States. Can three people from different parts of the world have anything in common?

Maninho

Maninho lives in the city of Cape Town in South Africa. He likes listening to hip-hop music. When he was just nine years old, he left his home country of Mozambique, which **borders** South Africa, because of family troubles. For five years, he has lived at Beth Uriel (which means "House of Light" in the Hebrew language), a shelter for young men aged sixteen to twenty-four. At Beth Uriel, young men live safely in a home where they also go to school, work, and participate in youth programs that help them reach personal goals. Maninho is in the tenth grade and loves learning English, Xhosa (a tribal language of South Africa), and math. He loves learning because it gives him the chance to talk with other people and share new ideas. He has not seen his real family since 2004; the young people he lives with now are part of his new family.

One challenge or difficulty he sees in his community is the way people treat each other. According to Maninho, "Sometimes you can interact or talk with someone one day and the next day they turn on you." Rather than getting upset, Maninho created a music group called *Young Soldiers* that focuses on **unity**. He refers to unity as the Uhuru Spirit, which means "one." The lyrics, or words, to the group's hip-hop music are positive and encourage people to work together and get along. Instead of creating wars, the Young Soldiers create music.

---

borders (v) – located next to another region or country (e.g., the United States borders Mexico)
unity (n) – the state of being together or in harmony

Maninho and Masakane, the Young Soldiers, use hip hop to create positive messages for youth.

1. Give students a few minutes to preview the reading, noting photos, titles, and subheadings.

2. Ask the students the following questions:
   - What do you think this reading will be about?
   - What is this article not going to be about?
   - Which words are bold-faced or in italics? Why do you think these words are emphasized?
   - What do you notice about the photos and illustrations in this reading?

3. Tell students that they will be searching for the main idea and supporting details as they read this selection.

- **Differentiated Instruction:** Provide sticky notes to students so they can flag possible supporting details.

- **Differentiated Instruction:** To see where there are gaps in comprehension for beginner students, photocopy the reading and have students use the *insert method*. They can insert the following codes when reading: a check mark (√) for facts or concepts they already know, a question mark (?) for facts or concepts they find confusing, an exclamation mark (!) for anything unusual or surprising, and a plus sign (+) for a fact or concept that is new to them.[1] ▶

Instructions, *continued*

4. Start by reading the first paragraph aloud.

5. Option: Use the following "think aloud" to model active reading:

"Wow, I can't believe Maninho had to leave his country when he was so young!

I wonder what happened to him and why he hasn't seen his real family since 2004.

I think the main idea of this section is introducing Maninho.

I believe this is the main idea because the reading states that (a) he lives in Cape Town, South Africa, (b) he loves to learn English, Xhosa, and math, and (c) he lives in a home for young men aged sixteen to twenty-four."

6. Continue reading the second paragraph:

"I know what he means about people not treating each other well. I have seen that same challenge in my own community.

Maninho started his own hip-hop group? That is so great!

I think the main idea of this paragraph is that Maninho knows there are challenges where he lives, but he also understands that there are solutions.

Details to support this idea include: (a) Maninho sees that people do not always treat each other with kindness, (b) he says that you can't trust some people, and (c) he created a hip-hop group known as Young Soldiers to promote unity." ▶

Raul

Raul lives in the town of Chinchero in Peru with his three brothers, one sister, mother, father, and grandmother. He loves life in Chinchero because it is peaceful; people are friendly and help each other. He also loves the mountainous environment.

Chinchero is famous for its **weaving**; boys and girls learn how to weave at a young age. Many people in Chinchero are farmers, and in addition to growing potatoes and lima beans, they raise sheep that provide wool for weaving blankets and clothes. The land is very important to the people in Chinchero because it provides food and a way to make money. The main language spoken in Chinchero is Quechua and the second language is Spanish. Raul can speak both.

One problem in Chinchero is that many people are not able to complete their education because they do not have enough money to finish school.

Students usually stop going to school by the time they are sixteen, and without a proper education they cannot earn enough money to support their families and take care of the land.

Raul is attending university now. His goal is to work in **tourism** so that he can help to strengthen his community's economy. Tourists support Chinchero's economy when they eat at local restaurants, take tours of the village, buy blankets or clothes, and rent hotel rooms. The money that local people make through tourism could help them to live sustainably. It could also help young people to complete their education. Raul also knows that it is important not only to earn money from tourism but to share his way of life. He wants to make sure that in fifty years his neighbors and his family have good opportunities in life.

---

weaving (n) – the process of making cloth (for blankets and clothing) by intertwining threads

tourism (n) – the business of providing tours, food, and lodging for people who travel

Raul poses with his family in Chinchero.

Maria

Maria lives in the city of San Francisco in the United States. She is nineteen years old and is in her second year of college. She loves learning about anything that challenges her ideas and helps her understand the world in a new way. The city where she lives has many small stores, restaurants, and student housing. She shares an apartment with two roommates. She loves the fact that her neighborhood has so many things happening: live music, street festivals, and dance shows. She also enjoys that people of all ages go to these events.

When she finishes college, Maria wants to be an urban planner so that she can help to design sustainable cities. Maria thinks that all people should have the chance to live in homes they can afford and have jobs to support their families. Right now, she **volunteers** with the group Habitat for Humanity. Habitat for Humanity works to end homelessness by building houses for families in need. Maria understands that if people do not have shelter and other basic needs, society will face many other problems.

Maria hopes that in fifty years people will understand what actions they can take to create a more sustainable world.

The World in Fifty Years...

When these three young people think about how to make their communities and the world better in fifty years, they are thinking about *sustainability*. They are taking action now to make sure the needs of people are met today and in the future. Even though they may be from different parts of the world and have very different lives, they have a common goal: to make sure the world is a great place for everyone. Maninho thinks about how his hip-hop music can help society by providing a positive message of peace. Raul thinks about how tourism can help support the local environment and boost the economy for the people in Chinchero. Maria thinks about how houses and jobs for everyone can help society. Together, these three young people from different corners of the world are working to create a bright future.

***

volunteers (v) – provides a service for free

Instructions, *continued*

7. Ask students if there is anything they notice about the first two paragraphs other than what you shared in the think aloud.

8. Have students read the rest of the article with a partner.

Maria builds homes with other Habitat for Humanity volunteers.

Reading Skill Follow-up

Instructions

1. After they finish the chapter reading, have students discuss with their partner what they think the main idea is.

- **Differentiated Instruction:** Once they believe they have identified the main idea, have pairs share their answers. Write the answers where everyone can see them. Have the class decide which one makes the most sense. Remind them that a main idea cannot exist without details to support it.

2. After determining the main idea, have each student write it in the center of the graphic organizer and let them work with their partner to figure out the supporting details.

3. **Additional Resource:** Allow students to explore resources from groups mentioned in the reading:

- Young Soldiers on MySpace: www.myspace.com/young soldierscapetown
- Minka Chinchero Cooperative: http://minkachinchero. interconnection.org
- Habitat for Humanity videos: www.habitat.org/ videogallery/default.aspx

Reading Skill Follow-up: Main Idea

Directions: Determine the main idea of the chapter reading. Then look for at least three details that support the main idea. Complete the graphic organizer with the main idea and three supporting details from the chapter reading.

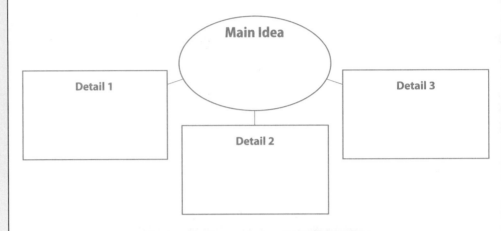

Community members from Chinchero show people how to weave.

Answers

Main Idea
Three young people around the world are working to make their communities more sustainable.

Detail 1
Maninho from South Africa created a hip-hop group that focuses on unity.

Detail 2
Maria from the United States volunteers her time building homes for people.

Detail 3
Raul from Peru is studying tourism to support his community.

Comprehension Questions

Comprehension Questions

Directions: Answer the following questions to support your comprehension of the chapter reading.

Understanding what you read

1. Identify the three countries where Maninho, Raul, and Maria live.

2. In Maria's story it states that she volunteers at Habitat for Humanity. Define the word *volunteer*.

Thinking about what you read

3. Read Maninho's story again. What exactly does Maninho want?

4. The title of the reading is "Been Around the World." Create a different title for this reading. Explain how your title reflects the main idea of the reading.

5. Explain how the following Chinese proverb connects to the reading:
"One generation plants the trees; another gets the shade."

Questioning what you read

6. Explain why you think the author wrote about these three young people.

Making connections to what you read

7. Do any of these stories relate to you and your life? Why or why not?

8. Evaluate the answers you gave in the Anticipation Guide before you completed the reading. Would you change any of your answers? Why?

Further discussion questions

9. How might a weak economy affect a society?

10. Can you think of an activity that harms the environment but helps the economy? How might you change this activity so that it does not harm the environment?

Instructions

1. Before students begin answering the comprehension questions, share with them the academic language that appears in many of the questions (see Appendix B).

2. Explain that the questions are divided into five sections according to the ways they support reading comprehension. (See Appendix B for a detailed explanation of each section.)

3. **Differentiated Instruction:** Differentiate the questions students must answer based on their reading levels. Support comprehension by working with students who may need more guided instruction.

Answers

1. South Africa, Peru, United States

2. To volunteer is to work or provide a service for free.

3. He wants people to treat each other fairly and with respect.

4. Example: "Three Young People Making a Difference"

5. These young people are working to make a better world not just for today but for the future.

6. All three are working toward sustainable solutions to problems in their communities. Their personal stories may inspire other young people to get involved.

7. Example: Yes, I agree with Maria's ideas about volunteering to help people in her society. I see people in my town who could live in better homes. I could see myself working with an organization like Habitat for Humanity.

8. Example: I would change my answer to the second statement. At first I said young people don't have the ability to make a difference in the world. After reading about these three people, I think we do.

9. People who do not have jobs are not able to afford things like homes, health care, and taxes that support public projects like parks. This could have a negative effect on a society.

10. One example is making material goods, like electronics. Buying these products might help a country's economy, but the natural resources used and the toxic waste produced would have a negative impact on the environment.

Instructions

1. Students will write a bio-poem about themselves and their vision for the future.

2. Before introducing the bio-poem, introduce them to the genre of poetry by reviewing the box at the top of the page.

3. **Option:** To immerse them in this genre, share different types of poems and discuss why people choose to write poetry.

What is a poem?

A poem is a personal expression of ideas and emotions.

Why write a poem?

A poem is an opportunity to express your ideas about different topics in a creative way. Poems allow you to personally express exactly what you are thinking. There are many different kinds of poems: some use words that rhyme, others focus on rhythm, and some use repetition. The more descriptive your poem is, the better.

You read about three young people from around the world and what they want for the future. Now you will be writing about yourself and the future you want by creating a *bio-poem*—a poem about yourself.

Example: Use the following structure for your bio-poem:

Name

Three words that describe you

Who loves…

Who thinks my family…

Who feels the environment should…

Who wants society to…

Who wishes school could…

Who believes money should…

Who dreams the future will be…

Name

Writing about Sustainability: Poetry

Writing about Sustainability

Directions: Before you write your own bio-poem, you will evaluate two others. When you evaluate writing, look carefully to see what the writer did well and how the writer could improve. Grade the poems on a scale of 1 through 3 (1 needs a lot of work, 2 is pretty good, and 3 looks great). Use the following questions to help you grade:

- Does the poet use the correct bio-poem structure?
- Does the poet use vocabulary words from this chapter?
- Does the poet use complete thoughts throughout the poem?

Instructions

1. Explain that before they write their own poem, they are going to analyze two other poems and grade them based on a few guidelines.

- **Differentiated Instruction:** To guide them through this process, complete one example with them.

Poem 1

Miguel Jordan
Hilarious, athletic, wise
Who loves any music that makes me dance
Who thinks my family deserves to live in a peaceful neighborhood where playgrounds replace broken glass
Who feels the environment should be full of lush forests and blue oceans, not polluted air
Who wants society to accept all different types of people
Who wishes school could teach me to speak three languages and fly airplanes
Who believes money should create jobs for all people so no one struggles
Who dreams the future will be full of poets, athletes, doctors, and lawyers
Miguel Jordan

What grade would you give this poem? Why?

Poem 2

Julie Li
Smart
Who feels the environment should not be destroyed
Who dreams the future will be a place of many opportunities
Who loves traveling but has only been to China and America
Who has two great parents
That's me

What grade would you give this poem? Why?

Instructions

1. Read through the writing steps with students.

2. **Grammar Suggestion:** Teach students how to incorporate meaningful adjectives to strengthen their poems.

3. **Differentiated Instruction:** For beginning students who may need more guidance, work with them in a small group and assist them in writing their poems. You can even write the poem with them as a shared writing exercise.

4. Share the Chapter 1 writing rubric with students. You may want to add relevant spelling and grammar components to the rubric.

Writing Steps: Poetry

Step 1: Use the Writing Organizer on the next page to help you write your bio-poem. Write complete thoughts, not just words, for each line that begins with "Who."

Step 2: Edit the poem using the Edit Checklist below.

Step 3: Have a classmate read and edit your poem using the same checklist.

Step 4: Correct and rewrite your poem.

Step 5: Share your poem with the class by reading it aloud.

 Edit Checklist

	Author Check	Peer Editor Check
Did you use the bio-poem structure correctly?		
Did you use chapter vocabulary words correctly?		
Did you write complete thoughts for each line?		

Chapter 1 Writing Rubric

Category	3	2	1
Organization	Uses the bio-poem structure correctly	Attempts to use the bio-poem structure	Writes a poem, but does not follow the bio-poem structure
Vocabulary	Uses all vocabulary words correctly	Uses some vocabulary words correctly	Does not use vocabulary words
Development	Includes a complete idea for each line of the poem	Includes a complete idea for some lines of the poem	Includes few if any complete ideas in the poem

Total = _____ / 9

Writing Organizer: Poetry

Your Name	
Three words that describe you	
Who loves...	
Who thinks my family...	
Who feels the environment should...	
Who wants society to...	
Who wishes school could...	
Who believes money should...	
Who dreams the future will be...	
Your Name	

Instructions

1. Students can use the graphic organizer to collect their thoughts.

2. **Option:** Before students begin writing, post the following words from the graphic organizer around the room on different pieces of chart paper: *family, future, environment, society, school,* and *money.* Have students brainstorm ideas that come to mind when they think of each word and then write these on chart paper. Now students will have a variety of words to work with when they write their poems.

3. When they finish writing their poems, students should exchange poems with a classmate, edit their peer's poem using the Edit Checklist (on the previous page), and then revise their own poem.

4. Have each student recite his/her poem to the class.

5. **Option:** Host a spoken word event. Have students practice and memorize their poems ahead of time.

Culminating Activity: Making Global Connections (20 minutes)

Overview
Students demonstrate the interconnectedness of global issues and solutions through a kinesthetic exercise using global issue cards and a ball of yarn.

Materials/Preparation
- *Global Issues Cards:* Cut out and distribute one card per student or one per student pair for larger classes. (**Note:** Cards should be printed double-sided so the front photos and back text are aligned.)
- Ball of yarn

Introduction
1. Ask students to recall from the writing warm-up what they consider to be the world's biggest problem.

2. Ask them if they think the problem they wrote about is connected to any other problem in the world.

3. Explain to students that they are going to do an exercise that will help them think about how global issues are connected to each other.

Steps
1. Have students stand in a circle. Pass out one *Global Issues Card* to each student/pair and keep one card for yourself.

2. For classes with more than 16 students, you can have students pair up so that each pair shares a card.

3. Read aloud the global issue on your card and then toss the ball of yarn to a student/pair across the circle.

4. Have the student read the global issue on his/her card and state how this issue could be connected to your issue. For example, health is connected to education because students cannot attend school if they are sick.

5. Once the student has stated how their issue is connected to the previous one, she/he holds on to a piece of the yarn and tosses the ball of yarn to someone else across the circle.

6. Continue the exercise until everyone has caught the ball of yarn, called out an interconnection, and is now holding a piece of the yarn. Have the last student throw the ball of yarn back to you. You should now have a representative global issues web with every student holding a *Global Issues Card* and a piece of the web.

7. Have everyone pull the string so that the web is taut.

8. Tug on your piece of the yarn and ask if anyone felt the tug. Have some others tug on the yarn and see who else feels it. Try tugging harder and see who feels it then. Ask what the tug might represent or indicate about the connections between global issues.

9. Help them to understand that all the issues on the cards are connected. Many global issues have related causes and solutions. Any issue, such as population growth, will have impacts on other global issues. A positive result of these interconnections is that working on a solution to one of the issues will likely bring positive benefits to other issues. For example, increasing access to education may improve health and slow population growth.

10. If time permits, you can ask students the following questions:

    - Why is it helpful to understand how and why global issues are interconnected?

    - Can you think of a solution to one of the global issues that would also help to solve another issue?

Global Issues Cards 1, front

Education

Conflict

Population Growth

Environment

Health

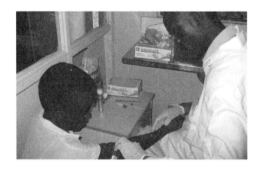

Food

Discrimination

Economy

Global Issues Cards 1, back

Conflict

fighting

war

disagreement

struggle

Education

school

teacher

learning

students

Environment

air

location

land

surroundings

Population Growth

more people

decreased space

many births

crowded

Food

vegetables

meat

fruit

bread

Health

medicine

well-being

feeling good

no illness

Economy

jobs

money

banks

finances

Discrimination

unfair

prejudice

racism

inequality

Global Issues Cards 2, front

Sustainability

Poverty

Society

Government

Migration

Consumption

Media

Water

Global Issues Cards 2, back

Poverty

poor

little money

hunger

struggling to survive

Sustainability

future

environment

society

economy

Government

leaders

President

laws

elections

Society

people

the public

culture

community

Consumption

resource use

buying and using things

shopping

garbage

Migration

journey

immigration

moving

relocating

Water

rivers

lakes

oceans

faucets

Media

newspaper

television

magazine

radio

Art Extension

Have students create a global issues mobile using photos or drawings that represent different global issues. Find photos or create drawings, glue the pictures onto cardboard, and cut them into shapes. Write the global issues on the back of the cardboard. Use either wire or string to attach the pieces to crossbars made of wooden dowels or sticks.

Action Project

Have students vote on a global issue they are most concerned about and then brainstorm solutions to this issue. On Global Youth Service Day, which takes place every spring, they can become involved in the issue they care about most along with millions of other young people around the world. Visit www.gysd.org for more information. (You could also challenge them to team up with students in other countries for their service project, perhaps through organizations such as Taking IT Global or iEARN.)

Additional Resources on Global Issues and Sustainability

Free the Children

www.freethechildren.com

Free the Children works to free children from poverty and exploitation and to free young people from the notion that they are powerless to effect positive change in the world. Through empowerment programs and leadership training, Free the Children inspires young people to become socially conscious global citizens and agents of change for their peers around the world. We Generation, the youth section of the site, features ways to connect with other young advocates for change.

What Kids Can Do

www.whatkidscando.org

What Kids Can Do is an organization that supports adolescent learning in and out of school. The organization brings youth voices to school, society, and world issues.

The Brower Youth Awards

www.broweryouthawards.org

The Brower Youth Awards were created in 2000 by the Earth Island Institute to create and call forth a new generation of leaders. Each year, the Brower Youth Awards honors six young people for their work in environmentalism and social justice. The website features the winners from each year through short films about their projects.

World Savvy

www.worldsavvy.org

World Savvy is a global education nonprofit with a mission to educate and engage youth in community and world affairs, and to prepare them to learn, work, and live as responsible global citizens in the twenty-first century.

Voices of Youth

www.unicef.org/voy

Voices of Youth is a UNICEF website that educates young people about global issues and what youth can do to take action.

Chapter 1 Student Assessment, page 1
Knowledge about Sustainability and Global Issues

Vocabulary

Directions: Read the sentence and circle the correct definition of the **bold-faced** word.

1. Eliza wants to live in a **society** that accepts people from many different cultures.
   a. a group of people that belong to a secret club
   b. a neighborhood that includes lots of people from all over the world
   c. a group of people that share common interests or a common background
   d. a lifestyle that allows you to choose your neighbors

2. When John grows up, he wants to move to a tropical rainforest and study the **environment**.
   a. everything in nature that surrounds us and supports our ability to live and grow
   b. rainforests that can be found near the equator
   c. the major oceans located around the world
   d. the way in which forests are cut down to provide people with more housing

3. During the 1930s, the American **economy** was not doing well. Many people could not find jobs.
   a. schools throughout a country
   b. the happiness of people in a society over a long period of time
   c. the way a community, region, or country makes and uses money, goods, and services
   d. the young people who work in a country

4. **Sustainability** is a goal for the town of Riverview. The town's mayor wants people to have good jobs, strong and peaceful neighborhoods, and plenty of green spaces like parks and nature trails.
   a. the ability to stay balanced
   b. the idea that the needs of people can be met now and for future generations
   c. the opportunity to have exciting adventures
   d. a town full of people who want to make a real difference in the lives of others

Chapter 1 Student Assessment, page 2

Content

Directions: Read the following sentences and choose the correct answer.

5. The Tamuk community has had some trouble lately. The freshwater from lakes they have used for over fifty years has decreased. They do not have a sustainable _____.
   a. economy
   b. environment
   c. society
   d. none of the above

6. A weak economy could hurt a society because _____.
   a. many people would be unemployed or out of work
   b. many people would use too many natural resources like water and energy
   c. the government would increase the number of jobs
   d. people would travel around the world to places they have always wanted to visit

Reading Comprehension

Directions: Read the paragraph below. For numbers 7 and 8, circle the correct answer.

In India, Jyoti lives in a mud house with her mother, father, two brothers, and sister. She gets up early every morning and milks the cow. Each of her sisters receives a few sips of milk while Jyoti's brothers receive a whole cup of milk each. Jyoti also has water to drink, which her mother draws every morning from the village well. After breakfast, Jyoti takes the cow out to the pasture while her brothers change into their school uniforms and walk to class. She wishes she could go to school too, but only a few of the girls in the village do. The reason Jyoti doesn't attend school isn't because her parents love her less—it's a question of money. There is no electricity or running water in her village. Jyoti and all the other villagers use the fields around the village as the bathroom. When someone gets sick, they are taken by bicycle to the doctor.

7. What is the main idea of this paragraph?
   a. Jyoti's brothers go to school and Jyoti takes care of the home.
   b. Since there is no electricity in Jyoti's village, everyone has to use the fields as the bathroom.
   c. Jyoti's parents love her, but don't have money to send her to school.
   d. Jyoti's life in a village in India has challenges.

8. What is the best title for this paragraph?
   a. Living in a Big City
   b. Surviving in the Village
   c. No School, No Problem!
   d. Traditions within India

Name _____ Class _____ Date _____

Chapter 1 Student Assessment, page 3
Outlook and Personal Beliefs

The answers to the following questions are based on your personal beliefs. There are no right or wrong answers.

Directions for 1 and 2: Place a check mark (√) in the box next to each statement that is true for you.

1. I know things I can do to live sustainably both now and in the future.
   ☐ True
   ☐ False

2. I want to live sustainably so that my children and grandchildren will live well.
   ☐ True
   ☐ False

3. **Complete the following sentence:**
   One way I can personally work on the issue of sustainability is by…

   _____

   _____

   _____

   _____

   _____

Directions for 4 and 5: Fill in the ovals below based on your level of agreement. 1 means you strongly agree. 7 means you strongly disagree.

1 = yes, definitely!   7 = no way!
⟵——————————————⟶

4. I believe my daily actions have an impact on people and places in other parts of the world.

   1   2   3   4   5   6   7
   ⬭ ⬭ ⬭ ⬭ ⬭ ⬭ ⬭

5. I believe I have the ability to help solve global problems.

   1   2   3   4   5   6   7
   ⬭ ⬭ ⬭ ⬭ ⬭ ⬭ ⬭

**Chapter 1 Student Assessment,
pp. 21G, 21H**

1. c
2. a
3. c
4. b
5. b
6. a
7. d
8. b

The Natural
World

Chapter

2

This chapter guides students in exploring how we use natural resources and the ability of the environment to provide these resources. Students begin by creating a caption for an environmental cartoon. Then, a writing warm-up prompts students to contemplate their daily use of natural resources. Students move on to a dialogue activity in which they use the iceberg model to discuss root causes of species extinction. After learning vocabulary relevant to natural resources, students read about different ecosystems and identify textual details that emphasize key pieces of information. Students then write a five-sentence paragraph about the food web of a forest-stream ecosystem. A culminating kinesthetic activity asks students to model consecutive seasons of harvesting fish, an important natural resource.

Possible Scope and Sequence
(based on one-hour class periods)

Day 1	Day 2	Day 3	Day 4
Activating Knowledge Writing Warm-up Expanding Vocabulary	Using Words in Context: *What's the Word?* Breaking Down the Meaning	Dialogue: *The Tip of the Iceberg*	Reading Skill Focus: *Textual Details* Pre-reading: *Anticipation Guide*

Day 5	Day 6	Day 7	Day 8
Chapter Reading: *The World Around Us* Reading Skill Follow-up	Comprehension Questions	Writing about an Ecosystem: *Five-sentence Paragraph*	Culminating Activity: *Fishing for the Future*

Time
Approximately eight one-hour class periods

Essential Questions
- What is biodiversity and why is it important in an ecosystem?
- How are natural resources connected to our everyday lives?
- What happens when a commonly-owned resource is overused?

Integrated Subject Areas
- Science
- English Language Arts

Content Objectives
Students will:
- Identify ways natural resources are connected to humans
- Explain the importance of biodiversity
- Analyze human impacts on natural resources and biodiversity

Language Objectives
Students will:
- Create a caption for a cartoon
- Write about natural resources they use every day
- Define and use new vocabulary words
- Discuss the iceberg model with a classmate
- Read about natural resources, biodiversity, and conservation

- Identify and interpret textual details in a reading
- Write a five-sentence paragraph

Key Concepts
- Ecological health
- Endangered species
- Resource consumption

Vocabulary
- Biodiversity
- Species
- Natural resources
- Ecological footprint

Standards Addressed
- TESOL standards
- NCTE standards
- NCSS standards
- NSES standards

* Please see Appendix A for a list of national standards addressed.

Assessment Option
Use the Chapter 2 assessments of student knowledge and outlook/personal beliefs as pre-tests for the chapter. Follow up with the same assessments at the end of the chapter to determine changes in knowledge and outlook/personal beliefs.

Introduction

1. Read the introduction with students.

2. Ask students what they think nature is. What do they think of when they hear the word *nature*?

3. **Option:** If students have lived in different places, ask them how the natural environment looks different here than where they used to live.

4. Ask students if they think living things from nature, like plants and animals, are important to them. Ask them how plants and animals might be connected to our daily lives.

5. Explain that, in this chapter, they will learn about the environment, how our lives connect to the natural world, and the impact humans have on natural resources.

Chapter

The Natural World

Have you ever thought about how important nature is? The natural world produces everything we need to survive: food, water, shelter, and energy.

Chapter 2 will encourage you to explore how we use Earth's resources and the ability of the environment to supply these resources. In this chapter, you will **speak** with your classmates about important resources that nature provides. You will **listen** to and then practice a dialogue about the root causes of species extinctions. You will also **read** about characteristics of healthy ecosystems and how you can contribute to a healthy environment. Finally, you will **write** a paragraph about a food web in a forest-stream ecosystem.

Mountains, soil, rivers, and sky are all part of the natural world.

A *caption* is an explanation of a picture. Each of the following images is accompanied by a caption.

Directions: Look at each image, and then read the caption below it. On the next page, you will create your own caption.

The snow leopard is an endangered cat species that lives in Asia.

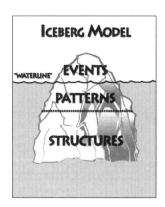

The iceberg model is useful for analyzing problems and solutions.

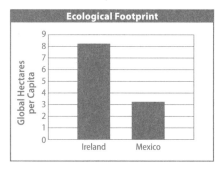

The average ecological footprint in Ireland is more than twice the size of the average ecological footprint in Mexico.

Instructions

1. Introduce the concept of a caption by reviewing the examples on the page.

2. **Option:** Have students identify captions in a magazine.

3. Ask students to consider what books and magazines might be like without captions. Would it be easier or more difficult to comprehend the meaning of photos without captions?

Instructions

1. Have students study the cartoon that is missing a caption. Ask them to write their own caption to explain the cartoon.

2. Students will work with a partner to complete the rest of the activity.

3. Ask for volunteers to share their captions with the class. You may want to write these captions on a board where everyone can read them.

4. Ask students if they found this cartoon to be funny. Why, or why not?

5. Reiterate that students will be learning about the environment and ways that our lives connect to the natural world. Ask students if they can recall the meaning of the word *environment* from Chapter 1.

6. Students may have encountered vocabulary related to this chapter in science courses. Ask students if they know any of the following words or how they are connected: *species, population, community, ecosystem.*

Directions: Study the cartoon image below, and then complete the steps that follow.

CHRIS MADDEN

1. Think of a caption for this cartoon. Write that caption as a sentence.

2. Exchange your caption with a partner.

3. Answer these questions together with your partner:
   • Did you both have similar captions?
   • If not, how were they different?

Directions: List seven things you use every day that come from nature. For an extra challenge, write what you think these things are made from. Use words from the word bank to help you with your list. An example is provided.

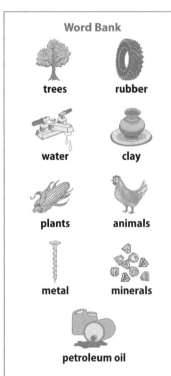

Word Bank

trees

rubber

water

clay

plants

animals

metal

minerals

petroleum oil

Instructions

1. Give students about 5 minutes to complete the writing warm-up. You may want to review the meaning of the words in the word bank with students before they begin.

2. Allow students to share their ideas with the class.

3. **Option:** On a large sheet of paper, record the natural resources that students identify and post the sheet of paper where everyone can see it. They can refer back to this list throughout the chapter.

4. Ask students if some of the natural resources they named are more important to them than others. Why? How would our lives change if these natural resources were to disappear?

Instructions

1. Have students study the four photos independently.

2. Have students share with a partner what they think each word means.

3. Discuss the definitions as a class.

4. **Option:** Copy this page onto an overhead or display it with a document camera. As students are brainstorming ideas for each vocabulary word, list these in the box with the photo.

5. **Option:** Review derivatives and word roots with students.

   • *biodiversity (n) – biology, biography, diverse, divide*

   • *species (n) – special, specific*

   • *ecological footprint (n) – ecology, ecosystem, foot, print*

   • *natural resources (n) – nature, source*

6. **Option:** Discuss the meaning of the following prefixes:

   • *bio – life*

   • *eco – from the Greek word* oikos *which means "house" or the place where something lives*

7. Have students share a sentence that uses the vocabulary word with either a partner or the class.

Directions: Look at the following images and vocabulary words. Guess what you think each word means based on the given images.

A	B

biodiversity	**species**
C	D

ecological footprint	**natural resources**

Using Words in Context: What's the Word?

Directions: Use the words in the box to fill in the blanks. Each word will be used once.

| biodiversity | diverse | species | ecological footprint |
| ecosystems | footprint | nature | natural resources |

Humans belong to the _____ *Homo sapiens.* Although humans are different from other animals, we still need things that come from _____, such as food and water. Humans live in _____ environments, from deserts to tropical rainforests to mountains. People who are surrounded by many different kinds of species live in ecosystems with high _____. Those ecosystems often have many _____, such as water, plants, and wildlife.

A _____ is the mark that your foot makes on the ground when you walk. People with small feet leave smaller footprints than people with big feet. When we use natural resources, we also leave a footprint on the earth. This is called an _____. If you were to take long showers every day, drive everywhere you needed to go, and never recycle anything, your footprint would be larger than someone who takes short showers, rides a bike instead of driving, and recycles. People who have bigger footprints have a bigger impact on Earth's _____, which include both environments and species that live in those environments. Thinking about the way you use natural resources can help to reduce your impact on the planet.

The gray wolf is a species related to dogs.

Instructions

1. Read the passage aloud to students.

2. As students listen, they can determine the appropriate vocabulary to fill in the blanks. Several of the words in the box have similar word roots.

3. Have students review their answers with a partner.

4. Ask a volunteer to read the completed paragraph aloud to the class.

Answers

1. species
2. nature
3. diverse
4. biodiversity
5. natural resources
6. footprint
7. ecological footprint
8. ecosystems

Instructions

1. Explain the directions. After reviewing the definitions, explain to students they will (1) answer the question, (2) create a sentence using the vocabulary word, and (3) choose the one word in the group that does not relate to the vocabulary word.

   • **Differentiated Instruction:** Demonstrate how the activity works by filling in one of the boxes.

   • **Differentiated Instruction:** Enlarge the four boxes to poster size and fill in one of the boxes. Work as a class to fill in answers for each box and write them on the poster. The poster can then remain hanging in the room throughout this unit of study.

2. This activity could be done independently, in pairs or small groups, or as an entire class.

3. **Option:** Have students search for and cut out magazine pictures that relate to each vocabulary word.

4. **Option:** As a homework assignment, have students write a single paragraph using the four vocabulary words.

Directions: Each box below includes one of the four vocabulary words from the previous page, as well as its definition. Below each definition:

1. Answer the question.

2. Write a sentence using the vocabulary word.

3. Choose the one word in the group that does not relate to the vocabulary word.

---

biodiversity

Definition: *numbers of plants, animals, and other living things*

1. What kinds of environments might have high biodiversity?

2. Use *biodiversity* in a sentence.

3. Which word does not belong?

   many   variety   same   species

---

species

Definition: *a group of living things that can produce offspring*

1. What is your favorite species to see at the zoo?

2. Use *species* in a sentence.

3. Which word does not belong?

   human   polar bear   insects   white oak

---

ecological footprint

Definition: *the area of land and water required to support a particular lifestyle*

1. What action could a city take to reduce its ecological footprint?

2. Use *ecological footprint* in a sentence.

3. Which word does not belong?

   lifestyle   land   resources   sunshine

---

natural resource

Definition: *materials we use that come from nature*

1. What is one natural resource you could not live without?

2. Use *natural resource* in a sentence.

3. Which word does not belong?

   plastic   water   trees   wildlife

Answers

biodiversity
1. tropical rainforests, coral reefs
2. A large number of different kinds of animals in a forest indicates high biodiversity.
3. same

species
1. e.g., tiger, giraffe, flamingo
2. The cheetah is a wild cat species.
3. insects

ecological footprint
1. e.g., create a public transportation system, teach people how to conserve water
2. A country that uses more land and water resources will likely have a bigger ecological footprint than one that uses fewer resources.
3. sunshine

natural resource
1. e.g., timber/trees, water
2. Water from rivers and lakes is an important natural resource.
3. plastic

Dialogue: The Tip of the Iceberg

An **iceberg** is a large piece of ice (frozen water) floating in the ocean. Only a small part of an iceberg is visible above water; most of it is below the surface and out of sight.

Directions: Study the iceberg model below, and then read the dialogue on the next page with a partner to learn more about the iceberg model.

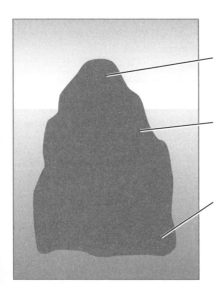

Tip of Iceberg (single event):
The snow leopard, which lives only in central Asia, is in danger of extinction.

Below Water Line (pattern):
The snow leopard isn't the only one in danger. As many as 27,000 species become extinct each year.

At Base (root causes):
Suspected reasons for species extinctions include environmental pollution, loss of habitat, and climate change.

Instructions

1. Give students a few minutes to study the iceberg photo. You may ask students to recall how an iceberg affected the *Titanic*.

2. **Option:** Show students an iceberg simulation. Fill a clear glass half-full with water. Place an ice cube in the glass. The cube will float near the surface but remain submerged.

3. Display the iceberg model with an overhead or a document camera. Ask students to comment on anything they notice about the iceberg model.

   • **Differentiated Instruction:** If students are confused about the model, discuss the significance of each component. If you did the ice cube simulation, ask students to relate the iceberg model to what they observed during the simulation.

4. **Option:** You may want to share an additional example: Iman has to walk four miles each day to fetch water (tip of the iceberg). No one in the region has close access to clean water (pattern). An ongoing conflict with a neighboring country has limited access to a nearby river (root cause).

Instructions

1. Read the dialogue aloud to students so they can hear proper pronunciation.

2. Divide students into pairs. Students will read the dialogue with a partner.

3. Have them read through the dialogue twice, switching roles the second time.

4. **Option:** Challenge students to analyze other problems using the iceberg model. They could use these scenarios or come up with their own:

   • If someone gets sick frequently, work to discover possible root causes of the illness (e.g., lack of sleep, lack of exercise, weak immune system).

   • If a number of teenagers in an area are not going to school, work to discover the root causes of this (e.g., they are working to support their family, they are taking care of a sick family member).

A: Why do you think this picture is called an *iceberg model?*

B: That's a good question. I don't know what an *iceberg* is, but I know what a *model* is. A model is an example to help you understand something.

A: I know what an iceberg is. It's a large piece of ice floating in the ocean. Only a small part of the iceberg can be seen above water. Most of the iceberg is below water where we can't see it.

B: Hmm…that gives me some idea of what an iceberg model is all about. It seems like you could use an iceberg model to think about what lies beneath the tip of things that you can see.

A: I bet you're right! Let's look a little closer at that iceberg model again.

B: Ok. In this example, the tip of the iceberg is the snow leopard in danger of extinction.

A: Right, and I know from science class that when an animal becomes *extinct,* it doesn't exist anymore. Below the tip of the iceberg, we see that many species become extinct each year.

B: Yes, the event at the tip of the iceberg is part of a *pattern*—something that keeps happening. The snow leopard is just one of many species that could become extinct in the future.

A: At the base of the iceberg, we see why species become extinct.

B: It looks like things such as pollution, habitat loss, and climate change can lead to extinctions.

A: I know that *pollution* results when we put harmful substances into the air, water, and soil. I wonder what *habitat loss* and *climate change* mean.

B: I remember learning about those in science class! A habitat is where an animal lives. Habitat loss happens when humans use land to build houses and roads. That can make it difficult for some species to survive. I think that climate change has something to do with weather patterns changing over time. I guess some species can only survive in certain types of weather and not others.

A: It seems that if we want to prevent more species from becoming extinct, we should reduce pollution, habitat loss, and climate change.

B: I agree. If we take action against these things, maybe species like the snow leopard will be able to survive.

A: It seems the iceberg model could be used to solve all sorts of problems, like finding out why people get sick.

B: Interesting idea! If a lot of people in a city have asthma, you could see if this is a pattern in other cities and figure out what is creating this sickness. You're right—the iceberg model would be really helpful for working on big problems.

Reading Skill Focus: Textual Details

Writers often use *textual details* to emphasize important information. The following textual details are all clues for important words or phrases.

- *italics:* Did you know that Mr. Parks is the *oldest* person in my church?
- **bold type:** This is our town's **first-ever** carnival.
- <u>underlining</u>: Mom, you're the <u>best</u>.
- "quotation marks": Brad called my new hairstyle "interesting."
- capitalization: Do NOT make a mark on the paper.
- punctuation (?!): I have never seen a cat with so much fur!

Example: Read the following paragraphs, looking for textual details that emphasize important information.

Until I started studying birds, I was never very excited about nature. In fact, I hated going camping and hiking every summer with my family. If my father said that being outdoors was "good for me" one more time, I thought I would scream! Last summer I took an ornithology class where we learned about all sorts of birds. Who knew there were so many interesting birds to learn about?!

A hummingbird in Peru

Did you know that there are nearly 10,000 bird species in the world?[1] Birds serve a **very** important purpose in their ecosystems. Many small birds, such as wrens, are a source of food for other animals. Other birds, such as eagles, eat small animals like mice and lizards. My favorite birds to watch are hummingbirds. Hummingbirds pollinate flowers so that the flowers can reproduce to create new flowers. These birds are so amazing to watch because they beat their wings up to 100 times PER SECOND!

Unfortunately, 12% of all bird species are in danger of extinction. Can you *imagine* what a loss of 1,200 bird species would be like? I would hate for that to happen. That's why I want to become an ornithologist when I grow up. I want to figure out ways to prevent more birds from becoming extinct.

Reading Skill Focus

Instructions

1. Ask students what they might do when they really want to get their point across to someone in a conversation. How would they emphasize important points?

2. Explain that writers can emphasize important facts or points by using *textual details*.

3. Tell students that the chapter reading contains a number of textual details. After learning more about them in this activity, students will use them to identify important information in the chapter reading.

4. Ask students to guess what textual details are, based on their knowledge of the words *text* and *details*.

5. As a class, review the definition of *textual details* at the top of the page. Then, read through the textual detail examples that follow.

6. Together as a class, read the first paragraph about bird species. Ask students to identify examples of textual details from the paragraph.

- **Differentiated Instruction:** Students can highlight or flag the textual details to help them remember how they have been used. ▶

Reading Skill Focus

Reading Skill Focus: Textual Details

Instructions, *continued*

7. Have students write this information in the table that follows the reading.

8. Continue reading the passage together as a class, or have students complete the passage in pairs.

Directions: Complete the following table with important information and textual details from the reading passage about birds.

Important Information	Textual Detail Clue	How This Textual Detail Emphasizes Important Information
The author hated going camping and hiking before he/she began studying birds.	quotation marks, punctuation	The quotation marks and exclamation point both convey how strongly the author felt.
There are many interesting birds.	punctuation	The exclamation point and question mark emphasize the author's disbelief at the number of birds.

Answers

Important Information	Textual Detail Clue	How This Textual Detail Emphasizes Important Information
Birds serve an important purpose in ecosystems.	bold type	Putting **very** in bold type emphasizes the important role birds play in ecosystems.
Hummingbirds are amazing because they beat their wings so fast.	capitalization	Capitalizing PER SECOND indicates that it is amazing how fast they can beat their wings.
Many bird species are endangered.	italics	Italicizing *imagine* makes it difficult to believe what would happen if that many bird species became extinct.

Pre-reading: Anticipation Guide

Directions: Read each statement below. Indicate whether you agree or disagree with each statement.

Statement	Agree or Disagree?
1. Protecting nature is important because it produces everything we need to survive.	
2. Some natural resources are used so quickly that they are difficult to replace.	
3. The world's biodiversity is disappearing.	
4. All parts of an ecosystem are connected.	
5. Present-day extinctions of plants and animals can happen because of human activity.	
6. I have the ability to help solve environmental problems.	

Instructions

1. If students are not already familiar with the prefixes *pre-* and *anti-*, which both mean "before," review them. Ask students what they think a pre-reading activity or an anticipation guide is.

2. As a class, read through the directions for the Anticipation Guide.

3. Read the first statement and pause to allow students time to consider whether they agree or disagree with the statement. Allow students to ask questions if they do not understand a statement.

4. Continue until all six statements have been read.

Instructions

1. Have students preview the reading by reading the title, subheadings, and images. Ask them what they think this reading will be about.

2. Remind students they will be searching for textual details throughout the reading. Ask a volunteer to recall how textual details can assist with reading comprehension. Ask for another volunteer to tell you how to recognize a textual detail.

3. Start by reading the first section aloud.

4. **Option:** Use the following think aloud to demonstrate how students can comprehend and analyze what they are reading.

"Hmm…**I have** heard that quote! I think I agree with it—nothing is really free. In order to get things in life, you have to work to earn them.

I wonder when the United States Environmental Protection Agency was started.

I think Mr. Ruckelshaus' quote is a textual detail that supports the main idea..

The quotation marks were a clue that this might be an important statement. I think the reading is going to be about how nature gives us free things every day, like trees and water, and how we need to control what we use if we don't want problems in the future." ▶

The World Around Us

Have you ever heard the saying, "There's no such thing as a free lunch?"

Consider this quote from William Ruckelshaus, the first director of the **United States Environmental Protection Agency**: "Nature provides a free lunch, but only if we control our **appetites** ."

Everything You Need

Can you think of anything you use that doesn't come from **nature** ? In some shape or form, nature provides us with everything we use. Earth produces everything that humans need to survive, including food, water, and shelter. We use natural resources every day to build our homes, to create electricity, and to make things like clothing and paper. Even man-made items such as computers or cell phones are made with resources that come from the earth!

How we use Earth's resources affects the present *and future* supply of those resources. To make sure that human needs can be met in the future, it is important to understand how people use natural resources. Many natural resources are replaced quickly after we use them. However, in some cases, we use resources so fast that they cannot be replaced.

One example of a nonrenewable resource, or a resource that is not replaced quickly, is petroleum. Petroleum is used to create many useful things, including gasoline and plastics. Because petroleum is created very slowly over the course of millions of years, it cannot be replaced quickly after we use it. What would happen if we didn't have any more gasoline? How would your life change?

One renewable resource is sunshine. The sun constantly produces solar energy in the form of heat and light. Solar energy can be converted to **electricity** by devices called solar panels. Solar energy is renewable because it is constantly replaced.

United States Environmental Protection Agency (n) – a government organization formed in 1970 to protect human health and the environment

appetite (n) – a strong desire, often for food

nature (n) – the outdoor environment and all the living things in it

electricity (n) – a form of energy used to heat and cool buildings, to power appliances and electronics, and to light buildings

Solar energy from the sun can be changed into electricity through solar panels.

Healthy Ecosystems

The health of the planet depends on the health of its many ecosystems. An ecosystem is a group of organisms (plants, animals, fungi, and bacteria) that works as a unit with its environment. All parts of an ecosystem are interconnected, which means they are all connected to each other in some way. One example of an ecosystem is a tropical rainforest. Tropical rainforests are usually located close to Earth's equator. They are warm, wet forests that contain many species of plants and animals. There are so many species in tropical rainforests that some have not even been discovered yet!

Some of the healthiest ecosystems have high biodiversity. Biodiversity refers to the number and variety of living things in a specific geographic region. An ecosystem with many different types of plants and animals, such as a rainforest, has high biodiversity. When there is high biodiversity in an ecosystem, the ecosystem is more likely to survive a damaging event like a hurricane or the spread of disease. For example, if certain insects spread disease to one tree species in a rainforest, the entire forest will not be destroyed because many other kinds of trees and plants will remain.

On the other hand, ecosystems like farms that grow only one kind of plant can easily have their plants destroyed by a single insect pest. For example, an insect called the boll weevil has destroyed cotton crops throughout the United States and put many cotton farmers out of business. However, growing different kinds of plants protects farmers from losing all of their crops even if one crop is destroyed by insects like the boll weevil.

Rainforests are habitats that have many different kinds of plants and species.

Unfortunately, the world's biodiversity is disappearing. Scientists estimate that there are as many as 10 million species on Earth.[2] Each year as many as 27,000 species of animals, plants, insects, and microorganisms disappear <u>forever</u>![3] There are many more that are endangered, which means they could be extinct soon. Learning about the root causes of extinction may help those species survive.

The number of **extinctions** has sped up a lot during the last 60 million years. Past extinctions have been blamed on natural events, such as volcanic eruptions or major changes in climate.

---
extinction (n) – the point at which no members of a species remain alive

Instructions, *continued*

5. Continue reading the second paragraph, using the think aloud if you choose:

"Well, I don't think my jeans came from nature.

On the other hand, if Earth produces everything that we need, they must come from nature somehow. What an interesting thought!

I see there is an exclamation point at the end of this paragraph. I think that is a textual detail used to point out that even man-made items originally come from nature. I can tell the author really wanted to emphasize this point."

6. Ask volunteers to share thoughts or questions about the reading that you did not share in your think aloud.

7. Have students complete the reading, taking turns reading either in pairs or in small groups.

8. Have them note textual details as they read.

• **Differentiated Instruction:** As students are reading, hand them sticky notes to flag textual details.

A fisherman in India uses a net to catch fish.

Most present-day extinctions, however, are thought to be the result of *human* activities, such as destroying natural habitats, overharvesting natural resources, and pollution.[4]

Marine Ecosystems

Oceans cover 70% of Earth's surface. Marine ecosystems, like oceans, often contain high biodiversity. Many different types of plants and animals, such as coral and fish, live in oceans. Almost *half* of all species in the world live in oceans.[5]

The oceans are so big that it might seem hard to believe that humans could have an impact on their health. The facts, however, tell us that we DO have an impact. Numerous species of fish are suffering because people have harvested too many fish, and species like cod and tuna have been caught faster than they can reproduce.[6] Harvesting species this way is not sustainable and could lead to species extinctions.

Biodiversity is important for healthy ocean ecosystems and marine food webs, but many human activities are causing damage to ocean ecosystems. The good news is that you have the power to improve the health of our oceans.

Water Pollution and Solutions

You may have seen a storm drain on the street with a stencil painted next to it that reads, "Dump No Waste: Drains to Stream". That stencil is there to remind us that much of the rain that falls on the ground ends up in the nearest body of water, like a stream or river. When that rain washes over the ground, it picks up everything that we have left behind: oil from a leaky car, agricultural or lawn chemicals, and animal waste. Eventually, every river—and its pollution—drain into an ocean and enter the marine food web. Toxic chemicals ingested by fish and other marine animals can then enter *our* bodies when we eat them.

Trash that enters the ocean is also considered pollution. Old tires, fishing nets, and plastic shopping bags can all be found floating in the ocean. This pollution can harm marine animals, including whales, fish, seals, turtles, sea birds, and corals. Animals can get tangled in trash or they might get sick when they try to eat it.

You can prevent marine pollution by throwing garbage in the proper place and not putting any waste in storm drains. If you have pets, cleaning up their waste will also help keep our waters clean. You could even label storm drains so that other people will know NOT to put garbage in them.

What's Your Shoe Size?

Different people use different amounts and types of natural resources. For example, while one person may drive to work, another person may take the bus. A person's ecological footprint is the amount of nature (land and water area) that is required to produce the resources he or she uses, and to absorb the waste he or she produces. In other words, an ecological footprint is a measure of a person's impact on the earth.

Think about the resources that you use every day. Land and water resources are required to grow food, to produce energy for electricity, to build roads and houses, and to haul garbage away. These activities all contribute to the size of our ecological footprint.

One way to stop garbage and toxics from entering oceans is to label storm drains.

By reducing big ecological footprints, we can make sure that more natural resources are available for humans and other species as well. Can you think of ways to reduce your ecological footprint? Can you think of ways that countries might be able to reduce their ecological footprint? Shrinking our footprint can actually *improve* our lives and the lives of other people on the planet!

Fish species like tuna are sometimes caught faster than they can reproduce.

Instructions

1. Have students work with a partner to determine what textual details were used throughout the chapter reading.

2. **Additional Resource:** Reinforce the idea of biodiversity by allowing students to explore sections of *Biodiversity,* a 112-page photo essay by Dorothy Hinshaw Patent and William Allen Munoz (New York: Clarion Books, 1996).

3. **Additional Resource:** Have students calculate their personal ecological footprints using an online calculator designed specifically for youth:

   • IslandWood's footprint calculator: www.islandwood.org/kids/impact/footprint.php

   • Zerofootprint KidsCalculator: www.zerofootprintkids.com/kids_home.aspx

Reading Skill Follow-up: Textual Details

Directions: Look for textual details in the article to identify five pieces of important information. Use this information to complete the following table.

Important Information	Textual Detail Clue	How This Textual Detail Emphasizes Important Information

Answers

See answers on page 44H

Comprehension Questions

Directions: Answer the following questions to support your comprehension of the chapter reading.

Understanding what you read

1. What is one way to keep oceans healthy?

2. Identify one of the vocabulary words from Chapter 2. How is the word used in the chapter reading?

Thinking about what you read

3. Explain why high biodiversity is important.

4. Create your own title for the reading. Explain how your title reflects the main idea of the reading.

Questioning what you read

5. How would you describe the author's perspective on the environment?

6. The article suggests that shrinking your ecological footprint can improve your life and the lives of others. Describe how reducing your impact on Earth's resources could **benefit** you or other people.

Making connections to what you read

7. Explain whether you think your friends and family have small or large ecological footprints. What evidence supports your explanation?

8. Review and reevaluate your original answers to the Anticipation Guide. After reading the chapter reading, would you change any of your answers? Why?

Further discussion questions

9. How might the number of people on Earth affect our combined ecological footprint?

10. How does our use of natural resources affect global sustainability?

Comprehension Questions

Instructions

1. Before students begin answering the comprehension questions, share with them the academic language that appears in many of the questions (see Appendix B).

2. Explain that the questions are divided into five sections according to the ways they support reading comprehension. (See Appendix B for a detailed explanation of each section.)

3. **Differentiated Instruction:** Differentiate the questions students must answer based on their reading levels. Support comprehension by working with students who may need more guided instruction.

Answers

1. Keep trash and chemicals out of storm drains. Clean up pet waste. Label storm drains.

2. Example: The word biodiversity was used in the chapter to describe ecosystems with many different species.

3. An ecosystem with high biodiversity is more likely to survive a damaging event.

4. Example: "Keeping our Environment Healthy"

5. The author thinks it is important that ecosystems have high biodiversity and that there are ways we can keep ecosystems healthy.

6. Example: Riding your bike or walking short distances could have health benefits.

7. Example: My friends and I have small ecological footprints because we take the bus to school.

8. Example: I would change my answer to the second statement. Resources can run out if we don't use them carefully.

9. More people will produce a larger ecological footprint.

10. If we use resources too quickly, some of those resources may not be available for future generations.

Instructions

1. Ask students if they have studied food webs in their science classes. If so, they will probably recognize the diagram as a food web.

2. Explain that, when they write about scientific topics, they must include evidence to support any statement they make.

3. Read through the directions at the top of the page.

Writing about an Ecosystem: Five-sentence Paragraph

Directions: Look at the following diagram. It shows a food web of organisms found in a forest-stream ecosystem. Write a paragraph that answers this question:

What would happen to other species in the ecosystem if the snake was removed?

Find at least three pieces of evidence from the food web to support your answer. Incorporate two or more chapter vocabulary words into your paragraph.

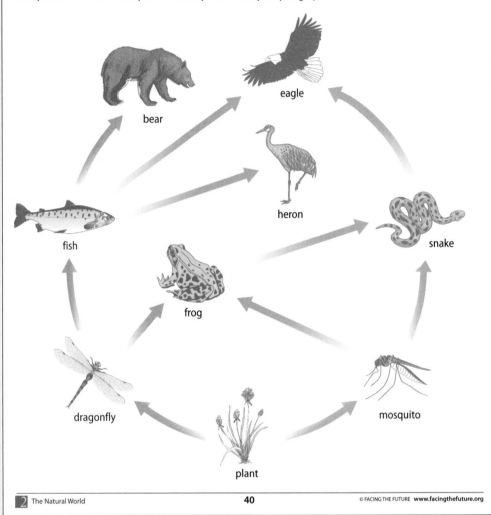

A five-sentence paragraph is exactly what it sounds like: a single paragraph of five sentences. It has the following structure:

Sentence #1: Topic Sentence

The topic sentence is the first sentence of a paragraph. It tells the **main idea** of the paragraph.

Sentences #2, 3, 4: Supporting Sentences

You need at least three **supporting** sentences. Each one provides details and examples that support the main idea of the paragraph.

Sentence #5: Closing Sentence

The closing sentence is the last sentence of a paragraph. It **summarizes** the main idea of the paragraph using different words than the topic sentence.

Example: The following paragraph is an example of a five-sentence paragraph.

The largest component of the world's ecological footprint is energy. Energy is required for everything we do! We use energy to make electricity so we can cook food, heat our homes, and watch television. We also use energy to travel from place to place in cars, buses, trains, and planes. By learning about the resources required for different types of energy use and the kinds of wastes that are produced, we can work to reduce our ecological footprint.

Riding bikes instead of driving is one way to decrease a person's ecological footprint.

Instructions

1. If necessary, review the paragraph structure and sample paragraph.

Instructions

1. As a class, review the basic steps students will follow to write their paragraph.

   • **Differentiated Instruction:** Work with students who may need more help incorporating transition words into their writing.

2. **Grammar Suggestion:** Guide students in incorporating punctuation that emphasizes important details. Differentiating between declarative, exclamatory, interrogative, and imperative sentences will help them to write a paragraph that uses textual details effectively.

3. After students construct their draft paragraphs, they will exchange paragraphs with a classmate, edit the paragraphs using the Edit Checklist, and then revise their own.

4. Share the Chapter 2 writing rubric with students. You may want to add relevant spelling and grammar components to the rubric.

Step 1: Think through your ideas using the Writing Brainstorm Page (see next page).

Step 2: Use the Writing Organizer to write a five-sentence paragraph.

Step 3: Edit your paragraph using the Edit Checklist.

Step 4: Exchange paragraphs with a classmate. Read and edit your classmate's paragraph. Ask him or her to review your paragraph.

Step 5: Revise and finalize your paragraph.

Transition Words

You can make your writing more sophisticated by including transition words that connect one idea in a paragraph to the next. You can try using one or two of the following transition words to strengthen your paragraph:

For example: ***For example,*** the golden toad is now extinct.

Additionally: ***Additionally,*** the snow leopard is an endangered species.

For instance: ***For instance,*** cars emit pollution into the air.

 ### Edit Checklist

	Author Check	Peer Editor Check
Did you use two vocabulary words from the chapter?		
Did you include a topic sentence, three details, and a closing sentence?		
Did you use transition words correctly?		

Chapter 2 Writing Rubric

Category	3	2	1
Answers question ("What would happen to other species...?")	Student answers the question and uses evidence from the diagram to support answer.	Student attempts to answer question, but answer does not make sense.	The paragraph does not attempt to answer the question.
Organization (structures paragraph properly)	Paragraph includes topic, supporting, and closing sentences.	Paragraph includes some of the correct structural elements.	Paragraph does not include necessary elements.
Vocabulary	Student uses two chapter vocabulary words correctly.	Student uses one chapter vocabulary word correctly.	Student uses no chapter vocabulary words.

Total = _____ / 9

1. What do you think the arrows in the food web diagram represent?

2. How is the plant connected to the bear?

3. What species depend *directly* on the snake? (Hint: Arrows connect the snake directly to these species.)

4. Do any species depend *indirectly* on the snake? (Hint: These species are NOT directly connected to the snake by arrows.)

5. Do any of the four chapter vocabulary words relate to the diagram? How?

• biodiversity:

• species:

• natural resources:

• ecological footprint:

Instructions

1. This page helps students to collect their thoughts about the food web prior to writing.

• **Differentiated Instruction:** For beginner students who may need more guidance, gather them into a small group and assist them with brainstorming. You can even write the paragraph with them as a shared writing exercise.

Instructions

1. This organizer will help to ensure that students are using the correct paragraph structure to draft their five-sentence paragraph.

2. Once they have written their five sentences, they should work through the remaining writing steps (edit and check, peer review, and revision).

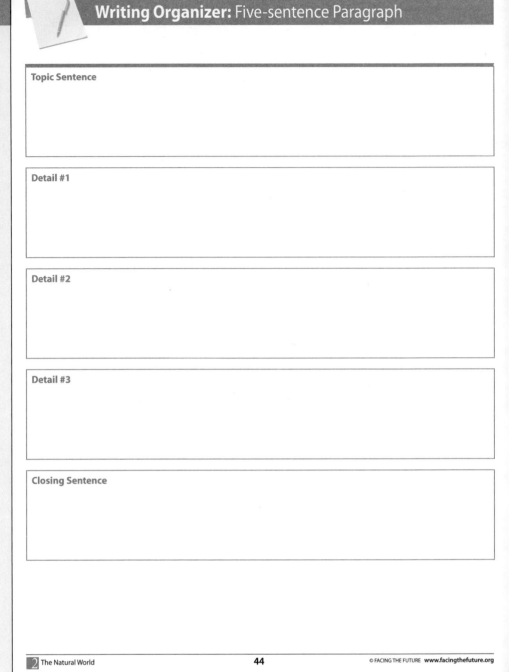

Writing Organizer: Five-sentence Paragraph

Topic Sentence

Detail #1

Detail #2

Detail #3

Closing Sentence

The Natural World   44   © FACING THE FUTURE   www.facingthefuture.org

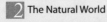

Culminating Activity: Fishing for the Future (45 minutes)

(Adapted with permission from "Fishing with Jim" by Jim Hartmann and Ben Smith)

Overview

Through a fishing simulation, students model several consecutive seasons of a fishery and explore how technology, population growth, and sustainable practices impact fish catch and fisheries management.

Materials/Preparation

- Plain, small candy-covered chocolate candies, one 16-ounce bag for up to 20 students (two 16-ounce bags for more than 20 students)
- Small plastic bowls, one per 4-5 students
- Put about twenty candies in one bowl per 4-5 students
- Spoons, one per 4-5 students
- Straws, one per student
- Watch, for timing activity
- Handout: *Fishing Log*, one per student

Steps

1. Explain the game rules:
   a. Each student will be a fisher whose livelihood depends on catching fish.
   b. The candies represent ocean fish, such as salmon or tuna.
   c. Each fisher must catch at least two fish in each round to survive (i.e., get enough fish to either eat or sell).
   d. When the fishing begins, students must hold their hands behind their backs and use the fishing rod (straw) to suck fish (candies) from the ocean (bowl) and deposit them into their boat (on the table in front of them).
   e. The fish remaining in the ocean after each fishing season represent the breeding population. Thus, one new fish (candy) will be added for every fish left in the ocean (bowl).

2. Divide the class into groups of four or five students. Have each group choose a name for their ocean (such as Mediterranean, Arctic, or Pacific).

3. Give each group one serving bowl, and give each student one straw and one copy of the handout *Fishing Log*.

4. Put one bowl with the candies next to each group.

5. Say, "Start fishing," and give the students about 20 seconds for the first season of fishing. They can use their straws but not their hands in this round.

6. Have each fisher count his or her catch and record the data in the Fishing Log.

7. Fishers who did not catch the two fish minimum must sit out the following round.

8. Add one new fish (candy from the bag) for every fish left in the ocean (bowl).

9. Allow fishers to use their hands on the straws during the second round to represent new technology (such as improved nets or fishing lines).

10. Say, "Start fishing," and allow another 20 seconds for the second season of fishing.

11. Have each fisher count his or her catch and record the data in the Fishing Log.

12. After the second fishing season, give one fisher from each group a spoon representing more new fishing technology, such as trawl nets, sonar equipment, etc.

13. Continue the game for round three.

continued ▶

14. Ask the students what happened when a group of fishers in one ocean runs out of fish. How are the fishers going to survive now? (One option is to move to another ocean.) Allow students to "invade" other ocean groups when their ocean is depleted, but do not tell them that they can do this beforehand. Fishers may either go as a group to another ocean, or they may disperse to other oceans by themselves.

15. Repeat fishing, recording, and replenishing fish stocks until either sustainable fishing levels are achieved (whereby oceans continue to have large numbers of fish) or until most groups have depleted the fish in their oceans.

16. Option: Repeat the activity after the class has experienced overfishing and resource depletion to see if they can harvest in a more sustainable manner. Tell students that their goal is to fish in such a way that the fish populations either remain at their current size or increase in size.

17. Discuss the following questions:

- How does this activity relate to conserving natural resources?

- What are other natural resources that might also be overharvested?

- How can technology be beneficial? How can it be harmful?

Fishing for the Future: Fishing Log

Ocean Name: _____

Fishers: _____

Directions: Record your group's catch and the amount of fish left in your ocean after each season.

Season	Catch	Fish Left in Ocean
1		
2		

Briefly describe what is happening to the number of fish in your ocean:

_____

_____

Season	Catch	Fish Left in Ocean
3		
4		

Briefly describe what is happening to the number of fish in your ocean:

_____

_____

How could you catch enough fish to survive each season and make sure that sufficient numbers of fish are left in the ocean?

_____

_____

_____

_____

Action Project

Have students research which kinds of fish are harvested in a sustainable manner and create an advertising campaign in their school to promote the consumption of sustainable fish and avoid the consumption of threatened fish. This might include researching the kind of fish served in your school cafeteria and then recommending a sustainable seafood purchasing program to cafeteria staff and the school principal. For recommendations about which seafood to buy or avoid, check out the Monterey Bay Aquarium's website, *Seafood Watch:* www.montereybayaquarium.org/cr/seafoodwatch.asp.

Additional Resources on Nature and Biodiversity

The Lorax, by Dr. Seuss

The Lorax is a classic rhyming tale of natural resource depletion. Technological advances and increasing consumption lead to the extinction of the Truffula Trees.

Earth Day Network
http://earthday.net/footprint2/index.html

The Earth Day Network Footprint Calculator lets students calculate their impact on Earth's resources.

Biodiversity and Conservation: The Web of Life
www.fieldmuseum.org/biodiversity

The Field Museum provides informative short readings on the importance of biodiversity, different kinds of diversity, the current status of the world's biodiversity, and ideas for protecting biodiversity.

IUCN Red List of Threatened Species
www.iucnredlist.org

The IUCN Red List website includes photos of threatened species from across the globe, paired with informative captions.

Discovery Channel
http://dsc.discovery.com

Students can watch video clips and view photographs from the series *Planet Earth.* Animal species are grouped by habitat.

Chapter 2 Student Assessment, page 1
Knowledge about Biodiversity and Natural Resources

Vocabulary

Directions: Read the sentence and circle the correct definition of the bold-faced word.

1. Healthy ecosystems often have high **biodiversity**.
   a. numbers of plants, animals, and other living things
   b. amounts of toxic chemicals
   c. cliffs made of rock
   d. types of trees

2. Researchers recently found a new fish **species** that is silver with a white stripe.
   a. a group of living things that live in one country
   b. a group of living things that can move very quickly
   c. a group of living things that can produce offspring
   d. a group of living things that need carbon dioxide to survive

3. Although the population of North America is fairly small, its **ecological footprint** is quite large.
   a. use of trees and water
   b. the area of land and water required to support a certain lifestyle
   c. size of land area needed to grow food
   d. ability to produce manufactured products

4. Trees are a **natural resource** used to make tables and beds.
   a. materials we use that come from nature
   b. tool to create furniture
   c. fuel for making a fire
   d. a source of energy

Chapter 2 Student Assessment, page 2

Content

Directions: Read the following sentences and choose the correct answer.

5. Tropical rainforests have high biodiversity. This means they _____.
   a. are visited by many tourists
   b. get a lot of rainfall
   c. have many different species
   d. are unusually hot

6. Trash and chemicals that are washed into a storm drain are considered _____.
   a. pollution
   b. nutrients
   c. species
   d. sustainability

7. Kirsten's family used to leave their computer and television on almost all the time. Recently, they have decided to turn them off when they are not using them in order to _____ the family's ecological footprint.
   a. increase
   b. maintain
   c. expand
   d. reduce

Reading Comprehension

Directions: Read the paragraph below. For numbers 8 and 9, circle the correct answer.

Did you know that more than half of all Americans drink coffee every day? During the late 1980s, forests in Latin America and other countries were cut down and replaced with coffee trees in order to meet the high demand. Destroying the forests had a **huge** effect on species living in the forest. Suddenly, animals depending on the shade of forest trees could not survive. Additionally, the chemicals used to grow more coffee beans increased pollution in nearby rivers. Because people realized how harmful this type of coffee farming was, they decided to make a change. Now people can buy "shade-grown" coffee. Forests do not have to be destroyed for shade-grown coffee, which helps encourage biodiversity.

8. Why does the author bold the word *huge*?
   a. To emphasize how many coffee trees were planted
   b. To emphasize how cutting down forests can reduce biodiversity
   c. To emphasize how much people in the United States love coffee
   d. To emphasize how destroying forests increases the amount of species

9. What is the main idea of this paragraph?
   a. People in the United States don't like drinking coffee.
   b. Buying shade-grown coffee reduces biodiversity.
   c. Buying shade-grown coffee increases biodiversity.
   d. Coffee comes mostly from Latin America.

Name _____ Class _____ Date _____

Chapter 2 Student Assessment, page 3
Outlook and Personal Beliefs

The answers to the following questions are based on your personal beliefs and experience; there are no right or wrong answers.

Directions for 1-3: Place a check mark (√) in the box next to each statement that is true for you.

1. I know how to keep bodies of water, like rivers and oceans, clean.
   - ☐ True
   - ☐ False

2. I take part in the following activities to protect the river and ocean health: (Check all that apply.)
   - ☐ I never throw garbage or chemicals (like paint and motor oil) into storm drains.
   - ☐ I only eat sustainably harvested fish and seafood.
   - ☐ I pick up my pet's waste and throw it in the garbage.

3. I think all species in an ecosystem are important.
   - ☐ True
   - ☐ False
   - ☐ Not Sure

4. **Complete the following sentence:**
   One way I can personally reduce my ecological footprint is by...

   _____

   _____

   _____

   _____

Directions for 5 and 6: Fill in the ovals below based on your level of agreement. 1 means you strongly agree, 7 means you strongly disagree.

1 = yes, definitely!   7 = no way!

◄——————————————►

5. I believe my daily actions have an impact on people and places in other parts of the world.

   1 **2** **3** **4** **5** **6** **7**
   ◯   ◯   ◯   ◯   ◯   ◯   ◯

6. I believe I have the ability to help solve problems related to the environment and nature.

   1 **2** **3** **4** **5** **6** **7**
   ◯   ◯   ◯   ◯   ◯   ◯   ◯

Reading Skill Follow-up, page 38

Important Information	Textual Detail	How Does This Textual Detail Emphasize Important Information?
1. Nature provides a free lunch, but only if we control our appetites.	Quote	The author uses this quote to let the reader know what the rest of the reading will be about.
2. Earth produces everything that humans need to survive.	Punctuation - !	An exclamation point emphasizes that even man-made materials require natural resources.
3. How we use Earth's resources affects the future supply of those resources.	Italics - *and future*	"And future" is in italics to emphasize that our actions have impacts on the future.
4. Petroleum is created so slowly that it cannot be replaced.	Underlining - very	"Very" is underlined to indicate the degree of slowness in replacing petroleum.
5. Tropical rainforests are very diverse.	Punctuation - !	An exclamation point emphasizes the large number of species in tropical rainforests.
6. Each year as many as 27,000 species of animals, plants, insects, and microorganisms disappear forever.	Punctuation - ! Underlining - forever	The author underlines "forever" and uses an exclamation point to illustrate the permanent impact of species extinctions.
7. Most present-day extinctions are thought to be the result of human activities.	Italics - *human*	The author wants to emphasize that humans, not natural events, cause most extinctions.
8. Almost half of all species live in oceans.	Italics - *half*	Italicizing "half" indicates that this is a large percentage.
9. Humans have an impact on oceans.	Capitalization - DO	Capitalizing "do" suggests that we need to be aware of our impacts.
10. We can ingest toxic chemicals when we eat marine animals.	Italics - *our*	Italicizing "our" emphasizes that we are also affected by toxins in marine animals.
11. Labeling storm drains lets people know not to put garbage in them.	Capitalization - NOT	Capitalizing NOT indicates how important it is to keep garbage out of storm drains.
12. Shrinking our footprints can actually improve our lives and the lives of other people on the planet.	Italics and Punctuation - !	The author wants to point out that your individual actions can benefit you AND others.

**Chapter 2 Student Assessment,
pp. 44E, 44F**

1. a	**6.** a
2. c	**7.** d
3. b	**8.** b
4. a	**9.** c
5. c	

Environmental Issues and Solutions

Brainstorm and writing activities

introduce students to thinking about environmental resources and possible problems. After learning vocabulary related to current environmental issues, students engage in a dialogue about freshwater scarcity. Students learn to identify cause and effect statements, and then use this skill during a jigsaw activity in which they read about three environmental issues: climate change, deforestation, and freshwater scarcity. Students are asked to consider their perspectives on climate change solutions by writing a persuasive essay. The chapter culminates with a hands-on collaborative activity in which they consider the impacts of everyday items on the environment.

Possible Scope and Sequence
(based on one-hour class periods)

Day 1	Day 2	Day 3	Day 4	Day 5
Activating Knowledge Writing Warm-up Expanding Vocabulary	Using Words in Context: *Concept Map* Breaking Down the Meaning	Dialogue: *How Do You Explain It?* Reading Skill Focus: *Cause and Effect*	Pre-reading: *True/False Quiz* Chapter Reading: *Environmental Issues and Solutions* Reading Skill Follow-up: *Cause and Effect*	Comprehension Questions

Day 6	Day 7	Day 8	Day 9
Writing about Current Environmental Issues: *Persuasive Essay*	Writing about Current Environmental Issues *(cont'd)*	Writing about Current Environmental Issues *(cont'd)*	Culminating Activity: *Watch Where You Step*

Time
Eight to ten one-hour class periods

Essential Questions
- What are some major global environmental issues?
- How are environmental issues and solutions interconnected?
- How can people take part in sustainable solutions to environmental issues?

Integrated Subject Areas
- Science
- Social Studies
- English Language Arts

Content Objectives
Students will:
- Identify current environmental issues: climate change, deforestation, and freshwater scarcity
- Determine the cause of environmental issues
- Consider solutions to environmental issues

Language Objectives
Students will:
- Discuss similarities and differences between two photographs
- Write an opinion on a statement about the environment
- Define and use new vocabulary words

- Discuss freshwater scarcity through a dialogue with a classmate
- Read about current environmental issues and solutions
- Use cause and effect to determine the meaning of a reading
- Write a persuasive essay

Key Concepts
- Environmental issues
- Personal solutions

Vocabulary
- Pollution
- Climate change
- Deforestation
- Freshwater scarcity

Standards Addressed
- TESOL standards
- NCTE standards
- NCSS standards
- NSES standards

* Please see Appendix A for a list of national standards addressed.

Assessment Option
Use the Chapter 3 assessments of student knowledge and outlook/personal beliefs as pre-tests for the chapter. Follow up with the same assessments at the end of the chapter to determine changes in knowledge and outlook/personal beliefs.

3 Environmental Issues and Solutions

What are the major environmental issues in the world, and what can we do to find solutions?

Chapter 3 will explore current challenges to the environment. In this chapter, you will **speak** to your classmates about the use of natural resources, such as water and forests. You will **listen** to and then practice a dialogue about the limited amount of water on Earth. You will **read** about current environmental problems, including climate change, deforestation, and freshwater scarcity. Throughout this chapter, you will learn about ways you can take action. At the end of the chapter, you will **write** a persuasive essay about whether or not people should take immediate action to limit climate change.

Melting glaciers like Exit Glacier in Alaska are a sign of environmental changes.

Instructions

1. Read the introduction with students.
2. Ask students the following questions:
   - *When you go outside, what do you notice most about the environment?* (If students do not remember the term *environment* from Chapter 1, you can share the following definition: *everything in nature that surrounds us and supports our ability to live and grow.*)
   - *What are environmental issues affecting the world today?*
3. **Option:** As students share their answers about environmental issues, write them on a board where everyone can see.
4. Ask students if any of the issues are connected to each other. If so, in what way are they connected? (For example, pollution might be related to species extinction.)
5. Explain that, in Chapter 3, they will learn more about different environmental issues and solutions to these issues.

Instructions

1. Review the two photographs of trees and the corresponding questions and answers.

2. Encourage students to share additional answers to the two questions.

Example: Look at the two photos and the answers to the questions below.

- How might the two photos be connected?
- What is different about the two photos?

- How might the two photos be connected?

  Both photos show trees.
  The photo on the left shows trees in a forest.
  The photo on the right shows trees that have been cut for lumber.
  Forests are an important resource for providing lumber for paper and furniture.

- What is different about the two photos?

  In the photo on the left, trees are alive and growing.
  In the photo on the right, trees have been cut down and are no longer alive.

Directions: Look at the two photos below. After you have looked at the photos on your own, brainstorm answers to the following questions with a partner.

- How might the two photos be connected?
- What is different about the two photos?

Phrases you could use to talk with your partner:

- Both photos show…
- The photo on the left shows…
- The photo on the right shows…
- I wonder why…
- I wonder how…

Instructions

1. Have students review the photos.

2. After they have had a moment to consider how these photos are connected and how they are different, ask them to work with a partner sitting next to them. Give students five minutes to discuss their reactions to the photos.

3. Ask each pair to share with the class how they think the two photos are connected. (One similarity: Both photos show people using water. One difference: On the left, the water is coming out of a faucet. On the right, the water is coming out of a well.)

Instructions

1. Read the italicized statement aloud to students. Make sure that all students understand what this statement means. You may want to go over the idea of *taking care of the environment*. What sorts of actions could be considered *taking care of the environment?*

2. Review the directions for the writing warm-up. In this case, there is one guideline (providing three reasons for agreeing or disagreeing).

3. Give students 5 minutes to respond to the writing prompt.

4. **Option:** Have students engage in a sides debate using the writing prompt. Everyone who agrees with the statement should stand on one side of the room; everyone who disagrees should stand on the opposite side of the room. Allow all students to voice reasons why they agree or disagree. If anyone changes their mind during the course of the discussion, that student may switch sides.

5. If not all students agree with the statement, return to the question at the end of the chapter to evaluate whether students have changed their perspective.

Do you agree with the following statement?

> *There are more important things to worry about than taking care of the environment.*

Directions: Provide a written response explaining whether you agree or disagree with the statement. Give three or more reasons why you agree or do not agree with the statement.

Tip: You can incorporate words from the question into your answer.

I agree with the statement because…

I do not agree with the statement because…

Directions: Look at the following images and vocabulary words. Guess what you think each word means based on the given image.

A	B
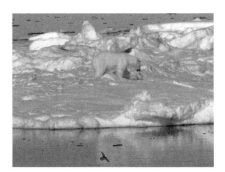	
climate change	freshwater scarcity

C	D

deforestation	pollution

Instructions

1. Have students study the four photos independently.

2. Have students share what they think each word means with a partner.

3. Discuss students' definitions and interpretations of the photos.

   • **Differentiated Instruction:** Copy this page onto an overhead or display it with a document camera. As students are brainstorming ideas for each vocabulary word, list these next to the photo in each box.

4. **Option:** Review the following derivatives:

   • *deforestation (n) – deforest*
   • *pollution (n) – polluting, pollutant*

5. **Option:** Review the following roots, prefixes, and suffixes:

   Deforestation is a good word to break apart: de-forest-ation

   • *de:* prefix meaning "opposite" (other examples: dehydrate, deconstruct)
   • *forest:* root word meaning "a large area of trees"
   • *ation:* suffix indicating a noun (other examples: magnification, colonization)

   Freshwater Scarcity

   • *freshwater:* a compound word (fresh + water) relating to water that is not salty; water people can drink
   • *scarce:* word meaning "insufficient to meet the demand or need"

Instructions

1. Read the concept map aloud.

2. Have students work either individually or in small groups on completing the concept map. The map outlines some of the causes and effects of climate change.

3. **Option:** Have students research specific greenhouse gases and the greenhouse effect. A potential starting place is EPA's website for kids: http://epa.gov/climatechange/kids.

4. **Additional Resource:** *Climate Change: Connections and Solutions* is a Facing the Future unit available for free on our website: www. facingthefuture.org. Lessons in this unit cover greenhouse gases and other relevant topics.

Using Words in Context: Concept Map

Directions: Complete the concept map using the four chapter vocabulary words. Each vocabulary word will be used once.

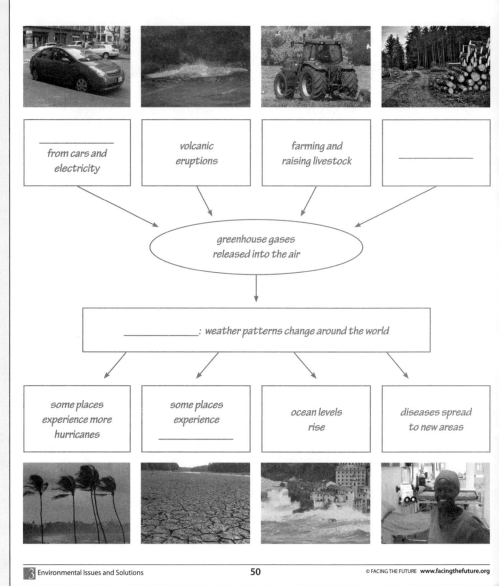

Answers

1. pollution
2. deforestation
3. climate change
4. freshwater scarcity

Directions: Each box below includes one of the four vocabulary words from the previous page, as well as its definition. Below each definition:

1. Answer the question.

2. Write a sentence using the vocabulary word.

3. Choose the one word in the group that does not relate to the vocabulary word.

climate change

Definition: *a change in long-term weather patterns*

1. What are possible signs that climate change is occurring?

2. Use *climate change* in a sentence.

3. Which word does not belong?

temperature	weather
long-term	sudden

freshwater scarcity

Definition: *the lack of safe and drinkable water around the world*

1. What are possible reasons that water is scarce in some parts of the world?

2. Use *freshwater scarcity* in a sentence.

3. Which word does not belong?

oceans   rivers   electricity   glaciers

deforestation

Definition: *removal of trees from an area*

1. How would an area look after deforestation has occurred?

2. Use *deforestation* in a sentence.

3. Which word does not belong?

growing   cutting   burning   harvesting

pollution

Definition: *substances that contaminate air, water, and soil*

1. What might be a source of water pollution?

2. Use *pollution* in a sentence.

3. Which word does not belong?

trash   waste   tree   smog

Instructions

1. Explain the directions. After reviewing the definitions, explain to students they will (1) answer the question, (2) create a sentence using the vocabulary word, and (3) choose the one word in the group that does not relate to the vocabulary word.

- **Differentiated Instruction:** Demonstrate how the activity works by filling in one of the boxes.

- **Differentiated Instruction:** Enlarge the four boxes to poster size and fill in one of the boxes. Work with students to fill in additional answers in each box. The poster can then remain hanging in the room throughout this unit of study.

2. This activity could be done independently, in pairs or small groups, or as an entire class.

3. Option: Have students search for and cut out magazine pictures that relate to each vocabulary word.

4. Option: As a homework assignment, have students write a single paragraph using the four vocabulary words.

Answers

climate change

1. warmer temperatures, more rainfall, less snow
2. Climate change has made Europe warmer now than it was 100 years ago.
3. sudden

freshwater scarcity

1. Droughts make it difficult for people to find drinking water.
2. If we can think of solutions to freshwater scarcity, then more people would have access to safe drinking water.

3. electricity

deforestation

1. All the trees would be gone and grass and soil would be exposed.
2. Deforestation sometimes occurs when land is cleared for agriculture.
3. growing

pollution

1. pet waste, motor oil, trash, pesticides
2. Exhaust from cars is a source of air pollution.
3. tree

Instructions

1. Ask students to study the graph on their own for a minute.

2. If students have any questions or are confused about the graph, urge them to ask questions.

3. Read the dialogue aloud so students can hear proper pronunciation.

   • **Differentiated Instruction:** If students are not familiar with reading numerals for different purposes (i.e., the year 1900 vs. a volume of 1,900 liters), pronounce the proper way to say each of the numbers.

2. Divide the class into pairs, and assign one person in each pair to role A and the other person to role B.

3. Instruct each student to read through the dialogue by himself/herself, and, where underlined choices are given, circle the correct answers for his/her role.

4. Have student pairs read the dialogue (with their circled answers) aloud together.

5. Close by asking a volunteer to summarize the main idea of the graph and the dialogue.

6. **Option:** Ask students to brainstorm the different ways they use water.

   • **Differentiated Instruction:** For advanced students, you may want to challenge them to think of hidden uses of water. For example, water is used in the manufacture of clothing, from irrigating cotton crops to dyeing fabric.

Dialogue: How Do You Explain It?

Directions: Study the graph below. What does it show? Before you read the dialogue below aloud with your partner, read through it on your own. Each time you see two choices underlined, choose the correct answer. After both you and your partner have done this, read the dialogue aloud together.

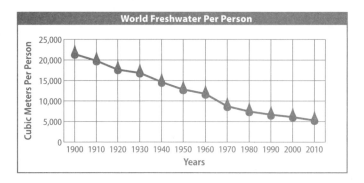

A: Do you know what the graph shows?
B: The graph shows the amount of water / raindrops per person available in the world.

A: It looks like the amount of water per person has increased / decreased over time.
B: How can you tell this from the graph?

A: Well, in 1900, there were more than 20,000 / 25,000 cubic meters of water available per person. Do you see what happens in 2000?
B: Yes, by 2000 only about 5,000 / 10,000 cubic meters of water were available per person.

A: Do you think that means there is less water in the world now than in 1900?
B: No, the total type / amount of water in the world is always the same.

A: So why do you think the amount per people / person has decreased?
B: The amount per person may have decreased because the number of people has increased.

A: Oh, I see. If more people / person are using the same amount of water, there will be less water for each person.
B: That's right. It is like when you and three friends plan to share a pizza. If another pizza / friend joins you, you will have to divide the pizza among more people. Now, you have five people who want to eat the pizza.

A: I see what you mean. If there were fewer / more people in the world, more water would be available for each person.
B: That's true, but there would also be more water available for other people if each person used less / more water.

Answers

B: water
A: decreased
A: 20,000
B: 5,000
B: amount
A: person
A: people
B: friend
A: fewer
B: less

Reading Skill Focus: Cause and Effect

Cause and effect means that one thing leads to another. A cause and effect relationship fits into the formula "**If…then…**."

For example: If my mother finds out I lost her favorite pair of earrings, **then** she will be angry.

Certain words can signal the presence of a cause and effect relationship:

as a result	therefore	consequently	because
for this reason	hence	due to the fact	so

Example: Take a look at the paragraph below. As you read, look for cause and effect relationships. Also look to see how signal words can be used to identify a cause and effect relationship.

Freshwater is a necessary resource around the world. We all need water for drinking, cooking, and bathing, as well as to grow food. Yet, many people have difficulty getting enough water. Because freshwater is scarce in many places, some people must walk miles to get drinking water. Often the water that is available is not clean. For this reason, people might become sick. Due to the fact that so little water is available in some places, some experts predict that future wars will be fought over access to freshwater.

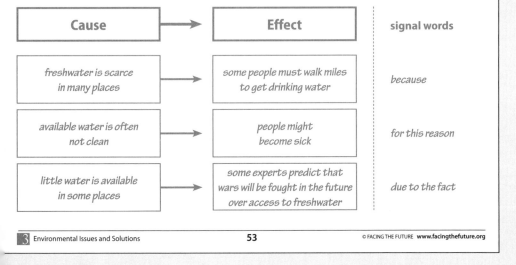

Instructions

1. Ask students: *If you overslept for school, what would happen?*
2. Explain that this is a cause and effect scenario. Oversleeping is the *cause* and being late to school is the *effect*.
3. Ask students to define the words *cause* and *effect*.
4. Read through the example together as a class.

Instructions

1. Have students read the passage either independently or in pairs.
2. The cause and effect graphic organizer will help to guide students.

Directions: Read the following passage. Use the graphic organizer to record cause and effect relationships.

The world's oceans, rivers, streams, and lakes are all aquatic ecosystems, or ecosystems located in water. Pollution is a major environmental problem that can damage these ecosystems. Whereas people may not put waste directly into our aquatic ecosystems, they do put it in storm drains. Have you ever noticed how many streets have storm drains to carry water off the street? Due to the fact that rain washes things from the ground into storm drains, motor oil that drips from cars onto the street can end up in rivers and lakes. Rain can also carry waste from dogs and other animals into storm drains. Because water flowing into storm drains and sewers usually empties into the nearest body of water, it is important to keep toxic, poisonous chemicals and garbage out of storm drains. If people dispose of motor oil, garbage, and pet waste properly, then we can keep aquatic ecosystems healthy.

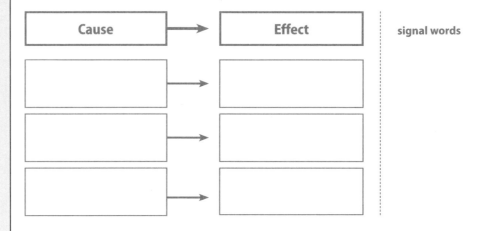

Answers

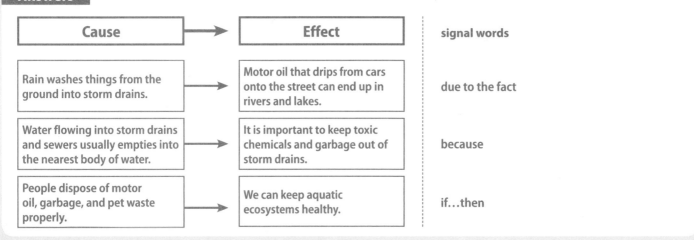

Cause	Effect	signal words
Rain washes things from the ground into storm drains.	Motor oil that drips from cars onto the street can end up in rivers and lakes.	due to the fact
Water flowing into storm drains and sewers usually empties into the nearest body of water.	It is important to keep toxic chemicals and garbage out of storm drains.	because
People dispose of motor oil, garbage, and pet waste properly.	We can keep aquatic ecosystems healthy.	if…then

Pre-reading: True/False Quiz

Directions: Take the following quiz about current environmental issues. Indicate whether each statement is *true* or *false*.

1. _____ Certain energy sources, like coal, release gases that contribute to making the earth warmer.

2. _____ One solution to climate change is to use more energy.

3. _____ Removing all the trees in an area is good for animals that live in forests.

4. _____ A common cause of deforestation is clearing land for growing food.

5. _____ It takes less water to raise a pound of beef than to grow a pound of corn.

6. _____ Most of the water in the world is salt water, found in oceans.

7. _____ The issues of climate change, deforestation, and freshwater scarcity are connected.

Factories can be a source of pollution related to climate change.

Instructions

1. Have students complete the quiz independently. If students are not familiar with a True/False quiz, review the directions with them.

2. **Option:** Go through the statements one at a time, asking additional questions for each statement, such as the following:

   • Does anyone know what gases make Earth warmer? (greenhouse gases like methane, carbon dioxide, and water vapor)

   • How is energy use related to climate change?

   • What are some ways that animals benefit from forests?

   • Could food be grown in a forest, or do trees need to be cleared?

   • Why do you think it takes different amounts of water to produce different kinds of food?

3. Let students know that they will return to this page after they finish reading the chapter.

Answers

1. true
2. false
3. false
4. true
5. false
6. true
7. true

Instructions

1. This reading can be done as a jigsaw activity. Divide the class into groups of six. Divide each group of six students into three pairs. Each pair will read about one of the environmental issues and then share the main idea from their reading with the larger group of six.

2. Give students a minute to preview the reading. Ask them to consider the title and the three main subtitles, as well as the photos.

3. Ask the following questions:

   • *What do you think the reading will be about?*

   • *What are your reactions to the photos in this reading?*

4. Remind students that they will be looking for cause and effect relationships as they read.

5. Ask volunteers to share ways they can identify causes and effects (i.e., signal words, fits the "if…then…" formula).

6. Have pairs read their assigned section.

7. Ask each pair to complete their portion of the cause and effect graphic organizer that follows the reading.

Environmental Issues and Solutions

Environmental Issue #1: Climate Change

Imagine you have lived on an island your entire life. You use resources from that island and had a peaceful childhood there. Recently, you noticed that the sea levels have been rising higher than usual, reaching further inland. Because of these rising water levels, some of your neighbors' houses have been destroyed. Salt from these rising waters has also damaged plants and trees around the area. Trees have started to die from too much salt. You have thought about moving and building your house on a higher foundation with walls around it to stop flooding during high tides and heavy rains. This move will cost you quite a bit of money. Your environment has changed so much during your lifetime that you fear what might happen in the future.

What's Happening?

Ben Namakin knows this story all too well because this scenario is happening where he lives in the Federated States of Micronesia (a Pacific island nation). He can remember his favorite place to spend time during high school, where he saw friends, snorkeled in the water, and camped. Unfortunately, the place has been destroyed by flooding as sea levels have risen. As an environmental educator, Ben teaches people of all ages about this environmental issue and the importance of creating solutions that will stop his island from being destroyed.[1]

Ben Namakin has seen the effects of climate change.

Around the world, people like Ben are observing the effects of climate change. Climate is the typical **weather** in an area over a period of time. When we talk about climate, we are not talking about what the weather is like on a single day. We are talking about weather patterns over a long period of time. For example, Alaska has a cool climate. Although there may be warmer days during the summer, the weather in Alaska is typically cool.

Climate change can have very different effects in different places. In some places, climate change may result in more rainfall and flooding. In other places, there may be less rainfall and droughts may increase. If the weather changed significantly where you lived, what might happen to people and to local environments?

weather (n) – outdoor conditions at a given point in time, including precipitation (snow, rain, ice), temperature, wind, and clouds

Sea levels are beginning to rise around the world. As water warms, it expands and takes up more space. Therefore, warmer oceans cause sea levels to rise. Also, some sea level rise is due to melting glaciers.

Our Place in the Story

There are many reasons why climate can change. Some climate change is natural and normal. For example, volcanic eruptions and ocean currents can affect climate change. However, the daily actions and choices of people can also affect Earth's climate.[2]

Think about all the times you turn a light on, use a computer, or watch television. One way that we contribute to climate change is through our energy use. We use energy for electricity and for transportation. **Electricity** is used to light our buildings, heat our homes, and power electronics like televisions and microwave ovens. **Transportation** is how we move from one place to another. Cars, trains, airplanes, and buses are all types of transportation.

Most of the energy we use comes from fossil fuels (materials such as **coal** and **oil** that were formed millions of years ago from ancient plants and animals). When we use fossil fuels, **carbon dioxide** and other gases are released into the air. These gases act like a blanket by trapping the sun's heat near the earth. Because of this, temperatures on Earth are beginning to rise. This process that warms the earth is called the *greenhouse effect*.

If we know that using fossil fuels for energy causes climate change, then we can help by reducing our use of fossil fuels for electricity and

Sea levels are beginning to rise all over the world.

transportation. Here are a few ideas:

- Travel less by car and airplane
- Use public transportation like buses and trains
- Turn off lights and unplug electronics when you are not using them

You could also help to fight climate change by planting trees and other plants. Did you know that plants actually *need* carbon dioxide to survive? They take carbon dioxide out of the air and use it to grow.

Whether you decide to take the bus more often or plant a tree in your yard, you are helping to reduce the effects of climate change. Just think what a large impact we could make if everyone did this!

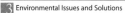

glaciers (n) – large masses of ice that remain frozen for many years

electricity (n) – a form of energy used to heat and cool buildings, to power appliances and electronics, and to light buildings

transportation (n) – the movement of people or things from one place to another

coal (n) – a black rock formed by decaying plants over millions of years; commonly used to create electricity

oil (n) – thick black liquid formed by decaying plants and animals over millions of years; commonly used to make gasoline and plastic

carbon dioxide/CO_2 (n) – a colorless, odorless gas made of one carbon atom and two oxygen atoms; a major component of Earth's atmosphere

Environmental Issue #2: Deforestation

Nelly Damaris Chepkoskei is fifty years old. She is a farmer in the western part of Kenya, a country in Africa. She grows maize and tea. She also raises a few cows that provide her with milk. During her lifetime, Nelly has seen bushes and trees completely cleared from forests in order to use the land to grow food and to make room for people to live. Growing food is important, of course, but so are forests! That is why Nelly works to educate people about forest **conservation** .[3]

Why Care?

You probably already know some reasons why forests are a valuable resource. Trees can be used to create many things we use every day, such as paper for books and magazines, building materials for homes, and fuel for firewood.

However, forests provide many other benefits that you might not think of. Did you know that forests help to keep soils healthy and streams clean? When trees are cleared, soil is left bare. With no tree roots to hold it in place, the soil washes away during the rainy season. This **eroded** soil may end up in streams and rivers, or it may be blown far away by winds. Soil erosion also has a negative impact on agriculture; without healthy topsoil, people cannot continue to grow food year after year.

Forests are also important for biodiversity because they are home to many species. In fact, the majority of all land animals and plants live in forests.[4] Approximately 13 million **hectares** are deforested each year. That means approximately 3% of the world's forests are lost every ten years.[5]

Nelly Damaris Chepkoskei plants trees in Kenya.

Complete removal of trees from an area is called *deforestation*. Why do you think people would want to cut down entire forests? It might surprise you to learn that the major reason for deforestation is to clear land for growing food and raising **livestock** . Forests can be cleared by cutting down the trees or by burning them.

Connecting Forests to Climate

During the past several years, Nelly has been facing a few problems that she thinks might be related to deforestation. First, the grass her cows graze on has been so dry lately that the cows haven't had as much food to eat. As a result, they have not been able to produce as much milk.

---

conservation (n) – the act of protecting something, like wildlife or forests

eroded (adj) – worn away, such as when rock or soil is worn away by constant exposure to wind or water

hectare (n) – a unit of measurement for land area; equal to 10,000 square meters, roughly an area the size of two football fields

livestock (n) – domestic animals, such as cows and sheep, that are raised to make money

Another problem she sees is that the amount of rainfall has decreased so much that crops have not been growing like they used to. Nelly has also noticed that warmer temperatures have led to an increase in mosquitoes. These mosquitoes can cause people to get sick from **malaria**. Could all these things—dry grass, reduced rainfall, and mosquitoes—be related?

The problems Nelly has been seeing are linked to climate change. Climate change is a change in long-term weather patterns, such as rainfall and temperature, in a region. **Carbon dioxide** is a gas that can cause climate change. When it is released into the air (from all sorts of events and activities, from volcanic eruptions to driving gasoline-powered cars), carbon dioxide contributes to the **greenhouse effect**, which makes temperatures on Earth warmer.

Deforestation is connected to climate change. Trees can take a lot of carbon dioxide out of the air, which is good news for us. In fact, trees need carbon dioxide to survive. Unfortunately, when trees are cut down or burned, all of the carbon dioxide they were holding is released into the air. Deforestation accounts for 20% of the carbon dioxide emissions from human activities.[6]

Getting Involved

We all benefit from the services provided by forests. As you already know, they take in carbon dioxide to help keep Earth a little cooler. Forests are also home to the majority of plants and animals that live on land. Plus, we use many products from forests, such as paper, fruits and nuts, spices, and medicines.

If you want to get involved, there are many ways that you can help to protect the world's forests.

Nelly tells other people about the environmental changes she has seen.

Here are a few ideas:

- Learn about the trees that are native to your region and plant them
- Reuse and recycle paper so trees do not have to be cut down
- Buy recycled paper products
- Avoid eating meat from animals raised in deforested areas

Can you think of other ways to help conserve forests? Thinking of these solutions now can help to prevent environmental issues in the future. Who knows—you could even educate other people about conservation, like Nelly Damaris does!

---

malaria (n) – a disease passed to humans by mosquitoes; symptoms include fevers, chills, and sweating

carbon dioxide/CO$_2$ (n) – a colorless, odorless gas made of one carbon atom and two oxygen atoms; a major component of Earth's atmosphere

greenhouse effect (n) – the process by which carbon dioxide and other gases in Earth's atmosphere trap heat from the sun that reflects off the earth, resulting in warmer temperatures on Earth

Environmental Issue #3: Freshwater Scarcity

Think of all the different times you use water throughout the day. Where does this water come from? What would you do if that water was no longer available? Could you survive?

Many people in the world struggle to find clean water for their daily needs. Gung Qiu Lai Jia lives in western China's Qinghai province. With his wife, he raises **yaks** for a living. Twenty years ago, a small stream ran near his house. It was about a foot, or twelve inches, deep. Water flowed through the stream all year long.

In recent years, the stream has become much smaller, and sometimes it completely dries up when rain has not fallen for a long time. Because of this, Gung Qiu Lai Jia's wife has to walk farther upstream to get water for the family. Gung Qiu Lai Jia worries how his five children will survive if their source of water disappears completely.[7]

Water: A Vital Resource

Water is an extremely important resource for all living things. Clean freshwater is a basic human need. We need it for daily activities, such as drinking, cooking, and cleaning. Unfortunately, there are many places in the world where clean freshwater is not easily accessible.

Today, about 25% of people in Africa live with water scarcity.[8] In places where water is not available, people have to walk miles each day to collect water. Spending time collecting water could be spent going to school or working to earn money. In some places, water may be

Gung Qui Lai Jia has seen the effects of water scarcity in China.

available, but it might not be clean. Water **contaminated** with garbage and bacteria can cause people to get sick from illnesses such as diarrhea. Diarrhea is a major cause of death worldwide, especially for children.

Increasing Freshwater Scarcity

Scientists predict that the number of people who have difficulty finding clean water will increase. This increase in freshwater scarcity is due to many reasons. Because all people need water, population growth (increasing numbers of humans on Earth) contributes to water scarcity.

Scientists also think that climate change is affecting water availability worldwide. Climate change is a change in long-term weather patterns, such as rainfall and temperature, in a region.

---

yaks (n) – a species of large animals that can be used for physical labor or to produce meat and milk

contaminated (adj) – foul or unclean due to introduced substances, such as dirt, toxic chemicals, or harmful bacteria

Right now Earth's climate is changing; overall temperatures on Earth are warmer than they used to be. Climate change can have very different effects on water resources in different parts of the world. In some areas, climate change may lead to more rainfall and flooding. (Rainfall has been increasing throughout North America and Europe.) In other places, rainfall may decrease, causing droughts. (Rainfall has decreased dramatically in West Africa over the past 100 years.)[9]

For Gung Qiu Lai Jia in China, rainfall has become unpredictable. Whereas rain used to fall continuously during the wet season in June, now it comes only in the form of sudden showers. The quick bursts of rainfall do not increase the amount of drinking water. Instead, they wash soil into the stream near Gung Qiu Lai Jia's home, making the water muddy and unsafe to drink.[10]

Using Less Water and Creating More Opportunities

Did you know that 70% of all freshwater use worldwide is for farming?[11] More freshwater is used for growing food than for any other purpose. Some foods require more water to grow than others. For example, it takes about thirty-seven times more water to produce 500 **calories** of beef than to produce 500 calories of corn.[12] That's not just because cows drink water; water is also used to grow the grain that the cow eats.

Because water is a shared resource, when we use less water we leave more for other people. There are many ways you can use a little less water every day:

- Take shorter showers and turn off the faucet when you brush your teeth

- Fix leaky faucets

- Eat food that requires less water to produce (such as vegetables, chicken, fish, and fruit)

---

calorie (n) – a measure of heat energy obtained from foods eaten

Gung Qui Lai Jia's wife collects water from a stream that she must carry back to her home.

Instructions

1. After each pair has read their article, give them time to share the information with their group of six.

2. Students should work together to complete the graphic organizer.

   • **Differentiated Instruction:** Write a sentence for each cause and effect relationship.

3. Have students return to the True/False Quiz. Would they change any of their answers based on the chapter reading?

4. **Additional Resource:** Watch a video or listen to a podcast from Ben Namakin (featured in the reading about climate change). Visit the World Wildlife Fund website (www. panda.org) and type "Ben Namakin" in the search box. His story is part of WWF's Climate Witness series.

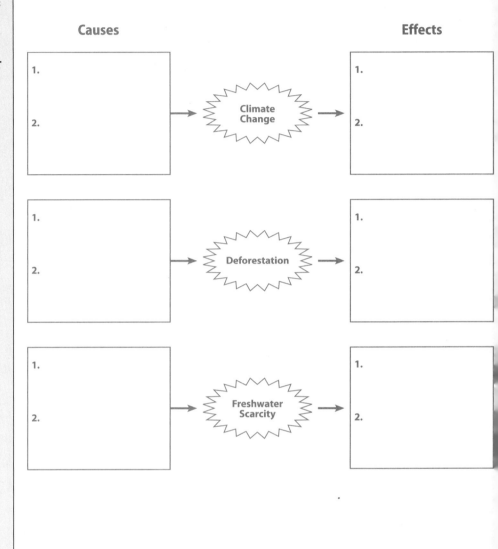

Directions: Record at least two causes and two effects for each of the environmental issues.

Causes — Climate Change — Effects

Causes — Deforestation — Effects

Causes — Freshwater Scarcity — Effects

1.
2.

Answers

Climate Change

Causes

1. natural causes: volcanoes, shifting ocean currents
2. human actions: energy use from fossil fuels

Effects

1. rising sea levels
2. changing rainfall patterns

Deforestation

Causes

1. cutting down trees for making paper and building homes
2. clearing trees for agriculture

Effects

1. soil erosion
2. release of carbon dioxide, which warms the earth

Freshwater Scarcity

Causes

1. reduced or more unpredictable rainfall
2. water contaminated by trash and bacteria

Effects

1. people have to travel farther to find drinking water
2. people get sick from drinking unclean water

Comprehension Questions

Directions: Answer the questions about the section you read to support your comprehension of the chapter reading.

Reading 1: Climate Change

Understanding what you read

1. Identify what country Ben Namakin is from.

2. What happened to Ben Namakin's favorite place where he used to spend time during high school?

Thinking about what you read

3. How might climate change have different effects in different parts of the world?

4. How does our energy use connect to climate change?

Questioning what you read

5. Explain why you think the author chose to write about climate change.

6. The author could have chosen to write about climate change without including the story of Ben Namakin. Why do you think the author chose to include his story?

Reading 2: Deforestation

Understanding what you read

1. Identify what country Nelly Damaris Chepkoskei is from.

2. What has Nelly seen in her lifetime?

Thinking about what you read

3. What benefits do forests provide us?

4. How is deforestation related to climate change?

Questioning what you read

5. Explain why you think the author chose to write about deforestation.

6. The author could have chosen to write about climate change without including the story of Nelly Damaris Chepkoskei. Why do you think the author chose to include her story?

continued ▶

Comprehension Questions

Instructions

1. Before students begin answering the comprehension questions, share with them the academic language they will see in many of the questions (see Appendix B).

2. Explain that the questions are divided into five sections according to the different ways they support reading comprehension. (See Appendix B for a detailed explanation of each section.)

3. Note that all students will answer six questions about the section they read. All students will answer the last four questions.

4. **Differentiated Instruction:** Differentiate the answers students must answer based on their reading levels. Support comprehension by working with students who may need more guided instruction.

Answers

Reading 1: Climate Change

1. Federated States of Micronesia

2. It was destroyed by flooding.

3. Some areas may have flooding and more rainfall, while others may have more droughts.

4. When we burn fossil fuels for electricity and transportation, greenhouse gases are released.

5. Climate change is an important environmental concern connected to people's lives.

6. The story connects the reader to climate change and shows how real people are affected.

Reading 2: Deforestation

1. Kenya

2. Nelly has seen bushes and trees completely cleared from forests in order to clear land for agriculture and to make room for people to live.

3. We can use materials from forests to make paper, build homes, burn firewood, and keep soils healthy and streams clean.

4. When trees are cut down, carbon dioxide is released into the air.

5. Deforestation is an important environmental concern connected to human well-being.

6. The story connects the reader to deforestation and shows how real people are affected.

Reading 3: Freshwater Scarcity

Understanding what you read

1. Identify what country Gung Qiu Lai Jia is from.

2. What percentage of people in Africa lives with water scarcity?

Thinking about what you read

3. What happened to the stream near Gung Qiu Lai Jia's house?

4. In places where water is not readily available, what do people have to spend their time doing?

Questioning what you read

5. Explain why you think the author chose to write about freshwater scarcity.

6. The author could have chosen to write about climate change without including the story of Gung Qiu Lai Jia. Why do you think the author chose to include his story?

All Readings

Making connections to what you read

7. Name one action you could take to help solve each of the following problems:
   a. climate change
   b. deforestation
   c. water scarcity

8. Do you see any environmental issues where you live? If so, what are possible solutions to these issues?

Further discussion questions

9. What are common causes of different environmental issues such as climate change and deforestation?

10. How could environmental issues like climate change, deforestation, and water scarcity be connected to conflict?

Answers

Reading 3: Freshwater Scarcity

1. China

2. 25%

3. The stream that once flowed by his house has become smaller; when there is no rain, it dries up completely.

4. People have to spend time collecting water.

5. Freshwater scarcity is an important environmental concern connected to human survival.

6. The story connects the reader to freshwater scarcity and shows how real people are affected.

All Readings

7. a. e.g., use less electricity by turning off lights

   b. e.g., use both sides of writing paper

   c. e.g., take shorter showers

8. Answers will vary

9. high rates of resource consumption, increasing population

10. When resources like land and water are scarce, people may fight over what little resources are available. Countries want to ensure that their people have essential resources for survival.

What is a persuasive essay?

A persuasive essay is an essay that attempts to persuade a reader to adopt a certain point of view.

Why write a persuasive essay?

Writing a persuasive essay allows you to create a solid argument for something that you strongly believe in. You might write a persuasive essay to encourage people to agree with you or to motivate them to do something.

You have just read about how three people's lives have been affected by climate change around the world. Imagine that a newspaper reporter has asked you to write an article to appear in the newspaper. The reporter asks you to answer the question:

Do you think people should take immediate action to stop climate change?

You will write a persuasive essay responding to this statement. You will be persuading or encouraging people either to take action or not to take action against climate change, depending on your opinion.

Tips for Writing

- Use the readings from the chapter to support your reasoning.
- Include at least three cause and effect statements in your essay.
- Use at least two chapter vocabulary words in your essay.

Instructions

1. Students will be writing an essay to persuade readers to take (or not take) action on climate change. Make sure that all students understand what climate change is and what actions could be taken to limit climate change.

2. Read through the page with students.

   • **Differentiated Instruction:** Review the idea of *persuasion* with students. Work with students to create a list of persuasive words they can use in their essay.

3. Share the Chapter 3 writing rubric with students. You may want to add relevant spelling and grammar components to the rubric.

Chapter 3 Writing Rubric
see p. 70l

Writing about Environmental Issues

Instructions

1. Grammar Suggestion:
Since students will be writing a persuasive essay with cause and effect statements, teaching students to identify independent and dependent clauses will help them to develop their writing.

Writing about Environmental Issues: Persuasive Essay

Use the information below to help construct your persuasive essay.

I. Introduction: Think about your reaction to the statement: *Do you think people should take immediate action to stop climate change?* Use your answer to write an introduction for your essay.

Begin this paragraph with an interesting **hook** so that readers will want to keep reading. A hook might be a sentence with an interesting fact or a question.

- Example: Climate change will affect people all over the world, from Kenya to China.
- Example: Did you know that forests have a major impact on Earth's climate?

End your introduction with a **thesis statement**. A thesis statement informs the reader what the essay is about.

- Example: Working to reduce climate change will benefit people all over the world.
- Example: People should *not* take action on climate change because there are more important problems in the world.

II. Body: Think of three reasons to support your answer. How do you think people can stop climate change?

- Example: Taking action on climate change is one way to protect Earth's freshwater resources.
- Example: Climate change will result in droughts in some places where water is already scarce.

III. Conclusion: Summarize your thoughts. This final paragraph should not provide new information. In a conclusion, you should restate your main ideas in a persuasive way. Remember: you are trying to encourage people to either take action or not take action against climate change.

The example on the following page is a persuasive essay that addresses the question:

Should there be a law against using disposable plastic bags?

As you read the essay, consider these questions:

1. What is the author trying to convince you to believe or persuade you to do?

2. Which statements in the essay are most persuasive?

3. Which statements in the essay are less effective at persuading you?

4. Do you agree with the author? If not, what would make you agree?

Instructions

1. Have students read the sample essay.
2. Discuss students' answers to the questions from the preceding page.

Should there be a law against disposable plastic bags?

Did you know that over 10% of the trash that ends up in landfills is plastic?[13] Not all of that plastic is disposable bags, but they are part of the problem. Disposable plastic bags add to the waste in landfills. Because taxpayers pay for landfills, anything that ends up in a landfill costs us money. Another problem with plastic bags is that they are made with petroleum—a nonrenewable resource. Also, plastic bags can harm marine animals. For these reasons, there should be a law against disposable plastic bags.

The first reason there should be a law against plastic bags is that most of them get thrown away. In fact, less than 1% of plastic bags are recycled.[14] The rest end up in the garbage or blowing around. The ones that end up in the garbage contribute to the problem of landfills. Landfills are places where trash is buried. When landfills get completely full, new ones have to be built. That's really expensive. Landfills can cost hundreds of thousands of dollars to build![15]

Another reason that there should be a law against plastic bags is that they are made from petroleum. Petroleum is a nonrenewable resource. That means that once we use it, it's gone!

It takes millions of years to create new petroleum. Based on the way we use petroleum now, there is only enough petroleum for forty more years! Why waste the petroleum on disposable bags when it could be used for more important things like medicines and safety equipment?

The last reason there should be a law against plastic bags is that they harm marine animals. Plastic bags can end up in the ocean.[16] Plastic bags have been found in the stomachs of sea turtles that tried to eat them. Eventually those plastic bags can kill ocean birds and marine animals. If the bags were outlawed, there would be one less threat to marine life.

While disposable plastic bags are a convenient way to carry your groceries home, people could start carrying their groceries in reusable bags. Most people have bags and backpacks that could be used to carry things. There should be a law against disposable plastic bags because they add to landfill waste, are made from petroleum, and harm marine animals. One solution to the problems of expensive landfills, using nonrenewable resources, and marine animal deaths, is to have a law against plastic bags. Our children will thank us for taking this step to clean up the environment.

Writing Steps: Persuasive Essay

Step 1: Think about your response to the question. Think of three or more reasons you feel this way.

Step 2: Write an essay using the persuasive essay structure that you have studied. You can use the Writing Organizer to get started.

Step 3: Edit the essay using the Edit Checklist below.

Step 4: Have a classmate read and edit your essay using the editing checklist.

Step 5: Revise the essay based on the peer edit.

 Edit Checklist

	Author Check	Peer Editor Check
Did you include a hook statement in your introduction?		
Did you include a thesis statement in your introduction?		
Did you write complete thoughts for each line?		
Did you use cause and effect statements correctly?		
Did you include a concluding paragraph?		
Did you use two chapter vocabulary words?		

Instructions

1. Review steps with students.
2. **Option:** Provide students with time and resources (Internet and print) to research supporting details. Information from the chapter reading could also be used.
   - **Differentiated Instruction:** For beginning students who may need more guidance, gather them into a small group and assist them with writing their persuasive essays. You can assign students one body paragraph to write instead of writing all three.
3. Once they write their essays, students will exchange them with a classmate, edit the essays using the Edit Checklist, and then revise their own.
4. **Option:** Have students type their essays and submit them to a local newspaper. Students could format them to look like newspaper editorials and even include small photos of themselves next to the byline.
5. **Additional Resource:** The U.S. Environmental Protection Agency's (EPA) Climate Change Kids Site, http://epa.gov/climatechange/kids/, includes interactive climate animations, an explanation of the difference between weather and climate, and ideas for reducing our climate impact.
6. **Additional Resource:** *You Can Prevent Global Warming (and Save Money!)* by Jeffrey Langholz and Kelly Turner. This 370-page book provides fifty-one tips for reducing greenhouse gas emissions at home while saving money.

Instructions

1. Use this organizer to help students structure their essays.

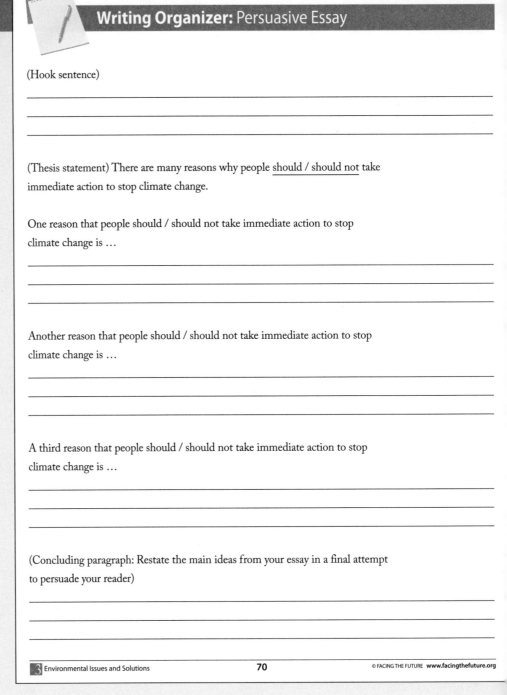

Writing Organizer: Persuasive Essay

(Hook sentence)

_____

_____

_____

(Thesis statement) There are many reasons why people should / should not take immediate action to stop climate change.

One reason that people should / should not take immediate action to stop climate change is …

_____

_____

_____

Another reason that people should / should not take immediate action to stop climate change is …

_____

_____

_____

A third reason that people should / should not take immediate action to stop climate change is …

_____

_____

_____

(Concluding paragraph: Restate the main ideas from your essay in a final attempt to persuade your reader)

_____

_____

_____

Culminating Activity: Watch Where You Step (60 minutes)

Overview

Students work together to identify the components of an ecological footprint by creating a web diagram of an everyday product. The activity emphasizes the interconnectedness of lifestyle, population, and environmental impacts, and focuses on solutions to reduce ecological footprints.

Materials/Preparation

- *Watch Where You Step* graphic organizers, one per group of 3-4 students

- Butcher paper or posters, one sheet per group

- Markers and other materials for decorating posters

- (Optional) Magazines with rich color photographs

Steps

1. Review the concept of *ecological footprint* with students. An ecological footprint is the area of Earth's surface needed to produce what we use. In other words, it's a measure of our impact on nature.

2. All of the environmental issues discussed in Chapter 3 are related to our ecological footprint. This activity asks students to consider how items they use every day may be related to three environmental issues: climate change, deforestation, and water availability.

3. Divide the class into groups of 3-4 students. In groups, students will identify resources and impacts associated with creating one item.

4. Provide each group with one of the graphic organizers (cheeseburger, car, or pants).

5. Tell them to write the number (1-8) from each impact in a circle connected to one of the item's components. For example, on the cheeseburger graphic organizer, #1 (diesel fuel made from petroleum was needed to run the machine that harvests grain) would go in one of the circles connected to the wheat. For answers, see p. 70I.

6. Encourage groups to think of additional impacts that are not listed, including environmental impacts related to using and disposing of the item. They can add these impacts to the graphic organizer by drawing additional circles and writing impacts in them.

7. After they have worked for about 15 minutes, tell them they will be creating an informative poster to share this information with others.

8. Pass out markers and a sheet of butcher paper or poster to each group. Ask them to create a visually appealing poster that will inform other people about the ecological footprint of their particular item. They will also be telling people about ways to reduce the ecological footprint of this item.

9. Instruct students to use a combination of pictures (either drawings or photos cut out of magazines) and words to draw a web diagram of their item and its associated environmental impacts. The poster should be eye-catching, informative, and easily readable. Students will use information from the graphic organizers to create these posters.

10. In addition to showing the negative impacts of their item, ask groups to save space on their posters to write three ways the item could have a smaller impact. Footprint reductions might be related to the way an item is made or how it is used. Be sure to emphasize that focusing on ways to reduce environmental impacts does not mean that people should give up everything they like. For example, rather than giving up cheeseburgers altogether, students might suggest that people eat one less meal with meat each week or only eat beef raised sustainably.

11. Have each group present their posters to the class.

12. **Option:** Display posters somewhere visible in the classroom or a school hallway.

Watch Where You Step
Group 1: What Does It Take to Make a Cheeseburger?

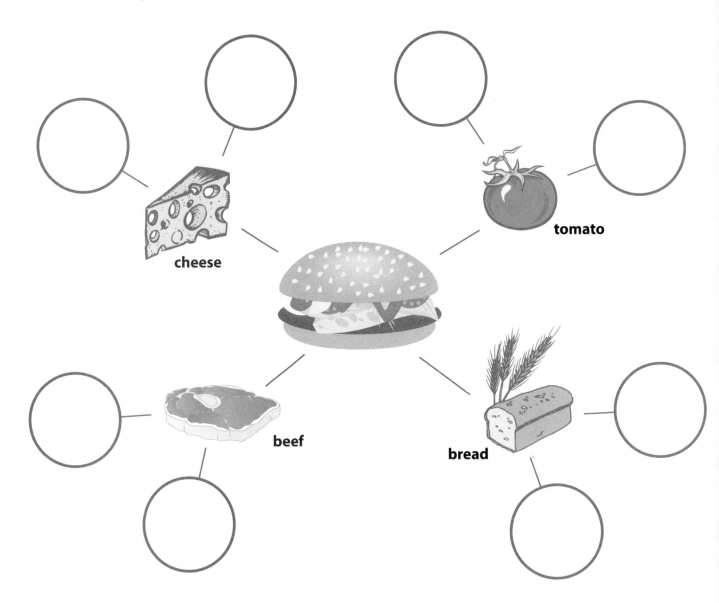

cheese

tomato

beef

bread

1. Diesel fuel, which is similar to gasoline and made from petroleum, runs the machine that harvests grain.

2. Water from an aquifer—a place deep underground that stores water naturally—is needed to help the tomato grow.

3. Cheese is made from cow's milk; methane gas from cows is a greenhouse gas that makes temperatures on Earth warmer.

4. One beef patty requires 600 gallons of water to be produced.

5. Gasoline from fossil fuels was needed to transport the wheat from a farm to a factory where bread is made.

6. Forests were cleared so that cows could graze, or eat grass in fields.

7. Chemicals used to kill insects on tomato plants can contaminate soil and water.

8. Electricity was needed to run the factory where cow's milk is turned into cheese.

Watch Where You Step
Group 2: What Does It Take to Make a Car?

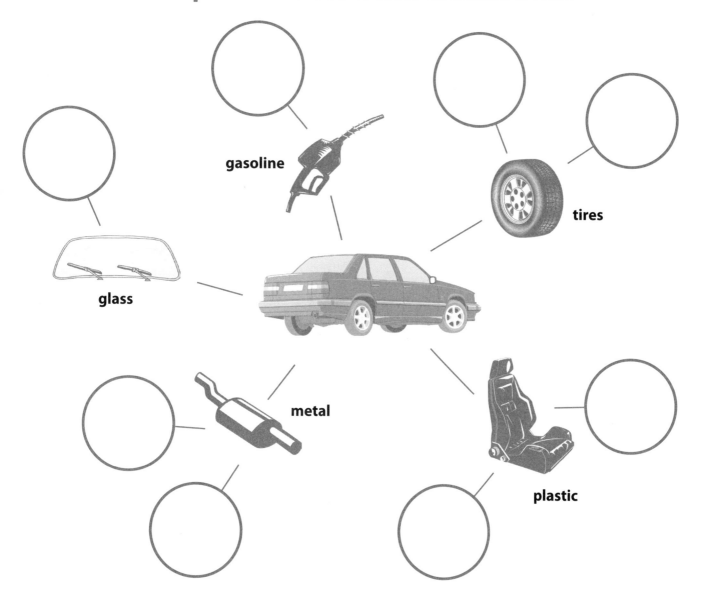

gasoline

tires

glass

metal

plastic

1. Steel is made of iron and other metals, which are mined, or extracted, from underground.

2. Plastic is made from petroleum (oil), a fossil fuel that took millions of years to form.

3. Car tires are made of synthetic, or man-made, rubber as well as other materials like steel belts.

4. Metals are often mined by first clearing all the trees from an area.

5. Synthetic rubber is made from petroleum-based chemicals.

6. Water is used in the process of turning petroleum into plastic.

7. Glass is made at very high temperatures, requiring a large amount of energy.

8. For every mile a gasoline-powered car travels, it emits approximately 1 pound of carbon dioxide (a greenhouse gas).

Watch Where You Step
Group 3: What Does It Take to Make a Pair of Pants?

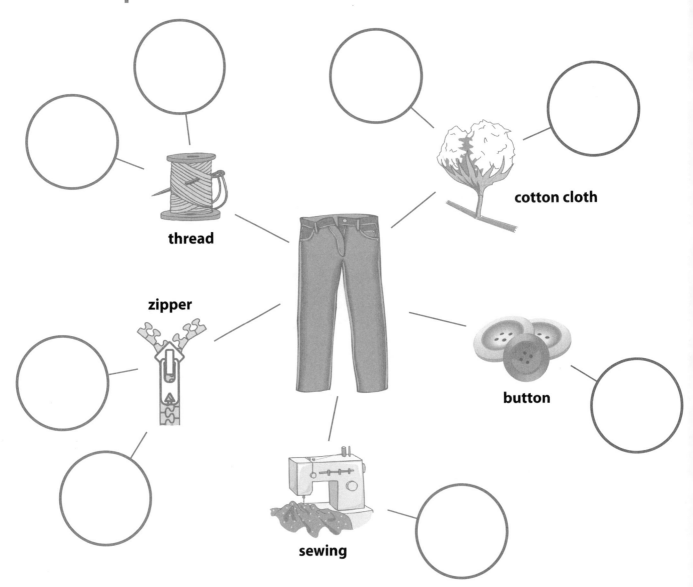

thread

cotton cloth

zipper

button

sewing

1. Polyester thread is made from petroleum.

2. A lot of water is used to irrigate, or water, cotton; 1 kg of cotton fabric represents 11,000 liters of water.

3. Zippers are made from metal that is mined, or extracted, from deep underground.

4. Chemicals used to kill insects on cotton plants can travel far by air and water.

5. Plastic buttons are made from petroleum, a liquid fossil fuel that takes millions of years to form.

6. Much of the world's petroleum (oil), used to create products like polyester, a man-made fabric, is transported great distances (such as from the Middle East to North America).

7. Fabric from the United States is shipped to another country such as Mexico to be sewn into clothing, and then it is shipped back to the United States to sell.

8. Mining metals destroys forests, soils, and other natural resources.

Chapter 3 Extension, Action Project, and Resources

Art Extension

Ask students to take photos of activities that contribute to environmental destruction and activities that reduce or prevent environmental destruction. Exhibit the photos in a large public area to educate people about everyday activities that harm the environment and ideas for reducing or preventing harm.

Action Project

Have students calculate their ecological footprint using Zerofootprint KidsCalculator (www.zerofootprintkids.com) to see how an ecological calculator works. Then, have students interview a classmate using questions from the KidsCalculator. After he/she has answered the questions, the student can enter that information into the online calculator to find his/her ecological footprint. Next, have students think of specific ways that their classmate can reduce his/her footprint. Finally, students should present their classmate with the footprint results and ideas for having a lighter impact on the planet.

Additional Resources on Environmental Issues and Solutions

Stuff: The Secret Lives of Everyday Things, by John C. Ryan and Alan Thein Durning
www.sightline.org/publications/books.stuff/stuff

Stuff reveals the natural resources required to produce things that a typical middle class North American consumes every day.

Water for Life
www.mtv.com/thinkmtv/features/global/water_for_life/

This interactive website allows viewers to read about rapper Jay-Z's travels highlighting water shortages around the world.

WWF Climate Witness
www.panda.org/climatewitness

Climate Witness is the World Wildlife Fund's initiative to document the personal experiences of people who are witnessing the impacts of climate change on their local environment. Scientific background information accompanies the climate witness testimonies.

Water Footprint Network
www.waterfootprint.org

The Water Footprint Network provides water consumption numbers for a variety of products, including foods and clothing. Their website also provides information about water footprints for individual nations.

Facing the Future
www.facingthefuture.org

From the homepage, click on *Global Sustainability*, then *Fast Facts & Quick Actions*, and finally *Deforestation*. Read a short list of facts about deforestation worldwide and simple actions you can take to reduce global deforestation.

Chapter 3 Student Assessment, page 1
Knowledge about Environmental Issues and Solutions

Vocabulary

Directions: Read each sentence and circle the letter next to the correct definition for each bold-faced word.

1. **Climate change** can have serious effects on natural environments, such as melting glaciers that have been frozen for thousands of years.

   a. a change in long-term weather patterns
   b. a change in weather from one day to the next
   c. a very hot day
   d. a lot of sunshine

2. Using too much water in irresponsible ways can lead to **freshwater scarcity** around the world.

   a. an increase in water polluted with trash and chemicals
   b. an increase in water available for people throughout the world
   c. a lack of safe and drinkable water for people throughout the world
   d. a lack of saltwater for fish and other species

3. Many animals might lose their homes as a result of **deforestation**.

   a. a lack of food and water
   b. planting forests
   c. building parks
   d. removal of trees

4. Both air and water **pollution** can make animals sick.

   a. substances that contaminate air, water, and soil
   b. substances that come from pollinating plants
   c. diseases spread by wind and water
   d. diseases caused by the growth of bacteria

Chapter 3 Student Assessment, page 2

Content

Directions: For each of the following statements, circle *True* if the statement is true and *False* if the statement is not true.

5. ***True or False:*** Natural events like volcano eruptions can cause climate change.

6. ***True or False:*** The total amount of freshwater in the world is decreasing.

7. ***True or False:*** One cause of deforestation is clearing land to grow food.

8. ***True or False:*** Pet waste is a source of water pollution.

Reading Comprehension

Directions: Read the paragraph below. For the questions that follow, circle the letter of the correct answers.

Worldwide, more than 600 million cars and trucks are in use today and nearly 50 million new ones are added each year. Most of these cars burn gasoline that can cause air pollution. In Mexico City, smog from pollution is sometimes so thick that schools and factories close and cars have to drive with their lights on. Pollution can make people sick and keep them home from work. When people are unable to work, the economy suffers. Estimates show that reducing air pollution could save the city millions of dollars every year!

9. What has been one of the effects of air pollution in Mexico City?
   a. Schools and factories have had to close because smog from pollution was so thick
   b. People have become sick and have not been able to go to work
   c. The city has lost money
   d. All of the above
   e. None of the above

10. Which of the following would be an appropriate title for this paragraph?
   a. Fresh Air, Please: The Dangers of Air Pollution
   b. Polluted Waters: Illness and Environmental Destruction
   c. Mexico City: Society, Environment, and Economy
   d. School Life in Mexico City

Chapter 3 Student Assessment, page 3
Outlook and Personal Beliefs

The answers to the following questions are based on your personal beliefs. There are no right or wrong answers.

Directions for 1 and 2: Place a check mark (√) in the box next to each statement that is true for you.

1. There is not much that young people can do to help the environment.
   ☐ True
   ☐ False

2. I can personally do things to reduce my contribution to climate change.
   ☐ True
   ☐ False

3. **Complete the following sentence:**
   One way I can personally work to solve an environmental issue is by …

   _____

   _____

   _____

Directions for 4 and 5: Fill in the ovals below based on your attitude. 1 means you strongly agree, and 7 means you strongly disagree.

1 = yes, definitely!   7 = no way!
⟵——————————————————⟶

4. I believe my daily actions have an impact on the environment.

   1   2   3   4   5   6   7
   ⬭   ⬭   ⬭   ⬭   ⬭   ⬭   ⬭

5. I believe I have the ability to help solve environmental issues such as climate change, deforestation, and freshwater scarcity.

   1   2   3   4   5   6   7
   ⬭   ⬭   ⬭   ⬭   ⬭   ⬭   ⬭

Writing a Persuasive Essay, p. 65

Chapter 3 Writing Rubric

Category	3	2	1
Answer Question "Do you think people should take immediate action…?"	Answers the question	Attempts to answer question, but instead answers another one	Does not attempt to answer the question
Introduction	Essay starts with an introduction including a hook and thesis sentence	Essay includes an introduction, but is missing a hook or a thesis sentence	The essay has no clear introduction
Body	There are at least three reasons given to support the author's thesis	Only two reasons are given to support the author's thesis	One or no reasons are given to support the author's thesis
Conclusion	The conclusion restates the author's argument	The conclusion somewhat restates the author's argument	The essay has no clear conclusion
Vocabulary	Uses two vocabulary words from the chapter	Uses one of the words from the chapter	No vocabulary words are used
Cause and Effect	At least three cause and effect statements are used correctly	One or two cause and effect statements are used correctly	No cause and effect statements are used

Total = _____ / 18

Watch Where You Step

Cheeseburger, p. 70B

cheese: 3, 8

tomato: 2, 7

bread: 1, 5

beef: 4, 6

Car, p. 70C

gasoline: 8

tires: 3, 5

plastic: 2, 6

metal: 1, 4

glass: 7

Pants, p. 70D

thread: 1, 6

cotton cloth: 2, 4

button: 5

sewing: 7

zipper: 3, 8

Chapter 2 Student Assessment, pp. 70F, G

1. a
2. c
3. d
4. a
5. True

6. False
7. True
8. True
9. d
10. a

Teacher Notes

Thinking about Consumption

Students use Venn diagrams to brainstorm similarities and differences in consumption around the world. In a writing activity, they contemplate the relationship between buying things and happiness. Students analyze an advertisement during a dialogue activity. After learning consumption-related vocabulary and derivatives, students learn more about consumer issues by reading about the life cycle of an everyday product: running shoes. Throughout the chapter, students practice sequencing. A writing activity focuses on creating a how-to guide for consumers. The chapter culminates with a hands-on activity in which students work in groups to create and present mock television commercials for products from two different points of view.

Possible Scope and Sequence
(based on one-hour class periods)

Day 1	Day 2	Day 3	Day 4	Day 5
Activating Knowledge Writing Warm-up Expanding Vocabulary	Using Words in Context: *Derivatives* Breaking Down the Meaning	Dialogue: *To Buy or Not to Buy?*	Reading Skill Focus: *Sequencing* Pre-reading: *Consumption Match-up*	Chapter Reading: *What to Buy?* Reading Skill Follow-up

Day 6	Day 7	Day 8	Day 9	Day 10
Comprehension Questions	Writing about Consumption: *How-to Guide*	Writing about Consumption *(cont'd)*	Culminating Activity: *Are You Buying This?!*	Culminating Activity *(cont'd)*

Time
Eight to ten one-hour class periods

Essential Questions
- What are the social, environmental, and economic impacts of resource consumption?
- What is included in a typical product's life cycle?
- How does advertising influence consumption?
- What are ways to consume with sustainability in mind?

Integrated Subject Areas
- Social Studies
- Science
- English Language Arts

Content Objectives
Students will:
- Evaluate the impacts of consumption
- Critically analyze an advertisement
- Identify the steps in the life cycle of a product
- Determine ways to become more critical consumers

Language Objectives
Students will:
- Compare and contrast ideas in two photographs
- Write a response to a prompt
- Define and use new vocabulary words
- Discuss and analyze advertisements through a dialogue with a classmate

- Read about the steps in a product's life cycle
- Sequence events in a reading
- Create a how-to guide on making better purchasing decisions

Key Concepts
- Resource consumption
- Consumerism
- Marketing and advertising
- Media literacy

Vocabulary
- Advertising
- Manufacturing
- Consumption
- Disposal

Standards Addressed
- TESOL standards
- NCTE standards
- NCSS standards
- NSES standards

* Please see Appendix A for a list of national standards addressed.

Assessment Option
Use the Chapter 4 assessments of student knowledge and outlook/personal beliefs as pre-tests for the chapter. Follow up with the same assessments at the end of the chapter to determine changes in knowledge and outlook/personal beliefs.

4 Thinking about Consumption

Instructions

1. Read the introduction with students. Ask them what kinds of products they buy and what effect these things might have on themselves, on other people, and the earth.

2. Explain that Chapter 4 will introduce them to how these things are made, and the possible impacts of using them.

What sorts of things do people buy, and why do they buy them? How do these decisions affect their lives, the lives of other people, and the environment?

Chapter 4 will introduce you to thinking about our consumption patterns and what it takes to make the things we buy. You will **speak** to classmates about how consumption differs in different parts of the world. You will **listen** to dialogue and then speak with a partner about how advertisements can convince us to make decisions about what we buy. You will **read** about the life cycle of an everyday item: running shoes. At the end of the chapter, you will use what you've learned to **write** a guide to help people learn how make better purchasing decisions.

Consumers have many choices at stores like this one.

Instructions

1. Ask two students who their favorite musicians are.

2. Ask the class to identify similarities and differences between the two musicians.

3. Explain that when students find similarities between two things, they *compare* them. For example, both musicians might play the guitar. When they find differences between two things, they *contrast* them. For example, one musician might sing rock and roll songs, while the other sings country music.

4. Read through the example on the page with students.

5. Have students review the two photos and the completed Venn diagram. Challenge them to add additional comparisons and contrasts. Ask them to use evidence from the photographs to make these comparisons and contrasts.

When you *compare* things, you find similarities among those things. When you *contrast* things, you find differences among those things.

Example: Look at the two photos on this page. Compare and contrast what you see in the photos.

The Venn diagram below the photos will help to guide you through this example. The middle section of the diagram shows how the two photos *compare*. The left and right sides show how the photos *contrast*.

Picture 1

Picture 2

Picture 1 shows food that looks:

- healthy
- like vegetables
- available at a market
- available during the fall

Both photos show food. The food appears to be for sale.

Picture 2 shows food that looks:

- processed
- like cereal
- packaged in boxes
- available at a grocery store
- like it all might taste the same

Directions: Use the Venn diagram to compare and contrast the following two photos. To *compare* the photos, think about what the people in the photos have in common. To *contrast* the photos, think about how their lives and the things they use might be different.

Picture 1

Picture 2

Activating Knowledge

Instructions

1. Explain that the photographs depict two families who live in different countries and own different kinds of items. The family on the left is from Japan, and the family on the right is from Western Samoa.

2. Have students work with a partner to complete the Venn diagram. Challenge them to identify at least two similarities and two differences between the families and their belongings.

3. Ask students to share their answers.

   • **Option:** Record all answers on a Venn diagram on the board.

4. Ask students why certain people from different countries may consume more than other people (i.e., why do they have more belongings?). (Possible reasons include differences in wealth or income, or societal influences). Ask students to make guesses about what life is like for the families in the pictures.

5. **Option:** Ask students: *If a photo were to show people in the United States with their belongings, what would be included in the photo?* If the students were not born in the United States, ask them to think about the kinds of things a typical family in their home country would own. How do these mental images compare? How do they contrast?

6. Explain that these photos are one indication of how people in different parts of the world consume, or buy and use, resources.

Instructions

1. To prepare students for the writing warm-up, ask them if they believe that people who own the most things are happiest. How might having some things make people happy? Could people be happy without these things? Could having lots of things actually make some people unhappy?

2. Have students respond to the writing prompt.

   • **Differentiated Instruction:** If beginner students are more comfortable writing in their native language, allow them to do so.

   • **Differentiated Instruction:** If beginner students are comfortable drawing diagrams to support their writing, allow them to do so.

3. Have students share their response with a partner.

4. Ask students to respond to this fact: In the United States, people have more things than ever, but only a third of people in the U.S. report being *very happy*. This is the same fraction of people who reported being *very happy* as in 1957, when people had half the wealth they do today.[1]

5. Ask students to share their responses with the class. Does this fact surprise them? Why, or why not?

Directions: Respond to the following question with a **free write**. When you free write, you write about an idea for a period of time without stopping. Write continuously and include every idea you can think of until you are told to stop.

Do you believe having more things can make people happier?

Tip: You might want to think about things that you have bought recently.

How do the things you buy make you feel?

Do they improve your life?

What are the things you need to be happy?

Directions: Look at the following images and vocabulary words. Guess what you think the words mean based on the given photos.

A

advertising

B

manufacturing

C

consumption

D

disposal

Instructions

1. Have students study the four photos independently.

2. Have students collaborate with a partner to come up with possible definitions for each word.

3. Discuss students' ideas.

   • **Differentiated Instruction:** Copy this page onto an overhead or display it with a document camera. As students are brainstorming ideas for each vocabulary word, list these next to the photo in each box.

4. **Option:** Review the following derivatives:

   • *advertising (n) – advertise, advertisement*

   • *manufacturing (n) – manufacture, manufacturer*

   • *consumption (n) – consume, consumer, consumable*

   • *disposal (n) – dispose*

5. **Option:** Review the following roots and prefix:

   • *manufacture – from the Latin words* manus *which means "hand" and* factus *which means "to be made"*

   • *dis – apart*

Instructions

1. Read the definition of *derivative* and the directions for the activity aloud.

2. Have students work independently or with a partner to complete the activity.

   • **Differentiated Instruction:** Read each statement aloud to students, pausing where a blank appears. As students listen, they can determine the appropriate vocabulary to complete the sentences.

3. Ask volunteers to read the completed sentences aloud to the class.

Using Words in Context: Derivatives

A **derivative** is a word that is created from another word. In this exercise, you will work with vocabulary words and their derivatives. Knowing derivatives can be useful when you want to use different forms of the word for speaking and writing.

Directions: For each of the sentences below, choose a word from the Word Bank to complete the sentence. Each word will be used once.

Word Bank	
advertising	advertisement
manufacturing	manufactured
consumption	consumers
disposal	disposing

1. My favorite _____ on television is the commercial where everyone is dancing around a car.

2. Hudson High School has trash cans in every room for waste _____.

3. In countries with high rates of _____, people buy many things.

4. Electronics _____ uses machines to do much of the work.

5. Instead of _____ of your aluminum can in the trash, why not recycle it?

6. Teenage _____ buy clothing and electronics.

7. _____ can persuade us to buy things we do not need.

8. The label on my shirt tells me what company _____ it.

Answers

1. advertisement
2. disposal
3. consumption
4. manufacturing
5. disposing
6. consumers
7. Advertising
8. manufactured

Directions: Each box below includes one of the four vocabulary words from the previous page, as well as its definition. Below each definition:

1. Answer the question.

2. Write a sentence using the vocabulary word.

3. Choose the one word in the group that does not relate to the vocabulary word.

---

advertising

Definition: *the practice of using messages to encourage people to buy or use something*

1. How does advertising influence what you buy?

2. Use *advertising* in a sentence.

3. Which word does not belong?
book   information   persuasive   sales

---

manufacturing

Definition: *the process of making or assembling a finished product*

1. What steps do you think are involved in manufacturing a wooden table?

2. Use *manufacturing* in a sentence.

3. Which word does not belong?
create   make   destroy   build

---

consumption

Definition: *the use of resources and products*

1. Which influences your consumption more: price or quality?

2. Use *consumption* in a sentence.

3. Which word does not belong?
buy   use   dispose   create

---

disposal

Definition: *the act of getting rid of something*

1. What are alternatives to waste disposal?

2. Use *disposal* in a sentence.

3. Which word does not belong?
trash   waste   garden   garbage

Instructions

1. Explain the directions. After reviewing the definitions, explain to students they will (1) answer the question, (2) create a sentence using the vocabulary word, and (3) choose the one word in the group that does not relate to the vocabulary word.

- **Differentiated Instruction:** Demonstrate how the activity works by filling in one of the boxes.

- **Differentiated Instruction:** Enlarge the four boxes to poster size and fill in one of the boxes. Work as a class to fill in answers within each box and write them on the poster. The poster can then remain hanging in the room throughout this unit of study.

2. This activity could be done independently, in pairs or small groups, or as an entire class.

3. Option: Have students search for and cut out magazine pictures that relate to each vocabulary word.

4. Option: As a homework assignment, have students write a single paragraph using the four vocabulary words.

Answers

advertising

1. TV commercials for restaurants often convince me to eat at those restaurants.

2. The advertising for that new movie makes me want to see it.

3. book

manufacturing

1. Wood must be cut into pieces for the table top and legs. Those pieces are joined together. The wood is sanded and stained.

2. Manufacturing usually involves large machines.

3. destroy

consumption

1. The price of something is what influences me the most.

2. Consumption around the world has increased over the last century.

3. create

disposal

1. Recycling and reusing items are alternatives to waste disposal.

2. My school provides trash cans for waste disposal.

3. garden

Dialogue

Instructions

1. Ask students to study the photograph independently.

2. Ask: *If this photo was an advertisement for a product, what do you think the product would be?*

3. Read the dialogue aloud so students can hear proper pronunciation.

   - **Differentiated Instruction:** For advanced speakers, choose two students to read the dialogue aloud to the class as an example.

   - **Differentiated Instruction:** Allow students to practice reading through this sample dialogue in pairs.

4. Ask students if there are any other considerations they would make before choosing to purchase the drink.

Dialogue: To Buy or Not to Buy?

Directions: Study the photograph below on your own for a minute. Then, read the dialogue that follows.

Thomas: If this photo were an advertisement, what do you think the ad would be selling?

Julia: I think the ad would be selling the sports drink in front of the runner.

Thomas: I agree with you. The message is: if you drink this sports drink, you could be a good athlete just like the man in the photo.

Julia: You're right. He looks like he has either just finished running or may be running soon.

Thomas: Do you think you would choose to drink this sports drink after seeing this advertisement?

Julia: I'm not sure. I would want to know more information before making a decision about the drink.

Thomas: What kind of information?

Julia: What are the ingredients in the drink? If the drink is just water with green food coloring and sugar, then I would rather drink water! But if there were healthy ingredients in the drink, I could be persuaded to drink it.

Thomas: I completely agree. I would also want to know if I could recycle the bottle and how much the drink costs. If it's more than a certain price, I'm not paying for it.

Julia: Great questions. It seems like price, where the bottle ends up, and what kinds of ingredients go into the drink can help us decide whether or not we would buy the drink.

Thomas: I guess when you ask more questions about a product, you can make better decisions before you actually purchase it.

Julia: Yes, I need to know more about a product than what is in the advertisement to decide whether or not I want to spend my money on it.

Dialogue: To Buy or Not to Buy?

Directions: You will review an advertisement. Use this page to create a dialogue with your partner, discussing what you think the message of the ad is, and what you would want to know before purchasing the product.

A: What do you think this advertisement is trying to sell us?

B: I think the ad is selling _____.
   What do you think it is selling?

A: I think the ad is selling _____.

B: What do you think about the advertisement? Do you like it?

B: I _____ like it because _____.
   (do or don't)
   How about you?

A: I _____ like it because _____.
   (do or don't)

A: What do you want to know that is not included in the ad?

B: I want to know _____.
   What about you? What would you want to know?

A: I want to know _____. If I had that information,
   it would help me decide whether or not I want to buy the advertised product.

B: Does the ad make you want to buy it?

A: _____ because _____.
   (Yes or No)
   How about you? Does the ad make you want to buy the advertised product?

B: _____ because _____.
   (Yes or No)

Dialogue

Instructions

1. Divide the class into pairs, and assign one person in each pair to role A and the other person to role B.

2. Each pair will work through this dialogue using a print advertisement. You might supply each pair with an ad from a magazine, or you could ask student pairs to choose their own ads. You could also display a single ad using an overhead or a document camera.

3. Have student pairs read through the dialogue aloud together, inserting their own ideas where there are blanks.

4. Have pairs share their advertisements and dialogues with the class.

Instructions

1. Ask students to recall the events in a story they may have recently read. Ask them what order the main events occurred—what came first, next, last?

2. Explain that when they recall events from a story in the order they occurred, they put together a sequence of events.

3. Ask if anyone is familiar with the term *sequence*. (A sequence is a series of things or a particular order in which things are arranged.)

4. As a class, review the transition words and read through the example paragraph.

5. Ask them how the story would be affected if the events were rearranged in a different order. Would the story still make sense?

When you **sequence**, you put things in order. Mathematicians might sequence numbers in order from least to greatest. Scientists may have to sequence steps in a lab experiment. Authors may sequence the order of events in their story to create a plot. Historians may sequence events in history in order to create a timeline.

The parts of the sequence must be told in the correct order to make sense. Certain *transition words* may be used at the beginning of sentences to indicate where they occur in the event or story. Here are some examples:

First (beginning)	Next (following)	Finally (end)
Then (following)	After (following)	Lastly (end)

Example: Read the following paragraph about how one teenager decided to speak out against toxics, or poisons, in makeup and other beauty products. Watch how the writer uses transition words to sequence the paragraph.

Jessica Assaf had no idea that some makeup products actually had toxics in them that could lead to cancer and other illnesses. She decided to take action. **First**, she worked with the Teens for Safe Cosmetics campaign and created *Operation Beauty Drop*, where large bins were placed in malls for teens to drop off beauty products that contained toxics. **Next**, the beauty products were sent back to manufacturers with a petition signed by teenagers demanding the products be made with safer chemicals. **Then**, Jessica and her friends asked their local senators to pass a bill in California requiring manufacturers to inform the Department of Health Services if their products contained toxics. **Finally**, after the bill was passed, Jessica held a **summit** to educate teenagers around the country about how they, too, could take action against toxic chemicals in beauty products.[1]

Jessica Assaf, member of Teens for Safe Cosmetics

---

summit (n) – a conference or meeting

Reading Skill Focus

Directions: Now it's your turn to sequence events! The photos in the left column are arranged in order showing the life cycle of an aluminum can. Each statement in the right column goes with one of the photos, but the statements are not in order. Determine which statement goes with each photo.

Instructions

1. The photos on the left are in correct sequential order, starting at the top and ending at the bottom of the page. The phrases on the right, however, are out of order. Ask students to match each photo on the left to its corresponding phrase on the right in order to correctly sequence the life cycle of an aluminum can. On a photocopied page, have students draw lines from the photos to the matching text phrases.

2. Ask for a volunteer to read the life cycle of an aluminum can in proper sequence.

Next, people buy and consume the soda in the aluminum cans.

The cans are later filled with soda and sealed.

Finally, the cans are disposed as garbage or recycled into new cans.

Then, the aluminum ore is manufactured into sheets of aluminum, which are cut to create cans.

First, aluminum ore (called bauxite) is mined from underground.

After the cans have been filled with soda, they are delivered to stores.

Answers

1. First, aluminum ore (called bauxite) is mined from underground.

2. Then, the aluminum ore is manufactured into sheets of aluminum, which are cut to create cans.

3. The cans are later filled with soda and sealed.

4. After the cans have been filled with soda, they are delivered to stores.

5. Next, people buy and consume the soda in the aluminum cans.

6. Finally, the cans are disposed as garbage or recycled into new cans.

Instructions

1. Photocopy the two pages and cut out the cards. There should be eighteen total cards. Note that this activity requires each student to have a partner. If you only have ten students, pass out five *Did You Know?* cards and the matching five *Hidden Impact* cards.

2. Explain to students that the goal of this activity is to talk to different students in order to share information with them about different products. Ultimately they want to find their partner (i.e., the person with the card that matches their own). Each Did You Know? card has a matching Hidden Impact card.

3. **Option:** Model how students might ask and answer questions to find their proper match.

   • *Student A: I have a picture of a pair of jeans on my card.*

   • *Student B: I have the words "cardboard box". We're not a match, but did you know that it takes 2–3 tons of trees to make 1 ton of paper?*

   • *Student A: Wow, that's a lot of trees! Well, did you know that the Levi Strauss Company first made its famous 501 style blue jeans in 1873?*

   • *Student B: I didn't know blue jeans had been around that long!* ▶

How much do you know about everyday products you use?

Directions: Review the information provided about the following products. Then, match each product with its hidden impact on the next page.

Did You Know?

1  Levi Strauss & Co. made their first famous 501 style blue jeans in 1873.	**2**  About 550 million Big Macs are sold by McDonald's in the United States each year.	**3**  The Coca-Cola Company sells products in over 200 countries.
4  Each year chocolate sales reach almost 60 billion dollars.	**5**  The first gasoline-powered automobile was built in 1885 and had three wheels.	**6**  All of the gold ever mined in the world could fit into two Olympic size swimming pools.
7 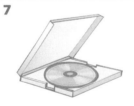 Music sales in the United States are shifting from CD sales to online or digital music sales.	**8**  More than 1 billion cell phones were sold worldwide in 2007.	**9**  About half of the paper produced in the world is used for packaging.

Hidden Impacts

A	B	C
Every gallon of gas burned in a car produces 20 pounds of carbon dioxide, a greenhouse gas that contributes to climate change.	To get enough gold to make one wedding ring, 250 tons of rock are removed from the earth.	It takes 2 to 3 tons of trees to make 1 ton of paper.
D	**E**	**F**
CDs and DVDs and their cases contain plastic, which may come from recycled plastic bottles or from petroleum oil.	Children as young as nine years old have been found working in sweatshops that make blue jeans.	It takes over 600 gallons of water to make one hamburger patty.
G	**H**	**I**
Many of the electronics (including cell phones and computers) recycled in the United States end up in Asia and Africa, where their toxic parts pollute the environment.	Chocolate is made from the cacao plant. Only about 7% of the money made from chocolate sales worldwide goes to cacao farmers.	Soda is made from corn syrup, which is sugar from corn plants. A diet high in sugar can cause obesity.

Instructions, *continued*

4. Distribute one card to each student.

5. Students will need to move around the classroom. At the end of the activity, students will be in pairs, equipped with an interesting fact and an impact associated with a particular item.

6. After all of the students have found their proper matches, ask them to share with the class facts they learned about their specific product. Ask student pairs what surprised them about the information on their cards.

7. Explain that the chapter reading will discuss the impacts of products (like the ones shown on the cards) in more detail.

Instructions

1. Give students a minute to preview the reading. Ask them to consider the title and subtitles, as well as any photos. What do students think the reading will be about?

2. Explain to students that, as they read, they will be learning about a particular sequence: the life cycle of a product.

3. Review transition words that will help students place events in a particular sequence. As they read, have them pay close attention to the life cycle of the product by identifying key sequence words.

4. **Differentiated Instruction:** As students are reading, hand them sticky notes to flag possible events during a product's life cycle.

What to Buy?

The average American child watches between 25,000 and 40,000 television commercials per year.[2] That's a lot of commercials! We see advertisements all around us: in magazines, on billboards, on buses, in stores, and possibly even at school. Do you think all these advertisements influence you in any way? What else might influence you to buy something?

People buy things for all sorts of reasons. Here are just a few reasons people might buy an item, like a new shirt:

- They need it.

- It is affordable or on sale.

- It makes people look or feel good.

- It is popular—almost everyone has one.

- It is made well and will last a long time.

- A famous actor, musician, or athlete advertises it.

There are many factors that a person might consider when deciding whether or not to buy something. Advertising companies spend millions of dollars trying to convince us that their product is the best. Advertisers may use famous people or **humor** to sell a product, or they might make the product appear to be very popular. Commercials and ads can influence the way we consume, but do they tell us the whole story about what we are buying?

humor (n) – the quality that makes something funny

Some people get rid of things they don't want by having garage sales.

Buy, Buy, Buy

In the last century, world consumption multiplied by sixteen times, from $1.5 trillion in 1900 to $24 trillion in 1998.[3] During the same period, world population **quadrupled**. That means that overall consumption has increased four times as much as the population has. People are buying a lot more stuff!

It is important for people to be able to buy what they need. All people have basic needs that must be met, like food, water, energy, and shelter. We also have other important needs like education and health.

Unfortunately, in some cases, overconsumption has led to problems around the world. Resources are being used up faster than they can replace themselves, which means we are losing many forests, natural areas, and species of plants and animals. Additionally, some people have gone into **debt**, believing they can spend more money than they actually have. Credit cards have allowed people to buy things they cannot afford.

When you think about the story behind the stuff we buy, you may start to wonder where it comes from and where it ends up after we use it. Were certain parts of the environment destroyed to make a particular product? Did the people who made the product earn enough money to survive? You may also start to question whether the product is healthy for you and the people you care about. Asking questions about consumption can be good for you, other people, the economy, and the environment.

---

quadrupled (v) – multiplied by four; became four times larger
debt (n) – the condition of owing money

Hides from cows are turned into leather for shoes and clothing.

The Life Cycle of a Product

A product's life cycle tells the story of how that product is made, how it is used, and what happens to it when it is no longer useful. Let's take a look at the life cycle of a running shoe.

Step 1: The first step in the life cycle is obtaining raw materials to create the product. You already know that everything we use comes from nature. Running shoes are made mostly of leather and petroleum-based chemicals. Leather comes from cows, and petroleum is drilled from underground.

The leather might come from cows raised in Texas. Hides from those cows are probably then shipped to another country to be treated with chemicals that turn them into useful leather. Petroleum-based chemicals are used to create the sole of the shoe. Much of the petroleum used in the United States comes from the Middle East and South America. After petroleum is drilled, it is broken down into many different useful products.

Container ships carry products around the world.

Step 2: Next, the materials are combined to manufacture a finished product. A factory in Hong Kong might **assemble** all the pieces of the running shoes (the leather, petroleum-based sole, and other components, such as shoelaces), with the help of people and machines. In some cases, workers in factories do not have safe working conditions, or they are not paid fairly for their work.

If you have ever bought running shoes, you probably know that each pair of shoes comes in its own box. Just like the shoes, the boxes have to be manufactured. Natural resources, like water and trees, are used to create them.

Step 3: After a product is assembled, it is **transported** to a place where it will be sold. Shoes from Asia travel by boat to the United States where they will be sold. A pair of shoes shipped from Hong Kong to a **distribution** center in Los Angeles, California, will travel over 7,000 miles (or almost 12,000 km). A distribution center will ship the shoes to stores all over the country.

Step 4: The next step in a product's life cycle is consumption. Consumption refers to buying and using goods and services. This step has a major influence on the entire life cycle of the running shoes. No company would make shoes if people didn't buy them.

Consumption is one step in a product's life cycle where you can have a big impact. You can influence the whole life cycle of a product by being a thoughtful consumer. For example, if lots of people buy running shoes that are made in factories where workers are paid low wages and exposed to toxic chemicals, companies will continue to make these shoes. On the other hand, if people only bought products that were produced sustainably—that is, products that are good for people, the environment, and economies— companies will respond by making products more sustainably.

assemble (v) – to put parts together
transported (v) – carried from one location to another
distribution (n) – delivering and handing things out to people

Step 5: The last step in a product's life cycle is disposal. One method of disposal is to throw things into the garbage. When you toss your used shoes into the garbage, they can no longer be used by anyone.

A different type of disposal is **recycling**. If you recycle your shoes instead of throwing them away, they can be used again. You might pass along your worn shoes to someone else who needs them, or the shoes could be turned into something completely new. For example, one running shoe manufacturer turns worn-out shoes into running tracks and playground surfaces.[4]

An alternative to disposal is to not discard materials at all. In some cases, we may be able to reuse items rather than throw away or recycle them. For example, you could save your old running shoes for when you might get dirty, like when you garden or paint. Also, buying running shoes that are meant to last a long time means that you won't have to buy new ones as often.

Asking Questions, Making Choices

We don't have to stop consuming, but becoming aware of what we buy and why we buy it is important. Sometimes it seems like we are surrounded by advertisements that try to persuade us to purchase more and more things. If we want a sustainable planet—one where our children and grandchildren can enjoy plenty of resources and a healthy environment—we have to think about what and how we are consuming. Asking questions about how products are made, if they are healthy for us, if the people who make them are treated fairly, and if they are healthy for the environment, are all ways we can be thoughtful consumers. Whether we wear designer brands or make our own clothes, or whether we use disposable or reusable cups, small choices that we make every day can have a big impact on the world.

***

recycling (v) – extracting useful materials from garbage or waste to use again

Old running shoes can be used to make running tracks.

Instructions

1. After students have finished reading, have them complete the reading skill follow-up activity.

   • **Differentiated Instruction:** For beginners, allow them to choose key words from each step and help them to create simple sentences using the key words.

   • **Differentiated Instruction:** Challenge students to come up with ideas for how the first step in the life cycle (extracting raw materials) could be eliminated. How might new shoes be manufactured without the first step? (For example, recycling shoes rather than throwing them away would provide materials that could be remade into new shoes.)

2. **Option:** Have each student determine the life cycle of a product he or she owns by researching what kinds of materials it is made from, and how the product is manufactured, distributed, consumed, and disposed of.

Directions: You have just read about the life cycle of a running shoe. For each box below, write one to two sentences explaining the sequence of this lifecycle using your own words.

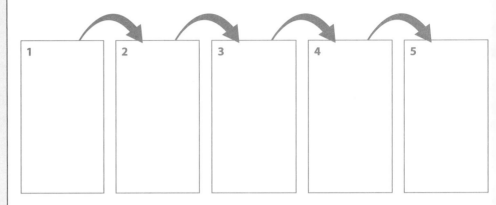

Answers

1. First, raw materials like leather and petroleum are gathered.
2. Second, people assemble the materials to create a running shoe.
3. Third, the running shoes are transported to different places where they will be sold.
4. Fourth, people purchase the running shoes. Then, they use the shoes.
5. Finally, the shoes are disposed of in the garbage or maybe recycled to create a running track.

Comprehension Questions

Directions: Answer the following questions to support your comprehension of the chapter reading.

Understanding what you read

1. In the example of the running shoes, the assembled shoes would have a label that says *Made in Hong Kong*. Identify other places where parts of the shoes were made.

2. According to the reading, what are two reasons people decide to buy something?

Thinking about what you read

3. Explain the reasoning behind the author's statement, "People are buying a lot more stuff!"

4. Create your own title for this reading. Explain how your title reflects the main idea of the reading.

Questioning what you read

5. What is the author's main message in this chapter reading?

6. Explain why you think the author begins the reading with the following fact: *The average American child watches between 25,000 and 40,000 television commercials per year.*

Making connections to what you read

7. What is one way you can help to reduce the environmental destruction caused by consumption?

8. How are people in other countries affected by the things we buy, use, and throw away?

Further discussion questions

9. Houses in the United States built 100 years ago had much smaller closets than houses built today. Why do you think closets today are much larger?

10. How are credit cards related to consumption?

Comprehension Questions

Instructions

1. Before students begin answering the comprehension questions, share with them the academic language they will see in many of the questions (see Appendix B).

2. Explain that the questions are divided into five sections according to the different ways they support comprehension. (See Appendix B for a detailed explanation of each section.)

3. **Differentiated Instruction:** Differentiate the questions students must answer based on their reading levels. Support comprehension by working with students who may need more guided instruction.

Answers

1. leather from Texas, petroleum from South America or the Middle East

2. Any of the following: They need it. It is affordable or on sale. It makes people look or feel good. It is popular. It is made well and will last for a long time. A famous actor, musician, or athlete advertises it.

3. Population has increased four-fold, but consumption has increased sixteen-fold.

4. Example: Sustainable Consumption Choices, Sustainable Lives

5. The author wants to inform the reader about what it takes to make the things we buy, and encourage people to think twice about what they buy.

6. The huge numbers grab your attention.

7. buy sustainably produced items, items that last a long time, or fewer new items

8. People in other countries might make the items. They earn money, but might also be exposed to toxic chemicals or other hazards. The use and disposal of items with toxic components, like electronics, may negatively impact the environment, affecting all people.

9. We have more stuff, like clothes.

10. Credit cards allow people to buy things even if they can't afford them, so people can buy more than they otherwise would.

Instructions

1. Students will write a how-to guide about making sustainable purchasing choices.

2. Read through the instructions and example how-to guide (see next page) with students. Their how-to guide will have a form similar to the sample how-to guide.

3. Share the Chapter 4 writing rubric with students. You may want to add relevant spelling and grammar components to the rubric.

> A **how-to guide** is a written manual that provides instructions for doing something. There are how-to guides for just about anything, from how to manage your time to how to eat healthy food.

Imagine an organization has been created to help consumers learn more about the products they buy. You have been asked by the organization to create a how-to guide that will help people to make smart purchasing decisions for themselves, for other people, and for the environment.

Your how-to guide should:

- focus on making a good purchasing decision about one type of product (choose one: food, clothing, electronics, toys, cleaning products, health and beauty products, or wood products)
- include at least five *tips* or ideas to help someone make good decisions
- include illustrations and/or pictures
- include at least two chapter vocabulary words
- use correct sequencing words, when appropriate

An example of a how-to guide is on the next page.

Chapter 4 Writing Rubric
see p. 93!

A how-to guide can help consumers make choices that are good for people and the planet.

How to Analyze a Commercial

Young people in the United States watch an average of 100 commercials per day. Instead of just watching advertisements without really thinking about their message, here are some things you can do to analyze a commercial:

1. First, when a commercial comes on, determine what product the company is trying to sell.

2. Second, carefully think about how the commercial is trying to convince you to buy their product. Is a famous person in the commercial? Is the commercial funny? Is the product supposed to make you sexier?

3. Third, decide who the commercial is targeting. Is the company trying to sell products to teenagers? Mothers? Grandparents?

4. Fourth, do some research to find out how this product compares to other products. Try to find information that was not included in the commercial.

5. Finally, share what you learn with your friends and family.

Following this guide can help you think critically about commercial advertising, and to buy products that are important to you—not just those that have great advertisements.

Writing Steps

Instructions

1. Review the steps with students.

2. Make sure that all students understand the choices: food, clothing, electronics, cleaning products, health and beauty products, and wood products. Each student will pick just one of these as the focus for his or her how-to guide.

3. **Grammar Suggestion:** Teach students how to write imperative sentences to include in their how-to guide.

Writing Steps: How-to Guide

Step 1: Decide which of the following types of products you will focus on: food, clothing, electronics, cleaning products, health and beauty products, or wood products.

Step 2: Think about what information would help people to make good decisions when they purchase a product. You want to help them to purchase things that are good for themselves, for other people, and for the environment.

Step 3: Research ideas for how people can make these decisions. You will need at least five ideas for your how-to guide.

Step 4: Use the Edit Checklist below to review and improve your guide.

Step 5: Come up with a title for your how-to guide. You will also want to include some introductory information and a closing sentence.

Step 6: Find or create pictures to include in your how-to guide.

Step 7: Put it all together. On a sheet of paper, include the title, at least five how-to ideas, and pictures to create an interesting how-to guide.

 Edit Checklist

	Author Check	Peer Editor Check
Did you select five or more ideas for how people can make good purchasing decisions that help themselves, other people, and the environment?		
Did you create a title for your how-to guide?		
Did you include pictures or other images in your how-to guide?		
Did you use at least two chapter vocabulary words?		
Did you use correct sequencing?		

Writing Organizer: How-to Guide

Title: How to _____

Introduction: Write two to three sentences about why people should care about making good purchasing choices when they are considering the type of product you selected:

_____

_____

_____

How-to Information: In your how-to guide, provide specific ideas for making smart purchasing choices. Here are some suggestions:

- Specific things people should know about these products
- What people should look for when they want to buy a product
- What people should avoid when they are thinking about buying a product
- Where people can find information to help them make informed purchasing choices

1. _____
   _____

2. _____
   _____

3. _____
   _____

4. _____
   _____

5. _____
   _____

Closing Sentence: _____

Writing Organizer

Instructions

1. Students can use this writing organizer to organize information for the how-to guide.

   - **Differentiated Instruction:** For beginning students who may need more guidance, gather them into a small group and assist them with writing their how-to guide.

2. Suggest resources that students may use to find consumer information. Here are some ideas to get started:

   - Cosmetics: Skin Deep Cosmetic Safety Database www.cosmeticsdatabase.com
   - Food: Local Harvest www.localharvest.org
   - Clothing: Sweatfree Communities www.sweatfree.org
   - General: GoodGuide www.goodguide.com
   - General: Environmental Working Group www.ewg.org

3. Once they finish writing their how-to guide, they should use the Edit Checklist and then exchange guides with a classmate. After the peer edit, students should revise their original drafts.

4. **Option:** Ask students to design real how-to guides (like tri-fold brochures) that can be used by community members. Each page might include a how-to step, an explanation of the step, and a photo.

Culminating Activity: Are You Buying This?! (1-2 hours)

Overview

Students work in groups to create and present mock television commercials for products linked to unsustainable or unhealthy behavior. Students first present the commercial as it would typically be seen on television, and then present it again incorporating the product's negative impacts.

Materials/Preparation

- *Product* and *Consequence Cards* – make one double-sided front-to-back copy with Products on one side and Consequences on the other. Cut into six individual cards.

- Blank paper and colored pens/pencils for creating props/signage

Introduction

1. Ask the class if they have seen a television advertisement recently that made them really want to buy a product. Ask them if they remember how the ad presented the product (this is an advertising technique).

   - Was a celebrity promoting it?

   - Did it feature people doing fun and exciting things?

   - Were there attractive models involved?

2. Tell the class that, in 2006, companies in the United States spent nearly $150 billion (that's $150,000,000,000!) to advertise their products.[2] The average young person views over 40,000 television ads each year, plus thousands more in magazines, billboards, and other outlets.[3]

   - **Differentiated Instruction:** Write these numbers on the board so that students can see them as you say them out loud.

3. Ask the class what important information they think is left out of most advertisements. (Most ads leave out any negative consequences tied to producing and consuming the product, and generally only include information on potential dangers if required by law, as with some advertising for prescription drugs. Typically, advertisers do not discuss the impact of their products on the environment or labor practices unless the product is being marketed as *eco-friendly* or *socially responsible.*)

4. Tell the class that they are going to try their talent at creating advertisements for products that are often marketed to U.S. consumers. However, they will not only have to create an ad that makes the product look good; they will also have to create a second ad that focuses on the product's less glamorous side.

Steps

1. Break the class into groups of 4-5 students. Distribute a *Product/Consequence* card to each group. One side of the card has some attractive selling points for the product. The other side has some of the negative consequences of consuming that product.

2. Tell the students that they will use these cards to create their two advertisements.

3. In order to sell their product effectively, each group will have to decide:

   - Who are they targeting? (who they think will buy this product)

   - What is the advertising technique they will use? (e.g., celebrity endorsement, humor, claims that using the product will make your life better)

4. Tell the students they have 20 minutes to create two commercials that they will act out in front of the class. One commercial will focus only on the attractive side of the product, and the other should focus only on the consequences. Both versions should attempt to sell the product. Students should use the same advertising technique for both ads. For example, if they are using supermodels to sell the attractive side of the product, they should also use supermodels to sell the negative consequences.

5. Tell the students that the ads have to be the same length as a regular television commercial, so each ad should be no longer than 1 minute.

6. After the groups put their ads together, have them present both commercials to the class, with the ad selling the attractive side of the product presented first.

7. Option: Have student groups create a third commercial for a sustainable alternative to the product they advertised in the first two commercials. They should focus the advertisement on how their new product will lessen the negative impacts the original item had on people, the environment, or the economy (local or global).

- The alternatives could be items/activities that already exist, or new inventions they dream up. For example, if their original item was *handi-lunches,* students might decide to make an advertisement for fruit picked from a local farm. They might focus on how the fresh fruit takes less water to produce than the processed handi-lunches, generates very little waste, and provides jobs for local farm workers.

8. Conclude the activity with a discussion, using one or more of the following questions:

- Do you think people know enough about the sustainability of their consumption choices?

- Should companies be required to share unsustainable or negative consequences associated with producing, consuming, or disposing of their products?

- Young people are a major target of many advertisements. Who should be responsible for regulating what young people consume: government, companies, or consumers?

- Often the true costs of a product are not included in its price; for example, when you buy a hamburger for $3 you may not be paying for all of the natural resources required to produce that burger. What are some costs that might not be included in the price of the things we buy? (Two examples are pollution and safety hazards.)

Are You Buying This?! Product Cards, front

Pine Valley Estates

- Beautiful all-wood dream homes
- Located in a quiet area
- 4,000-square-foot homes, plus 2 acres of private land
- Only a 30-minute drive from downtown

The Mega Burger

- Four beef patties, a half-pound of meat!
- Six slices of cheese
- Five strips of bacon
- Incredible low price of $1.99
- Available 24 hours a day

The Dominator XL SUV

- Over 12 feet long
- Fits eight people comfortably
- Four-wheel drive
- Includes CD player and TV
- Protects your family in case of an accident

Super Clean Car Wash Foam

- Keeps your car looking shiny and new
- Removes tough stains
- Protects your paint from scratches
- Makes every car look expensive

Handi-Lunches

- A complete pre-packaged lunch for kids
- Saves time spent preparing food
- Kids love the taste
- Includes healthy meats, cheese, snacks, and a drink

Way Cool Jeans

- Stylish
- Very hip—worn by famous people
- Flattering for all shapes and sizes
- Only $40 a pair

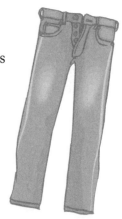

The Mega Burger

- It takes over 600 gallons of water to produce one beef patty
- Approximately 17% of U.S. children and adolescents are overweight
- Obesity is linked to diabetes—the yearly healthcare costs for a person with diabetes is more than twice the cost for a nondiabetic

Pine Valley Estates

- Over a 5-year period, 6 million acres of U.S. farmland—an area the size of the state of Maryland—were paved over for homes
- Trees are cleared to make room for houses and roads in new housing developments
- Deforested areas suffer from flooding and mudslides during heavy rains

Super Clean Car Wash Foam

- Washing your car at home puts harmful chemicals into streams, rivers, and oceans
- Runoff from car wash soap harms fish
- Washing your car at home while running a garden hose for 10 minutes uses 100 gallons of water; some commercial car washes recycle water

The Dominator XL SUV

- Air pollution from car exhaust contributes to the extinction of species and the destruction of natural environments
- Air pollution from car exhaust makes respiratory illnesses, such as asthma, worse
- Large automobiles often use more gasoline per mile than small cars

Way Cool Jeans

- Sewn in a sweatshop by 12-year-olds who work 16 hours a day and are not paid minimum wage
- Workers do not have time to go to school, so they cannot get better jobs
- Made from cotton; it takes 11,000 liters of water to produce 1 kilogram of cotton (approximately one pair of jeans)

Handi-Lunches

- Each food item is wrapped in plastic that cannot be recycled
- Most of the discarded plastic ends up in landfills where we bury trash
- In 2006, the United States threw away over 250 million tons of garbage

Action Project

Have students create a consumers' guide to locally available sustainable products—that is, products that promote long-term environmental, social, and economic health. Students should inquire about the sustainability of products sold in local stores, either in person or by telephone. Once they have compiled a list of all the neighborhood stores and restaurants that sell and/or use sustainably produced items, they can design a pamphlet, website, or poster to make this information accessible to the school or neighborhood community. If there are only a few sources of sustainably produced products available in your community, lobby one or more local business owners to offer more sustainable products or to use more sustainable practices.

Additional Resources on Consumption Issues

China Blue
www.pbs.org/independentlens/chinablue/

This film, part of the Independent Lens series on PBS, takes you inside blue jeans factories in China. The film focuses on a 17-year-old garment worker named Jasmine. (Micha Peled, 2005, Teddy Bear Films, 86 minutes)

Human Footprint, National Geographic Channel
http://channel.nationalgeographic.com

Short video clips (including a look at the United States' trash and car footprints), text, and interactive resources teach about the consumption habits of a typical American, and how that consumption impacts the environment.

Chew on This: Everything You Don't Want to Know about Fast Food, by Eric Schlosser

In this follow-up book to *Fast Food Nation*, Eric Schlosser provides an engaging exposé of the fast food industry, with a large section focusing on how junk food is marketed to youth. The book is intended for a pre-teen audience.

The Story of Stuff
www.storyofstuff.com

The Story of Stuff with Annie Leonard is a 20-minute online video. Annie's narration, alongside engaging graphics, walks viewers through the downsides of the *materials economy*, from extraction to production, distribution, consumption, and finally disposal. The movie is available in eleven languages. A fact sheet and an annotated script are also available on the site.

Chapter 4 Student Assessment, page 1
Knowledge about Consumption and Solutions

Vocabulary

Directions: Read each sentence and circle the letter next to the correct definition of the bold-faced word.

1. Billboards, television commercials, and newspaper ads are different forms of **advertising**.

   a. entertaining people
   b. a way that two people can speak to each other
   c. a written form of storytelling
   d. messages that encourage people to buy or use something

2. Both Ford and Chevrolet **manufacture** cars using an assembly line.

   a. paint
   b. sell
   c. make
   d. drive

3. The average person's **consumption** in North America is much greater than in Africa.

   a. use of medicine and clinics
   b. use of English language
   c. use of telephones and televisions
   d. use of resources and products

4. Many countries have huge landfills for the **disposal** of items that people no longer want.

   a. reduce, reuse, and recycling
   b. getting rid of something
   c. finding a new home
   d. turning trash into something people want

Chapter 4 Student Assessment, page 2

Content

Directions: Read the sentence and circle the letter next to the correct answer.

5. What is an alternative to throwing something away?

   a. finding another use for it
   b. putting it in a recycling bin
   c. giving it to a friend
   d. all of the above

Directions: Answer the following question by filling in the blanks with the correct information.

6. Compare and contrast the following two items:

   • Shirt A is a yellow cotton t-shirt. It was assembled in China and sells for $10.

   • Shirt B is a yellow polyester t-shirt made from petroleum. It was assembled in China and sells for $8.

   How do Shirt A and Shirt B *compare?*

   _____

   How do Shirt A and Shirt B *contrast?*

   _____

Reading Comprehension

Directions: For questions 7 and 8, circle the letter next to the correct answer.

7. Complete the following life cycle of an aluminum can:

   • First, metal is extracted from the earth.

   • Then, the metal is made into flat sheets that are cut to make cans.

   • Next, the cans are filled with soda or other liquid.

   • The full cans are then delivered to stores.

   • After that, people buy cans of soda at the store and drink the soda.

   • Finally, _____.

   a. the can is tossed into a garbage bin
   b. the can is refilled with new soda
   c. the sheets of metal are rolled into long tubes
   d. an advertising company creates ads to sell more cans of soda

8. Which step in the sequence would the following statement replace: *The can is placed in a recycling bin to be made into a new can.*

   a. the first step
   b. the third step
   c. the fourth step
   d. the last step

Chapter 4 Student Assessment, page 3
Outlook and Personal Beliefs

Answer the following questions based on your personal beliefs. There are no right or wrong answers.

1. Which of the following things do you think about when you purchase something new? (**Check all that apply**.)

☐ how well the people who made it were paid
☐ what kind of materials it is made of
☐ how much it costs
☐ how it affects the environment
☐ how far it traveled to reach you
☐ how long it will last or how much you will use it
☐ how using it will impact your health

2. Complete the following sentence:
One way I can personally work to be a thoughtful consumer is by …

_____

_____

_____

_____

Directions for 3 and 4: Fill in the ovals below based on your level of agreement. 1 means you strongly agree, and 7 means you strongly disagree.

1 = yes, definitely!   7 = no way!

⟵——————————————⟶

4. I believe my consumption decisions have an impact on people and places in other parts of the world.

1	2	3	4	5	6	7
⬭	⬭	⬭	⬭	⬭	⬭	⬭

5. I believe that I have the ability to help solve problems related to consumption.

1	2	3	4	5	6	7
⬭	⬭	⬭	⬭	⬭	⬭	⬭

Writing about Consumption: How To Guide, p.90

Chapter 4 Writing Rubric

Category	3	2	1
Content	Guide includes at least five ideas for purchasing items that are good for people and the environment.	Guide includes at least three or four ideas for purchasing items that are good for people and the environment.	Guide includes two or fewer ideas for purchasing items that are good for people and the environment.
Presentation	Guide includes title and photos and is easy to read.	Guide is missing title or photos.	It is difficult to read the guide or understand what it is about. No photos are included.
Vocabulary	Uses at least two chapter vocabulary words correctly	Uses one chapter vocabulary word correctly	Does not use chapter vocabulary correctly
Sequencing/ Logical Order	Presents information in a sequence and uses transition words correctly	Presents information partially in sequence and attempts to use transition words correctly	Does not present the how-to guide in a sequence and uses no transition words

Total = _____ / 12

**Chapter 4 Student Assessment,
pp. 93F, G**

1. d
2. c
3. d
4. b
5. d
6. compare: both are yellow t-shirts made in China

    contrast: shirt A is cotton and sells for $10; shirt B is polyester and sells for $8
7. a
8. d

Teacher Notes

5 Population around the World

During speaking and listening activities, students think critically about the potential impacts of population growth. After learning vocabulary relevant to population, students read about trends and effects of population growth and resource consumption around the world. Students predict the main idea of various reading passages, and then complete a writing exercise in which they write a five-paragraph essay detailing a community plan for growth. A culminating kinesthetic activity models the impact of changes in population growth rates and consumption patterns over time.

Possible Scope and Sequence
(based on one-hour class periods)

Day 1	Day 2	Day 3	Day 4	Day 5
Activating Knowledge Writing Warm-up Expanding Vocabulary	Using Words in Context: *Concept Map* Breaking Down the Meaning	Dialogue: *Immigration in the United States*	Reading Skill Focus: *Making Predictions* Pre-reading: *Fact and Opinion*	Chapter Reading: *People and the Planet* Reading Skill Follow-up

Day 6	Day 7	Day 8	Day 9
Comprehension Questions	Writing about Population: *Community Plan for Growth*	Writing about Population *(cont'd)*	Culminating Activity: *When the Chips are Down*

Time
Nine one-hour class periods

Essential Questions
- How does an increase in population affect people and resources around the world?
- What actions can people take to reduce impacts associated with carrying capacity?

Integrated Subject Areas
- Social Studies
- Science
- English Language Arts

Content Objectives
Students will:
- Explain how population has increased throughout time
- Make connections among environmental and social impacts related to population growth and resource consumption
- Identify solutions to population issues

Language Objectives
Students will:
- Discuss the effects of population growth around the world
- Write a response to a prompt about population growth
- Discuss changes in immigrant populations in the United States through a dialogue
- Define and use new vocabulary words

- Read about historic and current population trends
- Make predictions before and during a reading
- Write an essay outlining a community plan for growth

Key Concepts
- Population growth
- Carrying capacity
- Resource consumption
- Family planning
- Urban planning

Vocabulary
- Population
- Migration
- Carrying capacity
- Developing and developed countries

Standards Addressed
- TESOL standards
- NCTE standards
- NCSS standards
- NSES standards

* Please see Appendix A for a list of national standards addressed.

Assessment Option
Use the Chapter 5 assessments of student knowledge and outlook/personal beliefs as pre-tests for the chapter. Follow up with the same assessments at the end of the chapter to determine changes in knowledge and outlook/personal beliefs.

Instructions

1. Read the introduction with students.

2. Ask them if they have ever been in overcrowded places. Have they been in a crowded city, or even on a bus or train that was really crowded?

3. Ask students if they know which country in the world has the largest population. (China, with a population of over 1.3 billion people)

4. Ask them to consider what a more crowded planet would look like. How might the planet's resources be affected by an increase in human population?

Population around the World

How is population changing around the world? How does population growth connect to our lives?

Chapter 5 will introduce you to the effects of population growth around the world. You will **speak** to your classmates about what happens when the size of a population increases over a period of time. You will **listen** to and then practice a dialogue between two students learning about population growth among different immigrant groups in the United States. You will **read** about population growth over history and solutions to issues like overpopulation and overconsumption. Finally, you will **write** a community plan for growth that addresses overpopulation in your community in the future.

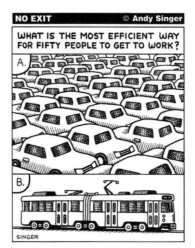

NO EXIT © Andy Singer

WHAT IS THE MOST EFFICIENT WAY FOR FIFTY PEOPLE TO GET TO WORK?

A.

B.

SINGER

Public transportation is one way to decrease pollution and traffic jams in heavily populated cities.

Activating Knowledge

Directions: A *caption* is a title or explanation for a picture. With a partner, match the photos on the left with the corresponding captions on the right, and then answer the questions that follow.

A.

B.

C.

1. One out of three people who live in the world's cities live in slums.[1] Slums are areas where many poor people live in crowded and often unclean conditions.

2. Less than 1% of freshwater is available for people around the world.[2] Freshwater is important for drinking, bathing, and cooking.

3. Mumbai, India, one of the fastest growing cities in the world, will have a population of over 27 million by the year 2015.[3]

Questions

- What do these photos have in common?

- Do these photos remind you of anything you have seen in your own life?

Activating Knowledge

Instructions

1. Have students work with a partner to match the photos with their corresponding captions.

2. Ask students to state the facts they learned in the matching activity. Did anything surprise them? What are their reactions to the photos and captions?

3. Ask students what a common theme might be for all of the photos. Explain that this chapter will focus on the issue of population growth.

Answers

A. 3
B. 1
C. 2

Instructions

1. Ask students if they know how many students attend their school.

2. Read the top portion of the page with them.

   - **Differentiated Instruction:** Before they begin writing, review the tripling diagram at the bottom of the page with students. Challenge them to explain how this diagram would look different for doubling and quadrupling.

3. For the writing warm-up, have students write independently about how their learning would be impacted by tripling the school's student population.

   - **Differentiated Instruction:** If beginner students are more comfortable writing in their native language, allow them to do so.

   - **Differentiated Instruction:** If beginner students want to draw diagrams to support their writing, allow them to do so.

4. Let students know that later in the chapter, they will have a chance to think about how a larger student population could be accommodated at your school.

Imagine you have just found out that, next year, three times as many students will attend your school. That means that the student population will *triple* (look at the diagram at the bottom of the page to see how tripling works). How will sharing books, seats, classrooms, and lockers with so many more students affect your learning?

Directions: Describe at least four different ways your learning will be affected if the student population of your school triples. Write in complete sentences.

Writing prompt: If my school population triples, my learning would be affected in many different ways.

How Tripling Works: The original population is multiplied by three.

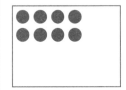

x 3 =

Directions: Look at the following images and vocabulary words. Guess what you think each word means based on the given photos.

A

population

B

migration

C

carrying capacity

D

developed country

developing country

Instructions

1. Have students study the four photos independently.

2. Have students share what they think each word means with a partner.

3. Discuss the definitions as a class.

4. **Option:** Copy this page onto an overhead or display it with a document camera. As students are brainstorming ideas for each vocabulary word, list these in the box with the photo.

5. **Option:** Review the following derivatives:

   • *population (n) – populated, overpopulation, populous, popular*

   • *migration (n) – migrate, migratory, immigration, emigration*

   • *developed and developing countries (n) – development, developmental*

   • *carrying capacity (n) – carry*

6. **Option:** Review the following word root:

   • *pop – people (other examples: popular, populist)*

Using Words in Context

Using Words in Context: Concept Map

Instructions

1. Read the activity aloud with students.

2. As students listen, they can determine the appropriate vocabulary for the concept map.

3. Have students work with a partner to compare and revise answers, if necessary.

4. Ask a volunteer to read the completed map.

5. **Differentiated Instruction:** Have students write a paragraph explaining the concept map in their own words.

Directions: Read the information in the *concept map* below, in order, from 1 to 5. Complete the map by filling in vocabulary words from the word bank. One word will not be used.

Word Bank				
developed	developing	migration	carrying capacity	population

Reasons for _____

1.
Lucy's family used to live in a _____ country where many people were not able to meet their basic needs. In some places, there wasn't enough food for everyone.

5.
Now, Lucy's family lives in another country and she and all of her siblings attend school. Her father would like to return to their country when it is safe again.

2.
The country where they lived did not have many opportunities.
The _____ was so large that there were not enough jobs for everyone.

3.
The country had reached its _____ with a population of 800 million people. In some cities, people started to get upset about the lack of opportunities. Conflict increased between different groups of people.

4.
Lucy's father decided it was time for their family to leave their country.

5 Population around the World   **98**   © FACING THE FUTURE www.facingthefuture.org

Answers

Reasons for Migration

1. developing
2. population
3. carrying capacity

Directions: Each box below includes one of the four vocabulary words from the previous page, as well as its definition. Below each definition:

1. Answer the question.

2. Write a sentence using the vocabulary word.

3. Choose the one word in the group that does not relate to the vocabulary word.

---

population

Definition: *the total number of people who live in an area*

1. What do you think the total student population is at your school?

2. Use *population* in a sentence.

3. Which word does not belong?
people   births   migration   conflict

---

migration

Definition: *movement from one place to another*

1. What evidence of migration have you seen where you live?

2. Use *migration* in a sentence.

3. Which word does not belong?
slum   movement
journey   resettlement

---

carrying capacity

Definition: *the maximum number of people that an environment can support*

1. What do you think might happen if the human population exceeds Earth's carrying capacity?

2. Use *carrying capacity* in a sentence.

3. Which word does not belong?
resources   population
food   festival

---

developed and developing countries

Definition: ***developed countries*** *have a high average per-person income;* ***developing countries*** *have a low average per-person income*

1. Do you think the United States is a developed or a developing country?

2. Use *developed* and *developing countries* in a sentence.

3. Which word does not belong?
wealthy   poor   economy   freshwater

Instructions

1. Explain the directions. After reviewing the definitions, explain to students they will (1) answer the question, (2) create a sentence using the vocabulary word, and (3) choose the one word in the group that is not related to the vocabulary word.

- **Differentiated Instruction:** Demonstrate how the activity works by filling in one of the boxes.

- **Differentiated Instruction:** Enlarge the four boxes to poster size and fill in one of the boxes. Work as a class to fill in answers within each box and write them on the poster. The poster can then remain hanging in the room throughout this unit of study.

2. This activity could be done independently, in pairs or small groups, or as an entire class.

3. Option: Have students search for and cut out magazine pictures that relate to each vocabulary word.

4. Option: As a homework assignment, have students write a single paragraph using the four vocabulary words.

Answers

population
1. Answers will vary. Example: The total student population of my school is 1,200 students.

2. Population around the world has increased in the last century.

3. conflict

migration
1. Answers will vary. Example: I have seen many people from the Dominican Republic migrating to my city.

2. Migration from rural to urban areas often occurs because of job opportunities.

3. slum

carrying capacity
1. Example: I think some people will be hungry if there are more people than Earth's resources can support.

2. An environment where it is difficult to grow food will have a lower carrying capacity than a place where food is plentiful.

3. festival

developed and developing countries
1. The United States is a developed country.

2. Developing countries have more people living in poverty than developed countries.

3. freshwater

Instructions

1. Give students a few minutes to study the chart. Ask them what they think the information represents.

   • **Differentiated Instruction:** Ask students to give a verbal summary of the information presented in the chart.

2. Read the dialogue to students to demonstrate proper pronunciation.

3. Divide students into pairs. Assign one person in the pair to read Ramon's part and one person to read Priya's part. As they read, each student should fill in the blanks in the dialogue.

   • **Differentiated Instruction:** If students need help analyzing the information in the chart in order to complete the dialogue, work with them in a small group.

4. Ask a set of volunteers to read the dialogue aloud to the class.

5. Ask students why they think different types of immigrants want to come to the United States. If they have immigrated themselves or know people who have immigrated, they can share specific reasons.

6. **Additional Resource:** Share an online interactive map of immigration trends created by the *New York Times* ("Remade in America," March 10, 2009): www.nytimes.com/interactive/2009/03/10/us/20090310-immigration-explorer.html?hp.

Dialogue: Immigration in the United States

Directions: Priya and Ramon have been learning about immigration to the United States in their history class. Complete their dialogue with a partner, using the chart below to help you fill in the answers. Once you have finished, read the dialogue with your partner.

The Largest Immigrant Groups in Counties within California and Maryland[4]

Locations in the United States	1880	1930	1970	2000
California (San Bernardino County)	Western European (1,094)	Western European (10,128)	Western European (37,335)	Latin American (318,559)
Maryland (Baltimore County)	Western European (9,864)	Russian, Eastern European (6,908)	Russian, Eastern European (22,842)	Asian, Middle Eastern (53,681)

Ramon: Hi, Priya! I missed class today. What did we learn?

Priya: Hi, Ramon. Mrs. Garcia shared a timeline with us about the largest immigrant groups in two different parts of the United States. I brought you the homework.

Ramon: Thanks, Priya. Can we work on this handout together?

Priya: Sure. By the way, tomorrow we're going to watch a movie about immigration.

Ramon: Let's look at this timeline. The title is: _____.

Priya: It looks like this chart shows different groups of immigrants living in two counties over a period of years.

Ramon: Yes, it looks like each immigrant group was the largest immigrant group in its county during a particular year. OK, let's get to work.

Priya: The first question we have to answer is: *How has the immigrant population of Baltimore County, Maryland, changed over time?*

Ramon: I notice in the year 1880, the largest group of immigrants in Baltimore County was _____ immigrants.

Priya: There weren't very many of them; in 1880, there were only _____. I wonder what countries Western Europe includes.

Ramon: Western Europe includes countries like Ireland, France, and Sweden.

Priya: OK, the second question asks which group of immigrants was the largest in Baltimore County in 1930, and exactly how large that group was.

Ramon: In 1930, _____ immigrants were the largest immigrant group in Baltimore County, with a total of _____ people.

Priya: Wow, if you look at how that number changed from 1930 to 1970, that population of immigrants increased dramatically!

Ramon: The last question about Baltimore County asks what the largest group of immigrants was in 2000.

Priya: By 2000, immigrants from _____ were the largest immigrant group in Baltimore County, with a total of _____ people. My grandparents are considered Asian immigrants because they moved from India.

Ramon: Why do you think Asian and Middle Eastern immigrants have become the largest group of immigrants in Baltimore County?

Priya: I'm not sure. Maybe it is because Western Europeans are not immigrating as much as they used to in the past.

Ramon: Or maybe it is because there are many more people in Asia and some of them want to move to a new place.

Priya: Maybe. Let's ask Mrs. Garcia tomorrow if she knows.

Ramon: The last question on the homework asks us to explain how immigration in San Bernardino, California, is different than immigration in Baltimore County.

Priya: Well, for one thing, the population size of the largest immigrant groups is much larger in _____ County.

Ramon: Yes, and the immigrant groups are from different regions. In 2000, the largest group of immigrants in San Bernardino was _____.

Priya: Wow, that is a large population— _____ is a lot of people!

Ramon: Do you know which countries are included in Latin America?

Priya: Latin America includes countries like Mexico, Cuba, and Venezuela.

Ramon: I wonder why certain immigrant groups that did not move to the United States in the past are moving here now.

Priya: Mrs. Garcia said that people immigrate to new countries for different reasons. Many people emigrate from their home countries to find jobs or educational opportunities, and to escape war and other kinds of conflict.

Ramon: This stuff is really interesting. I can't wait to see the movie about immigration tomorrow.

Priya: Then you'd better not miss class again!

Answers

Ramon: The Largest Immigrant Groups in Counties within California and Maryland.

Ramon: Western European

Priya: 9,864

Ramon: Russian and Eastern European; 6,908

Priya: Asia and the Middle East; 53,681

Priya: San Bernardino

Ramon: Latin American

Priya: 318,559

Instructions

1. Tell students that before you start the chapter reading, you want to go over the reading skill of making predictions. Making predictions encourages active reading. Students will be making predictions about the main idea of a reading passage.

   • **Differentiated Instruction:** Review the concept of main idea with students.

2. Review with students the definition of *prediction* at the top the page.

3. Have students, either independently or together as a class, read through the sample paragraph and the chart below the paragraph.

4. Discuss with students why the chart is filled out this way.

   • **Differentiated Instruction:** Use the following *think aloud* to demonstrate how to complete the chart:

   "I notice that the title of the paragraph is, 'We Keep Growing and Growing!'

   The first sentence says that in the year 2050, we will have a population of more than 9 billion people.

   I see why the student stated that the paragraph would be about population growth around the world; both the title and the first sentence are clues for this prediction. I also noticed that, after reading the entire paragraph, the student reviewed his/her prediction and wrote in the third box whether or not the prediction was correct."

When you make a **prediction**, you make an educated guess about what you think will happen based on evidence or clues. If you saw an article with the title, *Tokyo: 36 Million and Growing,* you might predict the article was about more and more people living in Tokyo.

These steps will help you to make predictions about the main idea of a reading passage.

   1. Read the title of the paragraph, section, or chapter.

   2. Read **bold-faced** words and words in *italics*.

   3. Read the first one or two sentences.

Example: Read the paragraph. Below the paragraph is a sample chart that demonstrates how to make a prediction and then evaluate it.

We Keep Growing and Growing!

Population studies estimate that, by the year 2050, there will be over 9 billion people living in the same area where 6.7 billion of us live now.[5] How and where will world population change? With almost half of the world's population under age twenty-five, the world's population will increase by several billion over the next few decades when those young people start having families.[6] Currently, 95% of all population growth occurs in **developing** countries. India is expected to soon replace China as the world's most populous country. Meanwhile, shrinking populations are predicted for some **developed** countries, such as Japan, Italy, and Germany.[7]

Prediction	Key Words / Evidence	Was your prediction correct?
I predict the paragraph will be about populations growing and growing around the world.	The title is: "We Keep Growing and Growing!" The first sentence points out that, by the year 2050, there will be many more people in the world than there are now.	Yes, the paragraph was about population growth around the world. However, the paragraph also mentions that population is actually decreasing in some developed countries.

5 Population around the World   **102**   © FACING THE FUTURE www.facingthefuture.org

Directions: Now it is your turn to make a prediction. Before you read, make a prediction about the main idea of the following reading passage. Use the chart below to write your prediction and identify the key words that helped you to make the prediction. Then, read the passage to see if your prediction was correct.

Curitiba, Brazil: Putting People First

Curitiba bus

Located in southern Brazil, the city of Curitiba has experienced much population growth over the last few decades. In 1968, Curitiba had a population of 350,000. Today, 1.8 million people live within the city limits and another 1.4 million in surrounding areas. To deal with its growing population, city planners in the 1970s began to think about how to design their city in a way that would make it livable for everyone. Since then, Curitiba has implemented a series of projects that have created a city built for *people*, not cars.

The first project began as a reaction to an idea to widen the streets of Curitiba and build a highway through its historic center to make room for more cars. An urban planner and architect, Jaime Lerner, thought that instead of making room for more cars, it would be better to design a city that put people first.[8]

Lerner, along with his co-workers, reorganized the streets of Curitiba to make bus-only express lanes with separate streets for cars. According to Lerner, the bus system was 500 times cheaper than building a subway system and 100 times cheaper than an aboveground train system.[9] When it was first created, the bus system could carry 54,000 passengers a day. During the 1990s, the city made changes that reduced the time it took passengers to get on and off the buses, and increased the number of passengers the system could transport. With these improvements, the Curitiba bus system now moves 2.3 million passengers a day. Due to this public transportation system, people who live in Curitiba use 25% less gas per person than the average Brazilian.[10]

Prediction	Key Words / Evidence	Was your prediction correct? *(explain why or why not)*

Instructions

1. Have students read through the passage and complete the chart. This can be done independently, in pairs, or together as a class.

Answers

Prediction

Example: The city of Curitiba has become more livable for its people.

Key Words / Evidence

Putting People First indicates that the city of Curitiba puts people first.

"People" in italics reinforces this idea.

Was your prediction correct?

Yes, this reading is about how the city of Curitiba responded to an increase in population by designing a city for people, not cars.

Instructions

1. Review the directions for the fact and opinion exercise.

2. Challenge students to come up with their own statements to illustrate fact and opinion.

3. Have students work with a partner to determine whether each statement is a fact or opinion.

4. **Option:** For every opinion that students find, they can substitute that opinion with a related fact from the chapter reading. Conversely, students can think of opinions related to those statements they identify as facts.

Directions: Read the information below to learn the difference between fact and opinion. Then, read the statements in the table that follows. Determine whether each statement is fact or opinion.

> A **fact** is something that can be proven, and an **opinion** is a personal belief that cannot be proven.
>
> **Fact:** Many people have migrated from Sudan to other countries in Africa because of war.
>
> **Opinion:** People from certain countries should not be allowed to use more than their share of resources.

Statement	Fact or Opinion?
1. The best part about New York City is its delicious pizza!	
2. New York City has a population of over 8 million people.	
3. Improved farming techniques is one reason population has increased around the world.	
4. People who live in the United States should reduce the amount of products they buy and consume.	
5. The country of Iran started to become so populous during the 1980s that it was running out of resources for its people.	
6. Girls don't need to be educated; they should stay home to cook and clean.	
7. People living in overpopulated cities can't do much to solve issues related to overpopulation.	
8. Much of the water used by people in Los Angeles comes from Mono Lake, a source of water that is 350 miles away.	

Answers

1. opinion
2. fact
3. fact
4. opinion
5. fact
6. opinion
7. opinion
8. fact

People and the Planet

Reading Skill Focus: As you read, stop when you reach a subheading to make a prediction for the main idea of the next section. Record your predictions in the table that follows the chapter reading, along with key words and evidence to support your predictions. After you read the entire passage, evaluate your predictions.

From Small to Large

New York City is famous for many things: pizza, the Yankees baseball team, migration from all over the world, hip-hop music, the Empire State Building…

Did you know that just 200 years ago, New York City was not a city at all? It was farmland![11]

What could have happened to transform farm-land into one of the biggest cities in the world?

In the 19th century, a number of events caused people to immigrate to New York City from other countries, increasing the city's population. For example, the Irish Famine of the 1850s forced many people in Ireland to leave their country to escape hunger and poverty.[12] Many Irish immigrants ended up in New York City. At the time, New York did not have enough safe housing for all the immigrants who were arriving, and they had to live in housing similar to **slums**. Today, New York City is home to over 8 million people, and the city has created ways for millions of people to live together comfortably and safely. How did the city increase from 6,000 people in the year 1690 to over 8 million people today?

_____
slums (n) – heavily populated areas where people live in poverty

New York City has a population of over 8 million.

Instructions

1. Have students preview the passage by reading only the title and subheadings. What do students think this reading will be about?

2. Remind students that they will be making predictions throughout the reading. Ask a volunteer to describe how to make predictions successfully. Explain that every time they come across a subtitle (these are the bolded words), they will stop and fill in a prediction about the section they are about to read. (They will do this using the table that follows the chapter reading.) They will also fill in any key words that helped them to make their prediction.

3. **Option:** Work with students to demonstrate how to make predictions. Start by reading the first paragraph aloud. Use the following think aloud:

   "I notice that the title of this section is, 'From Small to Large.'

   The first sentence discusses what New York City is famous for.

   I predict that this first section of the chapter reading will be about how New York City has grown from a small to a large city."

   After reading through the first section, confirm if this prediction was correct:

   "I was correct; the reading is about how the population of New York City has grown. I didn't realize that so many people from Ireland moved to New York City because of the Irish Famine." ▶

Instructions, *continued*

4. Have students complete the rest of the reading, taking turns reading either in pairs or in small groups. Every time they come to a subheading, they should stop and make a prediction about what they will read in the next section.

A Look Back at Population

For most of history, people have lived in **rural** areas, not cities. Living in small tribes as **hunter-gatherers**, early humans (about 50,000 years ago) followed the migrations of animals and the growth of plants. There were no restaurants or grocery stores, so people had to hunt for their food and search for land where food was available. Population during this time did not change much, with almost as many people dying every year as the number of people being born.

About 10,000 years ago, things started to change. Human populations began to increase as people learned how to grow plants and raise animals. Farming can produce up to 100 times as much food as will grow wild on the same amount of land. When people are able to grow more than enough food, they tend to stay in one place.

The stable food supply provided by farming led to the growth of towns and villages, and populations around the world grew quickly.

Population is still on the rise. Each year there are more and more people on Earth. In the year 2050, there may be over 9 billion people living in the same area where 6.7 billion of us live now.[13] Can Earth support this many people? Earth's carrying capacity is the maximum number of people the planet can support without resources being used faster than the planet can reproduce them. Consider what would happen if there were many more people living on the earth than there are now, but all of us continued to use the same amount of freshwater. At some point, there would not be enough freshwater to meet everyone's needs.

***

rural (adj) – countryside

hunter-gatherers (n) – people who survive by hunting, fishing, and living in nature

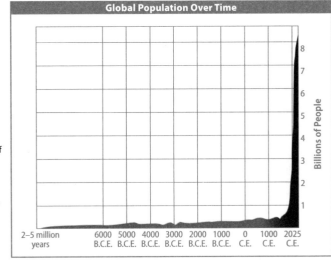

Global Population Over Time

It took nearly all of human history—about 50 million years—for the global population to reach 1 billion, but in only another 123 years it reached 2 billion.

Billions of People

2–5 million years | 6000 B.C.E. | 5000 B.C.E. | 4000 B.C.E. | 3000 B.C.E. | 2000 B.C.E. | 1000 B.C.E. | 0 C.E. | 1000 C.E. | 2025 C.E.

As population increases, the use of Earth's natural resources, such as food and fuel, also increases. These resources are limited; they will not necessarily always be available. At some point in the future there may not be enough resources to support our growing population. To address this challenge, many countries have developed strategies to ensure that their people's needs can be met.

Family Planning

Imagine you live in a small country. In only a few years, the population has grown very quickly. Suddenly there are not enough resources—from food to doctors—for everyone to live comfortably. Rapid population growth has many **consequences**. When a country becomes over-populated, it may be difficult for its **citizens** to find jobs, attend school, or maintain good health.

Some countries have developed successful population **policies** so that their citizens can live comfortably and not feel the pressures of over-population. In Iran before the 1980s, women were having on average more than six children each. The country began to feel the pressure of this growing population. Cities became crowded and polluted, and people were struggling to meet basic needs, such as food and water. The Iranian **government** decided to provide free family planning services to all citizens. Families were encouraged to space their children's births farther apart and they learned about the effects of population growth. The government also decided that mothers would only get time off from work after they gave birth to their first three children.

By 2000, women were having, on average, two children each, reducing Iran's demand for resources.[14]

Three generations of Iranian women

You Go, Girl!

There are many **benefits** to educating girls. Educated girls and women marry later and have fewer children. They seek medical attention sooner for themselves and their children. Mothers who learn about family planning and attend school often choose to have smaller families. When mothers make this choice, population growth and hunger often decrease. In addition, women gain skills they need to get jobs to support their families.[15]

---

consequence (n) – the effect or result of something that happened earlier

citizens (n) – members of a country who give loyalty to the country and receive privileges and protections from that country

policies (n) – rules that people follow

government (n) – the form or system of rule by which a country, community, etc. is ruled or administered

benefits (n) – advantages; things that are good or helpful

Batonga students at a school in Benin in West Africa.

In Ethiopia, the average number of children born to each woman is six. The literacy rate for women is 35%, which means that only thirty-five out of every 100 women are able to read and write.[16] Batonga is an organization working in Ethiopia and other African countries. This organization has a goal to make sure girls stay in school past eighth grade. Batonga works to keep girls in school through building more high schools, providing free school supplies, and helping young women to continue their education after high school. According to Batonga, "When a woman is educated, it changes not only her life but those of her children and her family."[17]

Using Less and Gaining More[18]

When a city's population grows, there is a danger of people overusing resources and not taking care of the land around them. However, with careful planning, resources like water, trees, and food can be used by many people. The management of Mono Lake in California is a good example of this kind of planning.

Northern California's Mono Lake is an important **habitat** for more than eighty species of migrating birds, and it supports a food chain of algae, shrimp, and insects. For most of the 20th century, a system of **aqueducts** delivered water from Mono Lake, located east of the Sierra Nevada Mountains, 350 miles across the desert to Los Angeles. However, a growing population in Los Angeles eventually needed more water than Mono Lake could supply without damaging the health of the plants and animals that depended on the lake for their survival.

In 1994, the California State Water Resources Control Board ordered Los Angeles to reduce usage of water from Mono Lake enough to return the lake to a healthy level. This required Los Angeles to conserve, or use less, water. The population in Los Angeles was high—over 3.6 million people—and growing more every year.[19] You can imagine how difficult it might be to reduce water usage in a city with so many people.

---

habitat (n) – the natural environment of an organism
aqueducts (n) – channels or pipes that carry water from one place to another

As it turns out, Los Angeles residents could save a lot of water by using low-flush toilets. The California Department of Water and Power worked with community volunteers to distribute new low-flush toilets in Los Angeles homes. Each low-flush toilet could save 5,000 gallons a year, reducing the use of water from Mono Lake.

Despite a 30% population increase, Los Angeles cut its water use by 15% to a level not seen since 1970. By using conservation methods like the low-flush toilets, more people are able to share the same resources.

Thinking about the Future

Population around the world continues to increase each year. With increased population comes a larger amount of people using the same resources. When these resources are overused,

people may face a number of problems. There are a number of things you can do to reduce your demand on Earth's resources. Here are just a few ideas:

- *Low-impact foods*—More water and energy are required to produce meat than plants. Cutting back on the amount of meat you eat would conserve these resources.

- *Low-flow*—Take quick showers and replace regular showerheads with low-flow shower heads to save water.

- *Alternative transportation*—Whenever possible, travel without using a car. Walk, ride a bicycle, skateboard, or take a bus to get around.

- *Energy conservation*—Use less electricity (and fewer natural resources) by turning off appliances like toasters and televisions when you are not using them.

Decreased water use by people of Los Angeles helped to keep Mono Lake healthy.

Instructions

1. After students have finished reading, have them complete the chart. They will be determining whether their predictions were correct and explaining why or why not.

2. Have them share the predictions they made before reading the various passages and whether their predictions were right. Which ones were easier to predict accurately, and why?

3. **Additional Resources:** Allow students to explore resources related to the reading.

   • Batonga Foundation website: www.batongafoundation.org

   • "How Low-Flow Toilets Work": http://home.howstuff works.com/low-flow-toilet. htm/printable

   • "Human Numbers through Time", an interactive map from NOVA: www.pbs.org/ wgbh/nova/worldbalance/ numbers.html

Directions: As you read, make a prediction for the main idea of each section. Use the table below to record your prediction, along with key words and evidence that support your prediction. After you read the entire passage, evaluate your predictions. Were they correct? Provide evidence that supports whether each prediction was correct or not.

Section Title	Prediction	Key Words / Evidence	Was your prediction correct? *(explain why or why not)*
From Small to Large			
A Look Back at Population			
Family Planning			
You Go, Girl!			
Using Less and Gaining More			
Thinking about the Future			

Answers

see p. 117H

Comprehension Questions

Directions: Answer the following questions to support your comprehension of the chapter readings.

Understanding what you read

1. How many people lived in New York City in the year 1690? How many people live in New York City now?

2. How many children did the average woman have in the country of Iran in 2000?

Thinking about what you read

3. Create your own title for this reading. Explain how your title reflects the main idea of the reading.

4. How is Batonga working to create a better future for women in different countries in Africa?

5. Explain how spacing children's births farther apart works to decrease overpopulation.

Questioning what you read

6. Explain why you think the author wrote this passage.

7. Why do you think the author begins the chapter reading with a focus on New York City?

Making connections to what you read

8. What are actions you can take now to address population growth?

Further discussion questions

9. How could overpopulation lead to conflicts between people in a country?

10. What actions could countries take now to deal with possible overpopulation in the future?

Comprehension Questions

Instructions

1. Before students begin answering the comprehension questions, share with them the academic language they will see in many of the questions (see Appendix B).

2. Explain that the questions are divided into five sections according to the different ways they support comprehension. (See Appendix B for a detailed explanation of each section.)

3. **Differentiated Instruction:** Differentiate the questions students must answer based on their reading levels. Support comprehension by working with students who may need more guided instruction.

Answers

1. 6,000 in 1690; over 8 million now

2. fewer than three

3. Example: *Population Increase: Problems and Solutions*

4. They are helping young girls to stay in school.

5. A woman who has a child every three years will have fewer children than a woman who gives birth to a child every year.

6. The author wants to educate the reader about the history of population growth and challenges and solutions related to rapid population growth.

7. New York City is an example of what is happening around the world. Its population has grown over time.

8. eat less meat, take alternative transportation, use less electricity, conserve water

9. People might fight over access to limited resources, including water, food, jobs, and health care.

10. Countries could institute population policies, ensure that girls are able to attend school, and encourage resource conservation.

Instructions

1. Read through the information in the box at the top of the page and the instructions for the example that follows.

2. Introduce the Chapter 5 writing rubric. You may want to add relevant spelling and grammar components to the rubric.

Have you ever thought that you could have the power to make changes where you live? There are many examples of people, from youth to the elderly, who work to make sure the schools, neighborhoods, towns, cities, and countries they live in are great places. Anyone can improve his or her community!

A **community plan for growth** is just what it sounds like: a plan that helps to prepare a community to grow over time. By creating a plan for growth, community members can make sure the place they live is sustainable in the future.

Example: Before you write your own community plan for growth, you will analyze essays by two students who came up with ideas and a plan for how their town could respond to an increase in population. When you analyze writing, read carefully to see what the writer did well and how the writer could improve. Grade the community plans for growth on a scale of 1 to 3 (1 needs a lot of work, 2 is pretty good, and 3 is great). Use the following questions to help you grade:

- Does the author include five paragraphs?
- Does the author provide a clear introduction and conclusion?
- Does the author provide three ideas for preparing for an increase in population?
- Are these ideas well-supported?
- Does the author use vocabulary words from this chapter correctly?

How would you plan for growth of your school community?

Chapter 5 Writing Rubric

Category	3	2	1
Organization of Information	Writes a plan that includes five paragraphs	Writes a plan that includes a few paragraphs	Does not write paragraphs and only includes ideas
Makes Predictions	Makes three predictions about what could happen to the school community	Makes two predictions about what could happen to the school community	Does not make realistic predictions about what could happen to the school community
Vocabulary	Uses two of the vocabulary words from the chapter correctly	Uses one of the vocabulary words from the chapter correctly	Does not attempt to use any of the vocabulary words from the chapter
Development	Offers three solutions to the challenges the school might face	Offers two solutions to the challenges the school might face	Offers no real solutions to the challenges the school might face

Total = _____ / 12

Instructions

1. Have students read the example and analyze which sample essay they believe to be stronger. What specific elements make this essay stronger?

Sample 1:

The town of Newberry has a population of 2,000 people. We are going to triple our size in a few years. This is going to change our town in many ways! Here are some solutions I suggest for accommodating this increased population.

First, there are going to be so many people that new homes and apartments will have to be built. Let's start building these homes and apartments now so there will be enough shelter for everyone.

Second, in order to cut down on pollution from cars, let's improve our bus system. More people will ride the bus if it's easy to use.

Finally, to make sure we have enough water, let's limit the amount each family is allowed to use each day.

Hopefully this community plan for growth can help Newberry in the future.

Grade for Sample 1: _____

Sample 2:

The town of Newberry has a population of 2,000 people. In a few years, we will triple our size. With the increase in population, our town could face a number of problems. However, if we think of ways that our town can prepare for this population increase now, we can prevent many problems from happening in the first place. I recommend a few ways we can work together to create a sustainable future for our community.

First, in order to deal with pollution from a growing number of cars, I suggest we create a bus system that is easy for everyone to use. If the bus system is convenient, fewer people will drive to school and work every day. Fewer cars mean less air pollution.

Second, in order to create a sense of community, I suggest we create more parks and recreational centers. With more places like these, people could spend time getting to know other people in the community. Additionally, young people would have places to go to after school where they could spend time playing sports, completing homework, or taking classes like art and dance.

Third, in order to manage the increase in garbage people will produce, I suggest we invest in a recycling plant. Garbage could be sorted and, instead of going to a landfill, bottles, cans, paper, and other recyclable goods would be sent to this recycling plant. No more landfills would have to be created, and increased recycling would keep the environment of Newberry clean.

In conclusion, the population of Newberry will increase in the next years, whether we are ready for it or not. While this population increase presents new challenges, we can still have the great town we have always had if we plan for these challenges. Creating an easy to use bus system, more parks, recreational centers, and a recycling plant will all help to support the needs of our growing community.

Grade for Sample 2: _____

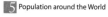

Instructions

1. Read through the scenario with students. Make sure that students understand the scenario, the possible challenges faced by a growing population, and their writing assignment.

- **Differentiated Instruction:** Discuss the potential challenges with students. Ask them to think of other potential challenges that are specific to your school. Work with them to brainstorm possible solutions.

Two Schools in One: How to Deal?

Do you know how many students are enrolled at your school? Is there plenty of room for everyone, or does it sometimes feel a little crowded?

Suppose that in the next ten years, a neighboring school combines with yours. All of the students from the neighboring school will be coming to your school. Since they have as many students as your school, that means your school's population will double.

The school district has already identified these potential challenges:

- No additional students can fit in the cafeteria at lunch time
- Crowded hallways could lead to fights between classes
- Currently there are not enough textbooks and computers for a larger population
- The amount of garbage will double
- The number of students in each class will double
- There will be increased competition to be in clubs and on sports teams
- There will be more cars dropping off and picking up students in the parking lot

Your challenge is to think of three ways that your school could plan for some of these challenges. At this point, money is not a consideration. First, your school must identify how it will deal with the biggest challenges. Later, money will be raised through taxes to deal with those challenges. Since you are a current student, you have a voice about how the school should plan for these challenges.

Directions: Make a prediction about what you think will be the **three** biggest challenges from the list above. Think of a possible solution for each of these problems. You will write a five-paragraph community plan for growth that will explain these challenges and solutions. For every solution that you create, you will need to include a few reasons why you think this solution is important and how it will meet the challenge at hand.

Writing Steps: Community Plan for Growth

You are going to write a plan for growth for your school. Your task is to create a plan that ensures your school will be a place where twice as many students can attend school in a safe learning environment.

Step 1: Use the Writing Brainstorm Page (see next page) to think about possible challenges and solutions for a larger student population.

Step 2: Write a community plan for growth (five-paragraph essay) using the Writing Organizer.

Step 3: Edit your essay using the Edit Checklist.

Step 4: Have a peer read and edit your essay using the Edit Checklist.

Step 5: Revise your community plan for growth based on the peer edit.

 Edit Checklist

	Author Check	Peer Editor Check
Did you write an introduction?		
Did you write three body paragraphs that include solutions to problems that are predicted to happen with a population increase?		
Did you write a conclusion?		
Did you use at least two vocabulary words from the chapter?		

Instructions

1. Review the basic steps to writing with students.

2. **Grammar Suggestion:** Review prepositions of location (i.e., above, across, behind, below, beside, between, outside). These words may be useful as students develop solutions to population issues in their school community.

Instructions

1. This page provides structure for students to brainstorm and collect their ideas.

2. Students may work through this page individually or collaborate with a partner.

1. How many students does your school have now?

2. How many students would there be if the population doubles?

3. Describe how it would feel to be a student at your school if there were twice as many students:

4. What are the three biggest challenges that may arise from your school's population doubling?

    1.

    2.

    3.

5. What are possible solutions for dealing with each challenge? How will each solution deal with a particular challenge?

    1.

    2.

    3.

Writing Organizer: Community Plan for Growth

Introduction

Hook Sentence (suggestion): An increase in our school's student population from _____ to _____ would pose many challenges for our school.

Thesis Statement (suggestion): Based on this increase in population, I propose a few suggestions for preparing us now so we can live sustainably in the future.

Body

First, in order to deal with the challenge of _____ , our school needs _____ .

    Reason A: _____

    Reason B: _____

    Reason C: _____

Second, in order to deal with the challenge of _____ , our school needs _____ .

    Reason A: _____

    Reason B: _____

    Reason C: _____

Third, in order to deal with the challenge of _____ , our school needs _____ .

    Reason A: _____

    Reason B: _____

    Reason C: _____

Conclusion

Restate your thesis.

Summarize your argument (the body of your plan).

Make a closing statement.

Writing Organizer

Instructions

1. Students can use the writing organizer to construct the first draft of their community plan for growth. (Note that this organizer includes specific structural elements for a five-paragraph essay, but students will need to develop their own connecting and supporting sentences for the introduction and conclusion.)

   - **Differentiated Instruction:** For beginning students who may need more guidance, work with them in a small group and assist them in writing their growth plan. You can even write the plan with them as a shared writing exercise.

2. Once they have written their essay, students should review the remaining Writing Steps: edit and check, peer review, and revision. Use the Edit Checklist for guidance.

3. **Option:** Invite the school principal to your class. Have students present their ideas to the principal.

4. **Option:** Use this writing exercise as a template for creating a community improvement plan. In their community improvement plans, students should think about the community/town/neighborhood where they live. How could it be improved for people who currently live there and for newcomers? What changes would improve living conditions for everyone?

Culminating Activity: When the Chips Are Down (45 minutes)

Overview

Students model three patterns of population and consumption growth over consecutive generations, using poker chips to represent ecological footprints. This activity provides a visual model for examining impacts of changes in population growth rates and consumption patterns.

Materials/Preparation

- Butcher paper: three sheets for a class of 20 or fewer, six sheets for a class of more than 20 (each sheet should be no larger than 25" x 30")

- Colored marking pens: twelve for a class of 20 or fewer, twenty-four for a class of more than 20

- Poker chips: 500 for a class of 20 or fewer, 1,000 for a class of more than 20

- Note: If you do not have poker chips, try substituting other similar-sized items, such as pennies. Or, you could give each group one quarter that they trace onto their maps. The number of poker chips required for that generation determines how many times the quarter should be traced.

- Count out the poker chips for each group and each generation according to the table below, and put the larger stacks in labeled plastic bags.

Generation	Group 1 (doubling)	Group 2 (tripling)	Group 3 (quadrupling)
1st	2	3	4
2nd	4	9	16
3rd	8	27	64
4th	16	81	256
Total Chips	30	120	340

Steps

1. Ask students warm-up questions around population and consumption:

   - Do more people live in cities or in rural areas? (cities)

   - Is most population growth occurring in developed or developing countries? (developing countries)

   - Where is consumption of resources higher—in developed or developing countries? (developed countries)

   - What is a tool for measuring our impacts on Earth's resources? (ecological footprint)

2. Introduce/review a few concepts with students by writing the following definitions on the board or on an overhead:

   - *ecological footprint:* the area of land and water required to support a certain lifestyle

   - *consumption:* using resources and products

   - *double:* to make twice as large

   - *triple:* to make three times as large

   - *quadruple:* to make four times as large

3. Read the following directions:

   "I am going to divide the class into groups. Each group will design and draw a map of your *ideal* country, including the following components: farmland, type of housing, available water, forests, parks, health clinics, schools, and roads." (Write these components on the board and review unfamiliar terms.)

   - **Differentiated Instruction:** Create a model of an ideal country that students can see before they get started.

Culminating Activity: When the Chips Are Down *continued*

4. Divide the class into three groups for a class of twenty or less, six groups for a class of more than twenty. (With six groups, you will need to double the number of chips indicated in the Materials/Preparation table. You will have two groups model doubling, two groups model tripling, and two groups model quadrupling).

5. Give each group a piece of butcher paper and four marking pens.

6. Have them brainstorm ideas, discuss the components to be included, and then draw their country maps. Instruct them to draw their map as if they were looking down on it from an airplane (e.g., small squares for houses and schools, areas for farming and forests). Encourage students to be creative and to think about everything they might want to include in their ideal country. Give them plenty of time to create their maps so they are proud of their country and have an emotional connection to it. Allow them to name their country and write this name on their map.

7. When the groups are finished creating their countries, have the groups place the maps side by side (with edges touching) on a large table or on the floor, and have each group (or two representatives from each group) stand next to their country maps. Be sure that all the students can see the maps.

8. With the students gathered around, have each group present their country map to the class, explaining what they included and why they chose to locate certain things where they did.

9. Read (or paraphrase) the following directions:

"You will model three different patterns of ecological footprint growth (based on population and consumption increase) over four generations, using poker chips to represent ecological footprints and the maps to represent countries. Each poker chip represents an ecological footprint. You will also be given information about the size of your ecological footprints. Larger populations have a larger footprint because more people require more resources to support them. Higher consumption lifestyles have a larger footprint because they require more resources per person to support those lifestyles."

10. Point to one map and tell them that this country represents a developing nation. The country is doubling in population each generation, but average consumption per person remains the same. Therefore, its ecological footprint is **doubling** each generation. Place two chips, representing the first generation, on this country.

11. Point to the next country and tell them that this country represents a more developed nation that has reduced its population growth rate, but is still experiencing a 50% increase in population and is doubling its consumption (meaning each person is using more resources). This country's total ecological footprint is **tripling** each generation. This is representative of some rapidly industrializing nations, such as Thailand. Place three chips, representing the first generation, on this country.

12. Point to the third country and tell them that this country represents a developed nation that is doubling both its population and its consumption each generation. Therefore, its ecological footprint will **quadruple** each generation. This is representative of wealthy countries such as the United States. Place four chips, representing the first generation, on this country.

13. Emphasize that chips cannot be placed outside the borders of countries and that chips cannot be placed on top of each other since an ecological footprint is a measurement of surface area and cannot be stacked. (Note: Be careful *not* to say that they must keep their chips on their own country. Placing chips, which represent ecological footprints, on other countries is allowed and even encouraged.)

14. Hand out the second generation of chips and have the groups place the chips on their maps, modeling one generation of ecological footprint growth at a time. After each cycle is complete, hand out bags of pre-counted chips (as indicated in the above table) for each generation. As you hand out the bags of chips, tell each group to decide where they want to place the footprints. As they continue through the generations, they will have to decide which resources they want to impact, or cover up, with the footprints.

15. Have the students stop briefly to observe the progression of the three models after each generation cycle. The group modeling a doubling of footprint size will finish its task quite soon, and with minimal difficulty. The group modeling a tripling of footprint size will probably take somewhat longer, and will confront decisions about how to handle growth and where to allocate impacts. The group modeling a quadrupling of footprint size will take much longer and need much more room. Allow enough time for students to consider alternatives, but force the play rapidly enough that there is a sense of urgency and stress.

16. Students modeling the faster growth patterns (tripling and quadrupling) will be forced to decide which resources to deplete to accommodate their needs, since not all of the chips will fit on their maps without overrunning the resource base. (Note: You may need to remind students that they cannot stack the chips or move them off the paper; however, there is no rule about putting chips on another country.) Situations that may arise include deforestation, loss of habitat, migration, and invasion of neighboring countries to support population and consumption needs.

17. Bring the class back together for the following reflection questions.

    - What two things can make a country's total ecological footprint, or impact on the environment, larger?

    - How does population growth affect a country's resources like forests and farmland?

    - How could lowering resource use affect the maximum number of people that a country could sustain?

    - What would happen if the game continued for two more cycles? What other decisions might each country have to make?

    - What different choices would you have made in your country if you had known what was going to happen?

Chapter 5 Extension, Action Project, and Resources

Math Extension

Have students investigate the population growth rate in the United States (www.census.gov). Compare birth rates to growth rates. If birth rates are not increasing, what other reasons might explain population growth in the United States (e.g., immigration)?

Action Project

Students could write and illustrate books about women's issues around the world. Sell the books as a fundraiser for an organization working to provide girls around the world with education, independence, and improved lives. Three such organizations are Work of Women (www.workofwomen.org), the United Nations Development Fund for Women (www.unifem.org), and Heifer International (www.heifer.org). Have students share what they learned by reading the books with younger students or hosting an assembly to raise awareness about the rights of women.

Additional Resources on Population

Population Reference Bureau
www.prb.org

Population Reference Bureau's website informs people around the world about population, health, and the environment, and empowers them to use that information to advance the well-being of current and future generations.

World in the Balance
www.pbs.org/wgbh/nova/worldbalance/

This video explores two different ways in which world population is changing. In Japan, Europe, and Russia, birth rates are shrinking and the population is aging. In parts of India and Africa, however, more than half of the still-growing population is under twenty-five. The video explores both of these population trends. (120 minutes, NOVA)

The Girl Effect
www.girleffect.org

This two-minute video, created by the Nike Foundation and NoVo Foundation, is about the powerful social and economic change that occurs when girls have the opportunity to participate in their society. Accompanying the video are ways to get involved with promoting *The Girl Effect*, as well as fact sheets and video clips about the effects of poverty on the quality of people's lives. Pause this fast-paced video frequently to help students interpret meaning.

Finding Balance
www.populationaction.org/Publications/Documentaries/

This nine-minute documentary includes interviews with women in Madagascar—a country where population growth, poverty, and deforestation are all connected. This video highlights interconnections among population growth and environmental destruction, and shows what Population Action International is doing to help.

Chapter 5 Student Assessment, page 1
Knowledge about Population around the World

Vocabulary

Directions: Read each sentence and circle the letter that corresponds to the correct definition of the **bold-faced** word.

1. In 1951, the **population** of the city of Dhaka in Bangladesh was 3.5 million people. Today it is around 13 million people.
   a. the total number of people who attend school
   b. a way in which the number of people is measured
   c. the total number of people who live in an area
   d. the total number of people who have jobs

2. Juan's family **migrated** from their village in El Salvador to San Salvador, the capital city, to find job opportunities.
   a. moved from one location to another based on weather
   b. moved from one country, region, or place to another
   c. worked to earn more money to support one's family
   d. traveled from one part of a country to another for vacation

3. The **developed** country had more people living with access to food, water, and shelter than the **developing** country.
   a. country with a high average per-person income / country with a low average per-person income
   b. country with a high rate of child birth / country with a low rate of child birth
   c. country with no highways / country with many highways
   d. country more likely to fight in a war / country less likely to fight in a war

4. Many people on the island died because the island had reached **carrying capacity**.
   a. maximum number of people that can live in an environment at one time
   b. maximum amount of water available to each person
   c. maximum area of land that can be used by one family without overusing the island's natural resources
   d. maximum amount of babies that can be born in a given year without making the island overpopulated

Chapter 5 Student Assessment, page 2

Content

Directions: Read the sentence and circle the letter that corresponds to the correct answer.

5. Teaching women how to space the amount of children they have over time is an example of _____.

     a. overpopulation   **c.** conflict
     b. family planning   **d.** migration

6. Reducing the amount of water you use when you brush your teeth, take a shower, and flush the toilet is an example of how to _____.

     a. educate girls
     b. use resources carefully
     c. increase population size
     d. consume as much as you want

7. Overpopulation can lead to a decrease in _____.

     a. conflict between religions
     b. environmental destruction
     c. migration to different countries
     d. resources like freshwater

8. As population increases in cities across the world, one way of carefully planning cities is by _____.

     a. allowing everyone to throw their garbage wherever they want
     b. building slums in the cities so that money does not have to be spent on new, safe housing
     c. creating a public transportation system that decreases traffic jams and air pollution
     d. decreasing the amount of jobs available to people so that only a small number of people have to work

Reading Comprehension

Directions: Read the paragraph below. For questions 9 and 10, circle the correct answer.

It took nearly all of human history—about 50,000 years—for the global population to reach 1 billion people, yet it only took 127 years for the population to reach 2 billion people. Population reached 3 billion people only thirty-three years after it reached 2 billion. Now we're adding another billion people every twelve to fourteen years! Nearly all of this population growth is occurring in Asia, Africa, and Latin America.

9. What is the pattern of population increase throughout human history?

     a. Population is increasing very slowly now compared to the past
     b. Population is increasing very quickly now compared to the past
     c. Population has increased at a very steady rate throughout history
     d. Population is now decreasing for the first time in history

10. If the pattern in the paragraph continues, what prediction could be made about population growth in the world twenty years from now?

     a. Population growth will decrease
     b. Population growth will increase, but at a slow rate
     c. Population growth will increase faster than ever
     d. Population growth will remain steady

Chapter 5 Student Assessment, page 3
Outlook and Personal Beliefs

Answer the following questions based on your personal beliefs. There are no right or wrong answers.

Directions for 1 and 2: Place a check mark (√) in the box next to each statement that is true for you.

1. I think overpopulation and Earth's carrying capacity are two issues that everyone should be concerned about.
   ☐ True
   ☐ False

2. I can personally do things to reduce my resource use so that more people can share resources.
   ☐ True
   ☐ False

3. **Complete the following sentence:**
   One way I can personally work to solve issues related to population growth is by…

   _____

   _____

   _____

   _____

Directions for 4 and 5: Fill in the ovals below based on your level of agreement. 1 means that you strongly agree, and 7 means that you strongly disagree.

1 = yes, definitely!   7 = no way!

←—————————————————→

4. I believe my daily actions have an impact on population around the world.

5. I believe I have the ability to help solve population issues.

Section Title	Prediction	Key Words / Evidence	Was your prediction correct?
From Small to Large	New York City has grown from a small to a large city.	- "From Small to Large" - New York City	Yes; the population of New York increased over time, largely due to immigration.
A Look Back at Population	Population grew slowly in the past.	- "A Look Back at Population" - The first two sentences tell us that population growth was slow.	Somewhat; population size on Earth increased slowly at first, but is now growing much faster.
Family Planning	Family planning is related to population growth and limited resources.	- "Family Planning" - The first two sentences paint a picture of limited resources and increasing population.	Somewhat; the section specifically refers to Iran as an example of a country whose family planning policies helped to slow population growth.
You Go, Girl!	Education of girls is important.	- "You Go Girl!" - Benefits of educating girls	Yes; if girls receive an education, they and their families will benefit in many ways.
Using Less and Gaining More	With careful planning, resources can be used by many people.	- "Using Less and Gaining More" - When populations grow, they can overuse resources.	Yes; large populations can share a common resource like Mono Lake if they use it carefully.
Thinking about the Future	In the future, population will continue to grow and people will continue to use resources.	- "Thinking about the Future" - Population is growing, and people are using more resources.	Somewhat; Earth's resources can support more people if we use those resources carefully.

Chapter 5 Student Assessment,
pp. 117E, F

1. c
2. b
3. a
4. a
5. b
6. b
7. d
8. c
9. b
10. c

Improving Our Quality of Life

Chapter

6

Students consider factors that contribute to a good quality of life and how these factors might differ between adults and young people. They contemplate their own ideas about quality of life during a dialogue. After learning vocabulary related to quality of life, they read a fictional story of three children struggling to improve their quality of life. Students are asked to draw conclusions to comprehend the reading. A writing activity asks students to write a conclusion to a realistic fictional story. The chapter culminates with students creating, administering, and analyzing a survey to measure quality of life based on peer responses.

Possible Scope and Sequence
(based on one-hour class periods)

Day 1	Day 2	Day 3	Day 4	Day 5
Activating Knowledge Writing Warm-up Expanding Vocabulary	Using Words in Context: *Filling in the Blanks* Breaking Down the Meaning	Dialogue: *Would You Rather…?*	Reading Skill Focus: *Drawing Conclusions* Pre-reading: *What's Missing?*	Chapter Reading: *Voices of Children* Reading Skill Follow-up

Day 6	Day 7	Day 8	Day 9
Comprehension Questions	Writing about Quality of Life: *Realistic Fiction*	Culminating Activity: *Living the Good Life*	Culminating Activity *(cont'd)*

Time
Eight or nine one-hour class periods

Essential Questions
- What kinds of things can improve quality of life?
- How does quality of life differ for people in different places?
- How is quality of life measured?

Integrated Subject Areas
- Social Studies
- English Language Arts
- Health
- Science

Content Objectives
Students will:
- Determine factors that contribute to quality of life
- Determine what prevents people from having a good quality of life
- Understand the connection between quality of life and sustainability issues like poverty and environmental pollution

Language Objectives
Students will:
- Discuss ideas that relate to quality of life
- Write a response to a prompt about quality of life
- Discuss quality of life through a dialogue
- Define and use new vocabulary words
- Read a radio drama
- Draw conclusions about the radio drama to aid reading comprehension
- Write a conclusion to a story

Key Concepts
- Quality of life
- Health and well-being

Vocabulary
- Quality of life
- Human rights
- Poverty
- Life expectancy

Standards Addressed
- TESOL standards
- NCTE standards
- NCSS standards
- NSES standards

* Please see Appendix A for a list of national standards addressed.

Assessment Option
Use the Chapter 6 assessments of student knowledge and outlook/personal beliefs as pre-tests for the chapter. Follow up with the same assessments at the end of the chapter to determine changes in knowledge and outlook/personal beliefs.

Chapter Introduction

Instructions

1. Read the introduction with students.

2. Ask them what it means to have a good life and what might be some reasons people are not able to *live the good life*.

3. Explain that, in Chapter 6, students will learn more about the concept of quality of life and what it means for them and for other people around the world.

Improving Our Quality of Life

What does it mean to live a good life? How can we work to ensure that people around the world are given the chance to improve their quality of life?

Chapter 6 will introduce you to what *quality of life* means. In this chapter, you will **speak** to your classmates about what *living the good life* means to you and other people. You will **listen** to and then practice a dialogue with a partner about making choices in life that contribute to your quality of life. You will **read** a fictional story about three children from around the world. At the end of the chapter, you will **write** a conclusion to a fictional story about quality of life.

Education can improve a person's quality of life.

Activating Knowledge

In this activity, you will brainstorm ideas about quality of life. When you brainstorm, you come up with possible answers to a question or problem.

Example: Look at the photo. What do you think is happening?

In this photo I see…

a family sitting together in the park. They look like they are having a picnic and eating sandwiches and fruit. The woman is laughing and the man is smiling.

Based on what I see in this photo, I can conclude the people in this photo feel…

relaxed and happy.

The people in the photo may feel this way because…

they are spending time with each other and enjoying each other's company.

Therefore, I imagine a caption below the photo would say…

"A Family Picnic"

Instructions

1. Review the photograph with students. Challenge them to answer the questions on the page before they review the answers provided.

2. As a class, review the answers provided. Discuss how they compare to students' ideas.

Instructions

1. Have students look at the photograph quietly by themselves. Ask them to think about what they see in the photo and how it makes them feel.

2. Have students work with a partner to complete the statements below the photograph.

3. Have students share their captions for the photo aloud.

   • **Differentiated Instruction:** Remind students that a caption describes or explains a photo.

4. Ask students how they think this photograph might connect to the phrase *quality of life*.

   • **Differentiated Instruction:** Break down the meaning of the words *quality* and *life* to construct a possible meaning for this phrase.

Directions: Look at the photo. Brainstorm ways to complete each sentence below the photo.

In this photo I see…

• Based on what I see in this photo, I can conclude the people in this photo feel…

• The people in the photo may feel this way because…

• Therefore, I imagine a caption below the photo would say…

Writing Warm-up

Writing Warm-up

Directions: Complete the Venn diagram by answering the questions within each circle. If you think that some things contribute to a good life for both young people and adults, write those things in the middle of the diagram, where the circles overlap. For things that only apply to young people, write them on the left side of the diagram. For things that only apply to adults, write them on the right side of the diagram.

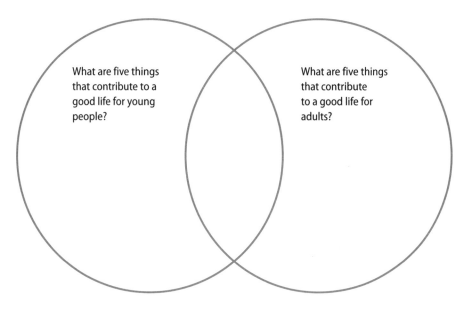

What are five things that contribute to a good life for young people?

What are five things that contribute to a good life for adults?

Instructions

1. To prepare students for this activity, ask them the following question: *Does living the good life mean the same thing for all people?*

2. Have students use the Venn diagram to answer the two questions.

   • **Differentiated Instruction:** Review how to use a Venn diagram to compare and contrast two things. Answers that compare should be written in the area where the two circles overlap.

   • **Differentiated Instruction:** If beginner students are more comfortable writing in their native language, allow them to do so.

   • **Differentiated Instruction:** If beginner students want to draw diagrams to support their writing, allow them to do so.

3. As a group, discuss what students thought living the good life means for young people and for adults.

4. **Option:** Use the following questions to generate a class discussion:

   • How is what you want now different than what you think you will want when you are older?

   • What things do you think are more important to your parents than they are to you?

   • Do we need different things to be happy at different times in our lives?

   • Why might we have different beliefs about what the *good life* is?

Expanding Vocabulary

Instructions

1. Have students study the four photos on the page independently.

2. Have students collaborate with a partner to come up with possible definitions for each word.

3. Discuss students' ideas.

   • **Differentiated Instruction:** Copy this page onto an overhead or display it with a document camera. As students are brainstorming ideas for each vocabulary word, list these next to the photo in each box.

4. **Option:** Review the following derivatives:

   • *quality of life (n) – living, lives*

   • *human rights (n) – humanity, humane, righteous, rightfully*

   • *life expectancy (n) – living, alive, expect, expectant, expecting*

Directions: Look at the following pictures and vocabulary words. Make a prediction about the meaning of the vocabulary words based on the given photos.

A	B

quality of life	**human rights**

C	D

poverty	**life expectancy**

Directions: Read the conversation between Oscar and Lisa. Fill in the missing vocabulary words.

quality of life	poverty	life expectancy	human right

"Hey Lisa," Oscar said, "I just saw this TV commercial that talked about the *good life*. What do you think the good life is all about?"

"I think the good life means having everything you need in life to be happy and healthy," Lisa said. "For me, the good life means having a good job, a comfortable home, time to spend with my family, and being healthy."

"Oh, that makes sense," Oscar said. "I thought it might mean something like that. The TV commercial had a bunch of people who looked really happy. If they had the things you mentioned— good jobs, homes, family time, and health—of course they would be living the good life."

"The good life means different things to different people," Lisa replied, "but most people would agree that it involves meeting basic needs, such as food and clean water. Unfortunately, people living in _____ struggle to meet those basic needs. For people living in poverty, access to things like food, water, and shelter would improve their _____."

"Those things are basics that everyone should have!" exclaimed Oscar. "Can you imagine not even having clean water to drink?"

Lisa replied, "I know; it's hard to imagine. I just read this story about a teenager who had to move to another country because her family wanted

her to have the chance at a better life. Because of widespread poverty, people in her country often died very young. The _____ of their home country was only thirty years!"

"I can't imagine what life is like in a country where many people only live to be thirty years old. It seems like everyone deserves to grow old and live a full life," said Oscar.

"Yeah," said Lisa, "and another crazy thing is, that teenager and her family couldn't even talk openly about the difficult circumstances that people in the country were facing. Their government wouldn't allow people to express their opinions publicly."

"Wow, having your own opinions is a _____! I thought everyone could express their opinions."

"I guess sometimes people don't have the basic things we assume everyone has. That's why I think it's so important to help people. My family serves food at a homeless shelter in our neighborhood. I feel like when we volunteer, we are not just helping others. Volunteering also improves our quality of life because it strengthens our community and makes us feel good."

"Really?" asked Oscar. "I think I'll have to check that out!"

Instructions

1. Read the instructions for the activity aloud to students.
   - **Differentiated Instruction:** Have two students with good pronunciation skills read this page aloud. One student will read Oscar's part; the other will read Lisa's part.
2. As students listen, they can determine the appropriate placement of the vocabulary words.
3. Have students review their answers with a partner.
4. Ask a volunteer to read the completed paragraph aloud to the class.

Answers

1. poverty
2. quality of life
3. life expectancy
4. human right

Breaking Down the Meaning

Instructions

1. Explain the directions. After reviewing the definitions, explain to students they will (1) answer the question, (2) create a sentence using the vocabulary word, and (3) choose the one word in the group that is not related to the vocabulary word.

   - **Differentiated Instruction:** Demonstrate how the activity works by filling in one of the boxes.

   - **Differentiated Instruction:** Enlarge the four boxes to poster size and fill in one of the boxes. Work as a class to fill in answers within each box and write them on the poster. The poster can then remain hanging in the room throughout this unit of study.

2. This activity could be done independently, in pairs or small groups, or as an entire class.

3. **Option:** Have students search for and cut out magazine pictures that relate to each vocabulary word.

4. **Option:** As a homework assignment, have students write a single paragraph using the four vocabulary words.

Directions: Each box below includes one of the four vocabulary words from the previous page, as well as its definition. Below each definition, do the following:

1. Answer the question.

2. Write a sentence using the vocabulary word.

3. Choose the one word in the group that does not relate to the vocabulary word.

---

quality of life

Definition: *the level of well-being and the physical conditions in which people live*

1. What is one thing you think would improve your quality of life?
2. Use *quality of life* in a sentence.
3. Which word does not belong?
   work   education
   happiness   video games

---

human rights

Definition: *the basic rights and freedoms to which all humans are entitled, often believed to include the right to life and liberty, freedom of thought and expression, and equality before the law*

1. Which human rights are most important to you?
2. Use *human rights* in a sentence.
3. Which word does not belong?
   rainforest   freedom   justice   equality

---

poverty

Definition: *the state of being poor and not having necessary resources*

1. Where might people live in poverty?
2. Use *poverty* in a sentence.
3. Which word does not belong?
   easy   food   water   shelter

---

life expectancy

Definition: *the age until which a person is expected to live*

1. What things do you think contribute to a long life expectancy?
2. Use *life expectancy* in a sentence.
3. Which word does not belong?
   average age   developing
   health   lifestyle

Answers

quality of life

1. Answers will vary.
2. John's quality of life improved when he started spending more time with his friends and family and less time worrying about his job.
3. video games

human rights

1. Answers will vary.
2. Marcella learned that practicing a religion is a human right that everyone should have.

3. rainforest

poverty

1. Answers will vary.
2. Living in poverty can make life very challenging for a family.
3. easy

life expectancy

1. Access to health care, education, food, and clean water could contribute to people having a long life expectancy.

2. The life expectancy of people around the world may depend on the type of health care available in the countries where they live.

3. developing

Dialogue: Would You Rather...?

Directions: Listen as the sample interview is read aloud. Then, you and a partner will take turns interviewing each other using the questions that follow. To respond to each question, choose a or b, then explain why you made this choice. After you work through the questions, read facts related to each question on the page titled *"Did You Know?"*

Sample Interview

Paul: Laila, would you rather...

   a. work long hours throughout the year, earn less vacation time, but receive more money, or

   b. work fewer hours throughout the year, earn more vacation time, and receive less money?

Laila: Paul, I would rather work long hours throughout the year, earn less vacation time, but receive more money so that I could save money for the future. I would deposit this money in the bank and use it to buy a home and to send my children to school.

1. Would you rather...

   a. work long hours throughout the year, earn less vacation time, but receive more money, or

   b. work fewer hours throughout the year, earn more vacation time, and receive less money?

2. Would you rather live...

   a. where we all use as many natural resources (like food, water, and energy) as we want, or

   b. where there are limits to how many natural resources could be used, but there is a cleaner and safer environment?

3. Would you rather live in a country that focused on...

   a. how happy its citizens are, or

   b. how rich its citizens are?

continued ▶

Dialogue

Instructions

1. Read the dialogue directions and sample interview with students.

2. Have students split into partners and interview each other using the *Would you Rather...?* questions. Explain that when they answer the questions, they need to explain why they chose one response over the other.

3. **Option:** Have the interviewer write down the interviewee's responses. They could write a summary of the interview like you might see in a magazine.

4. **Option:** Have partners introduce each other to the class and share facts about each other. For example, "This is Maria. She would rather...."

4. Would you rather live in a country where...

    a. you are able to vote for your leader or president, or
    b. where your leader is chosen for you?

5. Would you rather live where...

    a. all children receive an education, or
    b. half of the population of children receive an education?

6. Would you rather live in a community where...

    a. everyone speaks the same language, has similar beliefs, and eats the same food, or
    b. people speak different languages, have different beliefs, and eat different kinds of food?

7. Would you rather live in a country where...

    a. the life expectancy is over seventy years, or
    b. the life expectancy is under thirty-five years?

The life expectancy of a person born in Cambodia is 62 years old.

Dialogue: Did You Know?

 Income / Work: Europeans get five to six weeks of paid vacation, while the average American receives two weeks. The minimum wage in Europe is much higher than in the United States.[1]

 Environment: If all countries were to use natural resources like the United States did, we would need more than four planets to support everyone's needs.[2]

 Happiness: Costa Rica, a country in Central America, has been identified as a country with a very high life expectancy, a high level of life satisfaction, and a small ecological footprint.[3]

 Freedom: Women in the United States were not allowed to vote until 1920.

 Education: Over 93 million children around the world are not in school.[4]

 Culture: 18% of the U.S. population speaks a language other than English at home.[5]

 Health: The majority of the world's population (about 70%) lives in countries that have life expectancies between fifty and seventy-five years. These countries are located mostly in South America, North Africa, Eastern Europe, Asia, and the South Pacific.[6]

Instructions

1. **Option:** Have students read the facts about quality of life, either independently or with their partner from the dialogue activity. These facts will serve as an introduction to learning more about quality of life around the world.

2. **Additional Resources:** Allow students to research more information about quality of life, using the following resources:

   - The CIA World Factbook provides information about countries around the world, including literacy rates, education rates, health, and life expectancy: www.cia.gov/library/publications/the-world-factbook/index.html.

   - The New Economics Foundation website includes maps and data about life expectancy, life satisfaction, and ecological footprint for countries throughout the world: www.happyplanetindex.org.

Instructions

1. Explain that the reading skill for Chapter 6 is drawing conclusions. Ask volunteers to provide a definition for the word *conclusion*. How might drawing conclusions help you understand what an author has written?

2. Read the text from the box aloud.

3. Review the example together.

> You **draw conclusions** when you use your background knowledge and evidence from the text to determine the meaning of the text. It's like using clues to help you understand what you are reading. Clues can be found in words, phrases, sentences, and even pictures.

Example: Read the following paragraph and questions to learn more about drawing conclusions.

Janet had a huge smile on her face. She ran from school with a paper in her hand. Her paper had a shiny gold star on the top. When she got home, she immediately hugged her mother and said, " Mom, you'll never guess what happened!"

- What conclusion can you draw about how Janet feels? How do you know?
  Janet feels happy. She had a huge smile on her face and hugged her mother.

- Why do you think Janet feels this way? How do you know?
  She got a good grade on a test or paper in school. Sometimes teachers put gold stars on tests and papers when students receive a good grade.

Sometimes authors don't include all the information needed to tell the whole story. In the paragraph above, the author never said that Janet got a good grade in school. That is when you need to draw conclusions in order to make the reading meaningful.

Drawing conclusions sometimes requires you to act like a detective. Look for clues to figure out exactly what the author is trying to say.

Reading Skill Focus: Drawing Conclusions

Directions: Read the following paragraph. When you see a magnifying glass symbol ( ), stop to draw conclusions. The first one has been done for you.

Marisol Becerra lives in the neighborhood of Little Village in Chicago. She was a freshman in high school when she and her mother went through an environmental training program organized by the Little Village Environmental Justice Organization (LVEJO). During this training, Marisol and her mother took a tour of their neighborhood in Chicago to see what kinds of **toxics** were in the air. Marisol learned that 60,000 young people in her neighborhood lived close to coal power plants. They breathed heavily polluted and unhealthy air everyday. This fact enraged her; especially because these people in her community were developing health problems like asthma and giving birth to babies with defects. She decided to take action. She created a youth chapter of the LVEJO and decided to put together a map on the Internet that educated people in the community about toxics and pollutants in the neighborhood. She then motivated people to join campaigns for better air quality and cleaner neighborhoods. Through her work with environmental justice, people in her neighborhood were educated about their environment, their health, and their quality of life.[7]

Marisol Becerra campaigns for better air quality and cleaner neighborhoods in Chicago.

toxics (n) – chemicals that are poisonous and can cause harm or death

Based on the fact... ➡ I can conclude that...

Based on the fact...	I can conclude that...
In Marisol's neighborhood, 60,000 young people live close to coal power plants and breathe heavily polluted air.	*These people may develop health issues like asthma because they are breathing heavily polluted air.*
Marisol was enraged after hearing how many people in her neighborhood breathe polluted air.	
Marisol created a youth group of the LVEJO and put together a map showing toxics in her neighborhood.	
Marisol was able to motivate people to join campaigns for better air quality and cleaner neighborhoods.	

Reading Skill Focus

Instructions

1. Together as a class, read the paragraph about Marisol. Each time you come to a magnifying glass, stop to let students draw conclusions.

2. **Additional Resource:** Show students a short documentary about Marisol, who received a Brower Youth Award for her bold environmental leadership. Visit http://broweryouthawards.org and click on "Brower Youth Awards". Marisol's story is included with the 2008 Award Winners.

Answers

1. Marisol cares deeply about her community.

2. There was no youth chapter of the LVEJO before Marisol created one. She is committed to helping to improve quality of life for people in her neighborhood.

3. Marisol is a person who knows how to get others to care about important issues.

Instructions

1. Have students read through the page and fill in the appropriate answers. Each answer will be used once.

   - **Differentiated Instruction:** Have students work in pairs or small groups.

2. Ask students if they see any connections between different aspects of quality of life. For example, if Indira from India does not have water and food, what else might she not have? How could securing adequate water and food contribute to other aspects of Indira's quality of life?

Directions: Something important is missing from each of the people's lives below. Use words from the Word Bank to answer the questions.

Word Bank			
food and water	education	health care	work
clean environment	free time	help others	family and friends

1. Fatima lives in Sudan. Unfortunately, there has been a war in her country, and she hasn't been able to attend school during the war. What does Fatima need? _____

2. Raul lives in Mexico City. For the past two weeks, he hasn't been able to play outside because the air pollution has been so terrible. What does Raul need? _____

3. Teresa lives in California. Her dad recently lost his job because the economy wasn't doing very well. What does Teresa's dad need? _____

4. Lin lives in Beijing. He has been working very long hours and hasn't been able to play basketball. Before he started working, he played basketball three times a week. What does Lin need? _____

5. Indira lives in India. She comes from a family of farmers. Lately, there has been a drought in the area where they live and no crops have been growing. What do Indira and her family need? _____

6. Katy has been studying global issues. She has started to notice things around the world that do not seem fair. She wants to do something to improve people's lives. What does Katy need to do? _____

7. Heena lives in Egypt. She's started to feel very sick. The doctor only comes to her village once a month. If she needs to visit him during the month, she would have to travel 150 miles. What does Heena need? _____

8. John had to move to New York City to find a job. He doesn't know anyone there and has started to feel very lonely. What does John need? _____

Answers

1. education
2. clean environment
3. work
4. free time
5. food and water
6. help others
7. health care
8. family and friends

Voices of Children

Adapted from a radio drama by Karin Shankar, courtesy of UNICEF (www.unicef.org*)* [8]

Characters:
Kakooza, a 15-year-old boy in Uganda
Padmini, an 11-year-old girl in India
Amy, a 14-year-old girl in the United States
Narrator

Narrator: This is the story of three children—Kakooza, Padmini, and Amy—separated by thousands of miles of land and ocean.

Kakooza lives with his grandmother in a village in central Uganda. There are powerful thunderstorms and lots of rain here. Kakooza's village is small. The surrounding landscape is covered with lush, green rain forests.

Padmini lives with her family on the southeastern coast of India. This is a tropical land of coconut palms and old **temples**.

Amy is from a poor neighborhood in New York City in the United States. Her city of 8 million people is **bustling** and very noisy.

We travel between these three points on the globe, following three lives. This is a story told in different voices about similar situations. We begin in Uganda with Kakooza. He tells us about the person closest to him, his grandmother.

Kakooza lives in a village in Uganda with his grandmother.

Kakooza: My family is very small, we are just two: my grandmother, whom I call Nambi, and I. Nambi wakes up at sunrise every morning to cook breakfast and collect water. But one morning was different. Nambi did not wake up with the sun. She stayed in bed saying, "Kakooza, I feel very cold and I have a headache." I could see Nambi's small body shivering under the sheets so I covered her with another blanket. I dressed quietly for school and left. That evening, when I returned home, Nambi was still asleep. She said, "I'll be fine soon, Kakooza. Don't worry too much. Maybe I just need to rest." But I couldn't help worrying. Nambi usually had so much energy. And now, all she wanted to do was sleep.

---

temple (n) – a place of worship
bustling (adj) – full of energy or activity

Instructions

1. Give students a minute to preview the reading. Ask them what is unusual about the structure of this chapter reading. How do they think this reading would sound if it were read aloud?

2. Explain that they will be reading a radio drama that includes characters, a narrator, and scenes. This drama will be read aloud like a play.

3. Explain to students that the genre of this radio drama is *realistic fiction.* Ask them to recall the difference between fiction and nonfiction.

4. Remind students that the reading skill focus for this chapter is drawing conclusions. As they read, they will draw conclusions to comprehend the reading.

5. This drama could be read aloud together as a class, with four students assigned to each of the roles. Alternatively, divide the class into groups of four and have each group read the drama aloud.

6. **Option:** After students have read the radio drama once, have them take on the roles of characters and do a reenactment of the radio drama.

Padmini lives in a tropical area of South India with many coconut palm trees.

Narrator: We leave Kakooza for now and travel east, about 5,000 kilometers across the Indian Ocean to Padmini, in her village in the southern Indian state of Tamil Nadu. Padmini lives with her parents in a small house. She begins her story by telling us about the day her sister was born.

Padmini: My baby sister was born on the day of Pongal, the winter harvest festival. On Pongal morning, I woke up early. The house smelled like sweet coconut pudding that Amma, my mother, had cooked. I ran outside and found her decorating our front door with mango leaves and marigold flowers for the festival, like all the other houses in the village. She seemed very tired that morning; her eyes had dark circles underneath them. Amma said she was going to take a nap. I stayed outside, playing with the flowers and leaves. Suddenly, I heard her call out loudly to my father. I froze. I dropped the flowers I was holding as my father came rushing out the door saying, "Padmini, I am going to call the **midwife**. Stay with your mother till I get back!"

Narrator: More than 13,000 kilometers away from Padmini, in New York City, Amy's story begins in her public school classroom.

Amy: It was a rainy Wednesday afternoon. We were in my favorite class, Mrs. Travis's art class. Wednesday is also the one day during the week that my Mom gets off early from work to pick me up from school (usually I take the school bus). We only have each other, my mom and me. She has two jobs and works very hard for us, so I don't see her very much. In art class, I had been coloring a picture of the ocean when I started to feel a little stuffy. I got up from my seat and stood by the open window for a few minutes, but it didn't help. My cold from the day before had been getting worse all morning. I thought it was just because of the rain. I began coughing and felt like I would never stop. The back of my throat was itching and the coughing only made it worse. In between coughs I was **wheezing** for breath, but there wasn't enough air entering my lungs. I felt as if I was breathing through a straw. I started gasping to take in bigger gulps of air. Then my chest began to tighten. The other students around me thought I was just fooling around and told me to stop but I couldn't—I was having the biggest asthma attack that I had ever had! I was terrified.

Narrator: We return to Kakooza now, telling us how scared he was about his grandmother's health.

---

midwife (n) – a person trained to assist a woman during child-birth
wheezing (v) – breathing with difficulty

Kakooza: The third night of Nambi's weakness, I cooked dinner, katoogo, which is made from beans and bananas. But she refused to eat. That night, instead of shivering with cold, she felt very warm and was sweating. So, I opened the door for the cool night breeze to enter. I left the hut and began to cry quietly outside. Nambi was already looking weaker and so tired. I didn't want to lose her. I didn't want to be alone. Four years ago, when the violence came to our hometown, my parents sent me to live with Nambi in her village, many kilometers away. They were going to follow with my little brother, but they never did. The violence separated us. Now, Nambi's strange weakness was going to separate her from me also.

Narrator: Meanwhile, Padmini recalls how surprised she was when her father told her that her mother was going to give birth. The baby was not supposed to be born for another month.

Padmini: Some minutes later, I heard my father return with the village midwife, the dai. She was old. She had a kind face and wrinkled hands. Her hands had helped many, many mothers in our village give birth. They told me to wait outside the house. I tried to close my ears to the sounds that came from Amma's bedroom—cries of pain. I was so worried for her. I must have been outside for a few hours before I heard a new sound—a baby crying! The little baby was here! When they opened the door for me, I found Amma exhausted and half asleep in her bedroom, and there by her side was the little newborn. My baby sister was tiny; smaller and thinner than any baby I had seen, but I knew she would grow soon. My father said she was born a month early, which is why she was small. Over the next few days, my baby sister grew even smaller and my parents were very worried. The dai returned often during those days and I heard bits of their conversation: that the baby was losing too much water and that she could not keep any food in. She didn't even eat the honey that the dai suggested we feed her. My mother was also ill, tired and unable to feed the baby any milk. If my baby sister did not eat, wouldn't she die?

People wait to see a doctor in a clinic in Uganda.

Narrator: We hear from Amy again now, telling us how scary it was being unable to breathe.

Amy: I knew I had to remain as calm as I could and stop panicking because if I didn't, it would make my breathing even worse. I wished my mom was near. When I had an attack before, she sang a song to distract me while setting up the **nebulizer**. But my mom wasn't here and my **inhaler** was in my bag in another classroom. Now I had to concentrate on keeping myself relaxed. Mrs. Travis had realized that something was wrong. She got up from her chair and came closer. My breathing was now shorter and faster. Each time I tried to speak to explain, I started coughing. I felt like a fish out of water gasping for air. In all of this chaos, my chair was knocked over and I fell to the ground as the other children crowded around me. Mrs. Travis told them to clear the room and, at that point, I must have begun to lose consciousness. The last thing I remember is Mrs. Travis running to the telephone at the back of the room.

Amy lives in a neighborhood of New York City.

Narrator: Meanwhile, Kakooza resumes his story of how he realized a way to save his grandmother.

Kakooza: I knew from school that when a person has no energy, does not want to eat, and is very warm or very cold, this is no magic spell. They are ill and most illnesses can be treated in a health center. But where was the health center? I had never been to one. Maybe there was one in the next town? Dreadful thoughts filled my mind again, of losing Nambi, of being alone, and I started to feel hopeless. Who could I turn to, to help us? Then, I thought about my teacher in school. She knew a lot! She would know what to do. In school the next morning, I told her about Nambi. My teacher said she would take me to the health center because she thought Nambi had **malaria**. After school, we went on my teacher's bike to the health center, an hour and a half away. When we reached it, the health worker said that he would come to see Nambi soon. I wanted to cry out, "Soon? Why can't you come immediately?" But I looked around at the people in the small room, nearly twenty of them all waiting to be treated, and I understood. Nambi would have to wait. Late that evening, the health worker arrived at our hut. In the dim light of our kerosene lamp, he looked at Nambi and told us it really was malaria. Then he checked me to see if I had any signs of the disease. I didn't. He gave Nambi some medicine and also a bed net for us to sleep under every night. Before leaving, he took me aside and said that I had arrived at the health center just in time to save Nambi.

---

nebulizer (n) – a machine used to give medicine to people with asthma

inhaler (n) – a small device used to inhale or take in medicine

malaria (n) – a disease transmitted by mosquitoes that can cause chills, fever, and sweating

Narrator: We move to Padmini now and her recollections of what her family did to save her newborn sister.

Padmini: My little sister would die if she didn't eat or drink water. We all knew this, but we couldn't force her to eat. The dai, aunties, uncles, and neighbors all came to our house to tell us what to feed her, but my baby sister couldn't keep anything in her body. Finally, on the fifth day, my father decided that he would take my mother and the baby to the **government** health clinic a few kilometers from our village. We had never been there because there was always someone in our village to cure illnesses. We had also heard that the lines to see the doctor were very long there. Amma agreed to go, even though it is un-usual for a new mother to leave her home with her baby. We waited there for nearly two hours before a doctor could see us. He took one look at my baby sister and said that she needed to be fed only breast milk for six months. He also gave her a simple mixture made of salt, safe boiled water, and sugar.

Narrator: Amy speaks again now, remembering how she felt when she regained **consciousness**.

Amy: When I woke up again, I was in an ambulance and the **paramedics** were putting a mask on my nose and mouth. I was beginning to be able to breathe again. I could feel tears streaming down my cheeks and wished again that my mom was near. I didn't know where I was going and was happy, at least, to see Mrs. Travis in the ambulance. I had never had an attack this bad before. Last year I started swim-ming, which mom said was especially good for kids with asthma. I also started taking ballet les-

Padmini's father takes her mother and her baby sister to a government health clinic.

sons and doing everything the other kids did, so I became a little careless about taking my inhaler with me everywhere. When we arrived at the hospital, Mrs. Travis said that my mom had been called at work and would be here soon to take me home. When Mom finally arrived, she ran in and gave me a tight hug. She was crying.

Narrator: As Kakooza, Padmini, and Amy end their stories, they also face some difficult questions.

---

government (n) – the form or system of rule by which a state, community, etc., is ruled by a group of leaders

consciousness (n) – the state of being awake and aware of one's surroundings

paramedics (n) – people who are trained to give emergency medical treatment or to assist doctors in providing medical care

Amy is rushed to a hospital after her asthma attack.

Kakooza: What would I have done if Nambi had died? What would Nambi have done if I had fallen ill? What if my teacher had not known where the health center was? Why was our health so uncertain?

Padmini: Salt, water, and sugar—these were the things that would make her healthy? We nearly lost her for salt, water, and sugar? But we had these things at home! Why didn't Amma know? Why did the dai not tell us? Why was the life of my baby sister hanging on a last minute trip to the health center?

Amy: As my mom held me tight in the emergency room, I closed my eyes and thought how sad she would have been if anything had happened to me. The time I spend with her is important because she is always working. I know that she works so hard partly because of me.

She works so that I can go to swimming and ballet lessons, and she also works to pay for times like these when I have to go to the hospital.

Kakooza: I wish we had a health center in our village where Nambi and I could go when we get sick.

Padmini: I wish we had known the simple ways to help my little sister so that she wouldn't have had to suffer so much during the first days of her life.

Amy: I wish my neighborhood was less polluted. I think cleaner air would mean fewer asthma attacks.

Narrator: These three voices echo the voices of millions of other children across the globe with similar stories about how one of their most essential rights—the right to health and well-being—is **denied**. They are left asking questions that few adults, including their parents, teachers, and governments, can fully answer.

Kakooza: Why must the clinic be so far away?

Padmini: Why is it that we know so little about good health care?

Amy: Why should I have to breathe polluted air?

All three: How will you ensure that we have a healthy childhood?

_____
denied (v) – to withhold something from someone or refuse to grant a request

Directions: Read the following facts about the drama you just read, and then draw conclusions based on these facts. Return to the reading to gather more evidence to help you reach each conclusion.

Based on the fact... ➔ I can conclude that...

Based on the fact...	I can conclude that...
Kakooza's grandmother has to collect water.	
Padmini's mother is tired and has dark circles under her eyes.	
Amy starts to feel a bit stuffy in class. She begins coughing and thinks it will never stop.	
Kakooza's parents sent him to live with his grandmother in her village because it was unsafe for him in his own village. They were going to follow with his little brother, but he never saw them again.	
Padmini's baby sister looks smaller each day.	
When Amy loses consciousness, Mrs. Travis runs to the telephone.	
The doctor gives Kakooza's grandma some medicine and bed nets for both of them to sleep under.	
When Padmini and her family reach the health clinic, they have to wait in a line for two hours before they see the doctor.	
Amy's mom is always working.	

Instructions

1. Students may complete the table as they read or after they have finished reading the drama.

   • **Differentiated Instruction:** Have students complete the table in their reading groups.

2. Review answers with them. If students came up with different conclusions, discuss the differences. In some cases, there may be more than one correct conclusion.

Answers

1. Kakooza and his grandmother do not have water readily available from a faucet. She has to walk somewhere to collect it.

2. Padmini's mother must not be sleeping well because she is sick.

3. Amy is having an asthma attack.

4. Something must have happened that prevented Kakooza's parents and brother from reaching him. They may have died in the conflict, or they may have had to leave the country.

5. Padmini's baby sister is sick and gets worse each day.

6. Mrs. Travis runs to the phone because she is scared about what has happened to Amy. She is going to call someone for help.

7. Kakooza's grandma has malaria, a disease transmitted by mosquitoes. Bed nets will protect Kakooza and his grandma from mosquitoes while they sleep.

8. The health clinic has many patients and perhaps not enough doctors.

9. Her mother cares a lot for Amy and wants to make sure Amy can do everything she wants to in life. Her job may not pay very well.

Comprehension Questions

Instructions

1. Before students begin answering the comprehension questions, share with them the academic language they will see in many of the questions (see Appendix B).

2. Explain that the questions are divided into five sections according to the different ways they support comprehension. (See Appendix B for a detailed explanation of each section.)

3. **Differentiated Instruction:** Differentiate the questions students must answer based on their reading levels. Support comprehension by working with students who may need more guided instruction.

Directions: Answer the following questions to support your comprehension of the chapter readings.

Understanding what you read

1. Identify the country each character in the radio drama is from.

2. What important part of quality of life is uncertain in Kakooza's, Padmini's, and Amy's lives?

Thinking about what you read

3. Analyze how the following Arabian proverb connects to the lives of Kakooza, Padmini, and Amy: *"He who has health, has hope. And he who has hope, has everything."*

4. Amy mentions that she started coughing and *felt like a fish out of water.* Explain what Amy means when she uses this phrase.

Questioning what you read

5. Why do you think the author wrote this radio drama?

6. Explain why you think the author chose to write about three people from different places.

Making connections with what you read

7. What is one way you could improve your quality of life?

8. What is one way you could improve the quality of life for other people where you live?

Further discussion questions

9. How might air pollution be related to a person's quality of life?

10. How might world leaders and governments be able to improve the quality of people's lives?

Answers

1. Kakooza is from Uganda, Padmini is from India, and Amy is from the United States.

2. health

3. Health is an essential part of a good life. When a person is healthy, he can work, learn, and look forward to the future.

4. A fish cannot survive for long out of water because it is designed to breathe under water. When Amy started coughing, she was having difficulty breathing.

5. The author wants to show the connection between health and well-being, and how people in different places face different challenges.

6. The three stories show the different kinds of health issues people face and how poor health affects people's lives in different ways.

7. exercise, study, volunteer

8. recycle, volunteer, tutor

9. When people live in an area where there is a significant amount of air pollution, they could develop health problems, such as asthma. This can impact other parts of their life: it might be difficult to play or exercise outside, or they might be too sick to work.

10. There are a number of possibilities, such as giving all children the ability to go to school, providing all people with opportunities to work, and making resources like food and water available for everyone.

What is realistic fiction?

If a story is **fiction**, it is not true. **Realistic fiction** is a type of fiction that is not true, but it could happen in real life. You just finished reading a drama that is realistic fiction. The characters had to deal with real-life problems in settings that were also realistic. Improving in math because a genie suddenly gives you magical powers is NOT realistic fiction. Improving in math because a tutor helps you IS realistic fiction.

Throughout this chapter, you have read about quality of life and what can sometimes prevent people from improving their quality of life. You will now read the beginning of a story about quality of life and determine a realistic conclusion to this story.

Example: Read the following two examples. Which story do you think is a better example of realistic fiction? Why?

Story A:

Last year, Angela was pretty lonely. She spent a lot of time by herself. Her mother and father worked almost all the time. They made a lot of money, which is how they bought a really big house. Angela liked her house and her neighborhood, but it was hard for her to enjoy spending so much time alone.

Now Angela sees her mother a lot more because her mother decided to get a different job so that she works fewer hours. Their family had to move into a smaller house in a different neighborhood, but Angela is much happier. Now she doesn't have to spend her afternoons alone.

Story B:

George and his family used to live in a small apartment. George's father worked most of the time, so George didn't get to see him very much. George's mother stayed home to take care of George and his brother and two sisters.

All of that changed two months ago when George's father won the lottery. He won $3 million dollars! After that he quit his job, and George's family moved into a big house. Now George and his siblings get to spend a lot more time with their dad.

Instructions

1. Explain to students that they will write a conclusion to a realistic fictional story.

2. Review the description of realistic fiction. Ask them to explain why improving in math because a genie gives you magic powers is NOT realistic fiction.

3. Have students read through the two sample stories and decide which is the better example of realistic fiction. Why is this story a better example?

Instructions

1. The beginning and middle sections of a short story about quality of life are provided. Students will develop a realistic conclusion to this story.

2. Have students read these sections either independently or with a partner.

3. **Grammar Suggestion:** Ask students to identify what tense the story is written in (past tense). Students will need to write the conclusion to this story in the past tense. Teach them how to differentiate between the past tense of regular and irregular verbs.

Directions: Read the following beginning and middle sections of a story. Your job is to finish the story. For the conclusion of this story, you will write two paragraphs. Your conclusion should explain how the Thompson family worked to solve their problems.

The Eye of the Storm

BEGINNING:

Mr. and Mrs. Thompson moved to the neighborhood of Gulfstown with their children five years ago. They developed a strong community with the people who lived near them. They would have monthly block parties, and children were often seen playing outside with each other. Crime was rare because everyone looked out for each other. The Thompson's house was never empty. Mrs. Thompson had weekly coffee time with neighbors to talk about ways they could improve their neighborhood. The Thompson children had friends who came over on the weekends.

Last year, Najma was thirteen years old and was going to enter the eighth grade. Her middle school was only three blocks away from their house. Tony was fifteen years old and was going into tenth grade. His high school was five blocks away. A week before they started school, the weather in Gulfstown was really severe. There were heavy rains, and winds swept through the area at 160 miles per hour. Gulfstown had been hit by a hurricane. The mayor declared a state of emergency and told everyone they needed to leave the city. Some people left and never returned. After leaving for several months, Mr. and Mrs. Thompson, Najma, and Tony decided to come back to Gulfstown.

MIDDLE:

When Mr. and Mrs. Thompson's family returned to their neighborhood, things had changed. There was water damage in their home. The floors were sagging, and the carpet was ruined. Many houses in their neighborhood were empty because their neighbors had moved to different cities and towns. Najma and Tony's schools were both destroyed by the hurricane. They had to take two buses to get to their new schools, making them exhausted by the time they returned home at night. Mr. Thompson lost his job, and now Mrs. Thompson was the only one making money. She had to work additional hours during the weekend to make sure the family could pay for food, electricity, and water.

The family was troubled by the fact that their neighborhood had changed so much. The quality of life they were used to—a safe home, good jobs, and a close community of good friends—seemed to be a part of their past rather than their future. After the hurricane, no children played outside and people kept to themselves. The Thompsons decided they needed to improve their life. They did not want to live like this anymore.

How does the story end?

Writing Steps: Realistic Fiction

Step 1: After reading the partially completed story, use the Writing Brainstorm Page on the next page to write a conclusion to the story. Your conclusion should include a solution that will help the family improve their quality of life.

Step 2: Edit your conclusion using the Edit Checklist below.

Step 3: Have a classmate edit your conclusion using the same checklist.

Step 4: Revise your conclusion based on the peer edit.

Step 5: Share your conclusion with the class.

Instructions

1. Review the steps with students.
2. Share the Chapter 6 writing rubric with them. You may want to add relevant spelling and grammar components to the rubric.

✔ Edit Checklist

	Author Check	Peer Editor Check
Did you write two paragraphs for your conclusion?		
Did you use at least one chapter vocabulary word?		
Is your conclusion realistic?		

Chapter 6 Writing Rubric

Category	3	2	1
Organization of Information	Writes two paragraphs for the conclusion of the summary	Attempts to write two paragraphs for the conclusion of the summary	Does not attempt to write two paragraphs for the conclusion of the summary
Development of Information	Writes a realistic conclusion	Writes a somewhat realistic conclusion	Does not write a realistic conclusion
Vocabulary	Uses chapter vocabulary correctly	Uses at least half of chapter vocabulary correctly	Does not attempt using chapter vocabulary

Total = _____ / 9

Instructions

1. Students can use this page to develop their ideas for the conclusion.

   • **Differentiated Instruction:** For beginning students who may need more guidance, work with them in a small group and assist them in writing their story conclusion.

2. **Additional Resource:** Allow students to research what people have done to improve their neighborhoods after Hurricane Katrina hit New Orleans. A few stories can be found on the following websites: CNN Heroes (www.cnn.com/SPECIALS/cnn.heroes) and Habitat for Humanity New Orleans (www.habitat-nola.org/index.php).

3. **Option:** Have students share their conclusions with each other to see how many different conclusions the story can have.

4. **Option:** Rewrite this story as a play that students can act out, similar to the *Voices of Children* drama.

What are some ways the Thompson family could work to solve their problems and improve their quality of life?

Your summary could include answers to one or more of these questions:

- How do they bring their neighbors back to the community?

- How do they make the neighborhood feel safe for people to go outside again?

- How does Mr. Thompson find work?

- What happens so that Mrs. Thompson does not have to work on the weekends?

- How are the children able to go to school closer to where they live?

How will the story conclude in a realistic way?

Culminating Activity: Living the Good Life
(2 hours, plus time outside class to survey peers)

Overview

Students use indicators to measure quality of life and conduct a survey to obtain data for these indicators. Students compare their own performance as measured by the quality of life indicators against peer averages determined by the survey results.

Materials/Preparation

- Clear a large space where students can stand in a circle
- *Quality of Life Sample Survey*, displayed on an overhead or with a document camera
- *Quality of Life Survey*, two per student

Introduction

1. In a cleared space, ask all students to stand in a circle. Tell them that you will be reading several statements one at a time. Students who agree with a particular statement should take one step inside the circle. Those who disagree with a statement should remain in the outer circle. After each statement is read and students have responded, all students should return to the outer circle.

2. Read the following statements one at a time:
   - Good friends are an important part of quality of life.
   - Making more than enough money to pay your monthly bills is an important part of quality of life.
   - Graduating from college is an important part of quality of life.

3. Ask the class: *If everyone in the world was "living the good life", what would we have in common?*

Steps—Day 1

1. Ask students: *What is one way you can find out how people rate their own quality of life?* (e.g., surveys, interviews, polls)

2. Give the definition of a **survey** (a sampling of information taken from a group of people to see what they believe about a certain topic).

3. Explain to students that they will survey other students to learn about their quality of life. In order to do this, they will use *indicators*. Indicators will allow students to quantify and evaluate survey data.

4. Explain that students need to create indicators that are easy for people to understand. Ask students which of the following indicators makes the most sense, and discuss why:
   a. The number of seconds students watch TV per week
   b. The number of hours students watch TV per week
   c. The number of hours students watch TV per year
   d. The number of minutes students watch TV per month

5. Share the *Quality of Life Sample Survey* with students. Go over each category and sample indicator. Note that each indicator will result in a numerical answer. Also note that for each indicator, a higher number relates to higher quality of life.

6. Explain that, as a class, you will create your own list of indicators to measure quality of life. You will use these indicators to see how your life and the lives of other students stack up.

   - **Differentiated Instruction:** Instead of having students develop their own indicators, allow them to use the Quality of Life Sample Survey to survey themselves and their peers.

7. Pass out two *Quality of Life Survey* handouts to each student. Display one copy on an overhead or with a document camera.

8. Guide students in developing each of the indicators. Students can even vote on which

indicator makes the most sense for each part of the survey. They should write the final indicators on both of their blank *Quality of Life Survey* handouts.

9. Each student will administer one survey to himself/herself and one to another student outside of class in order to assess their quality of life as defined by these indicators. They will share and analyze their results during Day 2 of this lesson.

10. Tell students to be aware of problems they may encounter when conducting their surveys, which could make the data they collect less accurate. Typical issues to be aware of when conducting a survey include:
   • Do people understand the questions?
   • Do people have enough information to give an accurate answer?
   • Are the people surveyed being honest?
   • Are people surveyed individually, rather than in groups? (People tend to adjust their answers based on what they hear their peers saying.)

Steps—Day 2 (after surveys have been administered)

1. Prepare a blank table on the board or an overhead where student groups will share their data. It might resemble the following table:

Quality of Life Category	Survey Results from Class	Survey Results from Interviewing Peers
Family		
Friends		
Health		
Rest/Relaxation		
Recreation		
Creative Pursuits		
Work/Earn Money		
Volunteer/Help Others		
The Environment		

2. Ask the students how their surveying went and if they think the data they collected are accurate.

3. Have each person write the numbers from their two completed surveys in the corresponding cells of the table you prepared on the board or overhead. Have each person write a comma after the numbers they report to differentiate their answers from others.

4. Ask them what kinds of calculations they might make in order to summarize the data. In this case, you will find the average for each group. To find the average, add up all responses for a category and divide by the number of responses. So, if you collected data for the Family category from fifty students, you would add up each of their individual responses and divide the total by fifty.

5. Have students calculate the average response from the class and from the peer interviews for each indicator. You could assign pairs of students to calculate different averages and report their answers to you. Write the answers where everyone can see them.

6. Ask them to talk to a partner about what they notice about the results. It might help to pose the following questions:
   • What is surprising about the results?
   • How do class members' assessments of quality of life compare to their peers?
   • In what ways do people seem to be doing well? (i.e., which indicators scored the highest?)
   • What could people do differently to change or improve their quality of life? (i.e., which indicators scored the lowest?)

Quality of Life Sample Survey

Quality of Life Category	Indicator
Family	Number of times you eat dinner with your family per week Answer:
Friends	Number of friends you talk to on the phone per week Answer:
Health	Number of hours you exercise per week Answer:
Rest/Relaxation	Number of hours you sleep per night Answer:
Recreation	Number of hours you spend watching movies or playing games per week Answer:
Creative Pursuits	Number of hours you spend doing creative activities per week Answer:
Work/Earn Money	Number of dollars you earn per week Answer:
Volunteer/Help Others	Number of times you help someone or volunteer your time per week Answer:
The Environment	Number of cans and bottles you recycle per week Answer:

Quality of Life Survey

Survey administered by (your name): _____

Person being surveyed is: ☐ a member of the class   ☐ not a member of the class

Quality of Life Category	Indicator
Friends	Number of _____ per _____ Answer:
Health	Number of _____ per _____ Answer:
Rest/Relaxation	Number of _____ per _____ Answer:
Recreation	Number of _____ per _____ Answer:
Creative Pursuits	Number of _____ per _____ Answer:
Work/Earn Money	Number of _____ per _____ Answer:
Volunteer/Help Others	Number of _____ per _____ Answer:
The Environment	Number of _____ per _____ Answer:
Other	Number of _____ per _____ Answer:

Action Project

Have students develop an *Alternative Holiday Catalog* with ideas for gifts that improve the quality of life of individuals in your local community and in other parts of the world. Gifts might improve quality of life for both the giver and the recipient. Distribute the catalogs at school events and in the community.

Additional Resources on Quality of Life

Think Impact
www.studentmovementusa.org

Think Impact is a leadership development organization that provides students in the United States with ideas, leadership, and funding to effect positive change and help alleviate poverty in different regions of the world.

United Nations CyberSchoolBus
www.un.org/Pubs/CyberSchoolBus

Cyberschoolbus is a global education website for teachers and students with links to information about the Convention on the Rights of the Child, Model UN Headquarters, and teaching human rights.

United for Human Rights
www.humanrights.com/#/videos

Thirty short videos teach about each of the thirty human rights in the Universal Declaration of Human Rights.

YES! magazine
www.yesmagazine.org

This magazine often includes articles about quality of life issues, including positive stories from scientists, writers, sociologists, religious leaders, and others working to improve quality of life. There is a free one-year subscription for educators.

Global Campaign for Education
www.campaignforeducation.org

The Global Campaign for Education is a movement that strives to make free quality public education available to all. Students can get involved with promoting universal education during Global Action Week, held each April.

Chapter 6 Student Assessment, page 1
Knowledge about Improving Quality of Life

Vocabulary

Directions: Read each sentence and circle the letter which corresponds to the correct definition of the **bold-faced** word.

1. Many people think that strong relationships with friends and family improve a person's **quality of life**.

   a. how much money a person makes
   b. the type of job and house a person has
   c. the well-being of an individual
   d. how many friends a person has

2. **Human rights** of all people around the world include the right to practice religion and the right to education.

   a. things every person in the world deserves to have access to
   b. the right to food and water
   c. having equality and freedom
   d. practicing any religion and belief you want

3. People living in **poverty** may not have enough water, shelter, and food.

   a. areas of town that do not have services
   b. the state of being poor and living without necessary resources
   c. the state of being too rich and having too many things
   d. living with hardly any food to eat

4. The **life expectancy** of a person who lives in Japan is eighty years, while the life expectancy of a person who lives in Malawi is thirty-nine.

   a. a person's health
   b. the age until which a person is expected to live
   c. a person's family characteristics
   d. the age a person is supposed to start having children

Content

Directions: For each of the following statements, circle *True* if the statement is true and *False* if the statement is not true.

5. **True or False:** Everyone is born with basic human rights.

6. **True or False:** A high life expectancy means a person is likely to live a long life.

7. **True or False:** A high quality of life is only meant for those who make millions of dollars.

8. **True or False:** People who struggle to meet basic needs have a high quality of life.

Chapter 6 Student Assessment, page 2

Reading Comprehension

Directions: Read the paragraphs below. For numbers 9 and 10, circle the correct answer.

In the country of Kenya in Africa, a young boy named Bati gets up each day before the sun rises. He wears thin, patched shorts passed down from his two older brothers. Bati helps his mother start the wood fire to cook breakfast for him and his four brothers and sisters. His sisters gather water from a river two miles away. Twice a day, Bati and his family eat green peas and corn boiled with salt. Bati's house is made of mud bricks and has a roof of leaves. Chickens sleep under the bed he shares with his two brothers. His mother and two sisters sleep in the other room. Because his father works as a laborer in a town twelve hours away, Bati only sees him twice a year.

Bati goes to school a few months every year but is always behind because he misses classes often. His family can only afford to send the oldest son to high school. Bati was very sick last year. He had to be carried to a health clinic six hours away. He received medicine and got better, but now his mother can't buy the goat she was saving for because she spent the money on the medicine.

9. What conclusion can you make about Bati's life?
   a. Bati lives a very easy life and can get all the food, water, and shelter he needs to survive.
   b. Bati lives in poverty. He doesn't eat much food, and basic needs like water are difficult to obtain.
   c. Bati lives with his family and therefore lives a life filled with love.
   d. Bati lives a privileged life. He knows he can have a very successful future.

10. What is the main idea of these two paragraphs?
    a. Bati has many hopes and dreams, but he may not be able to fulfill them.
    b. Living in Kenya can be a challenge for certain families.
    c. Bati's family struggles to meet their basic needs. Their life is difficult.
    d. Bati's mother hopes to earn a lot of money by buying a goat.

Chapter 6 Student Assessment, page 3
Outlook and Personal Beliefs

Answer the following questions based on your personal beliefs. There are no right or wrong answers.

Directions for 1 and 2: Place a check mark (√) in the box next to each statement that is true for you.

1. I have the ability to improve my own quality of life.
   ☐ True
   ☐ False

2. I have the ability to improve the quality of life of other people.
   ☐ True
   ☐ False

3. **Complete the following sentence:**
   One way I can personally work to improve quality of life for myself or others is by…

   _____

   _____

   _____

   _____

   _____

Directions for 4 and 5: Fill in the ovals below based on your level of agreement. 1 means you strongly agree, and 7 means you strongly disagree.

1 = yes, definitely!   7 = no way!

⟵————————————————————⟶

4. I believe my daily actions have an impact on people and places in other parts of the world.

   1   **2**   **3**   **4**   **5**   **6**   **7**
   ◯   ◯   ◯   ◯   ◯   ◯   ◯

5. I believe I have the ability to help solve quality of life issues.

   1   **2**   **3**   **4**   **5**   **6**   **7**
   ◯   ◯   ◯   ◯   ◯   ◯   ◯

Answers

Chapter 6 Student Assessment,
pp. 142 F, G

1. c
2. a
3. b
4. b
5. True
6. True
7. False
8. False
9. b
10. c

Teacher Notes

Chapter 7

Peace and Conflict

Students think critically about the meaning of conflict during introductory speaking and writing activities. After learning vocabulary relevant to a study of peace and conflict, students work to understand the meaning of a poem. In a jigsaw activity, students read about four different examples of real-world conflicts, identifying the theme of each reading section. Students take on the role of an advice columnist in a final writing activity. The chapter culminates with an activity in which students role-play different scenarios and resolve conflicts.

Possible Scope and Sequence
(based on one-hour class periods)

Day 1	Day 2	Day 3	Day 4	Day 5
Activating Knowledge Writing Warm-up Expanding Vocabulary	Using Words in Context: *Multiple Choice* Breaking Down the Meaning	Dialogue: *Funny, Isn't It?*	Reading Skill Focus: *Identifying Theme* Pre-reading: *What Would You Do?*	Chapter Reading: *Stories of Conflict* Reading Skill Follow-up

Day 6	Day 7	Day 8	Day 9
Comprehension Questions	Writing about Peace and Conflict: *Advice Column*	Culminating Activity: *To Fight or Not to Fight?*	Culminating Activity *(cont'd)*

Time
Eight or nine one-hour class periods

Essential Questions
- What are some different types of conflict?
- What are some root causes of conflict?
- What are ways conflicts can be resolved in peaceful ways?

Integrated Subject Areas
- Social Studies
- English Language Arts

Content Objectives
Students will:
- Understand the meaning of conflict and identify different types of conflict
- Identify root causes of conflicts
- Develop ideas for resolving conflicts

Language Objectives
Students will:
- Analyze words related to peace and conflict
- Write a response to questions about conflict
- Discuss a poem about conflict through a dialogue
- Discover the meaning of a poem using reciprocal reading
- Read different scenarios of real-world conflicts and resolutions
- Identify the theme of a reading selection
- Define and use new vocabulary words
- Write an advice column

Key Concepts
- Conflict
- Peace
- Bullying

Vocabulary
- Stability
- Conflict
- Tolerance
- Violence

Standards Addressed
- TESOL standards
- NCTE standards
- NCSS standards
- NSES standards

* Please see Appendix A for a list of national standards addressed.

Assessment Option
Use the Chapter 7 assessments of student knowledge and outlook/personal beliefs as pre-tests for the chapter. Follow up with the same assessments at the end of the chapter to determine changes in knowledge and outlook/personal beliefs.

7 Peace and Conflict

How can individuals and countries work to create a peaceful world?

Chapter 7 will introduce you to different types of conflicts happening around the world and how people are working to resolve these conflicts. In this chapter, you will **speak** to your classmates about the differences between peace and conflict. You will **listen** to a poem and work with your classmates to uncover the meaning of the poem. You will **read** about different types of conflicts and ways people are working to resolve them. After learning about conflict and solutions, you will **write** an advice column to a student who is going through a conflict and needs your help.

Instructions

1. Read the introduction with students.
2. Ask students if they can think of conflicts (like wars) happening around the world right now. Alternatively, ask them if they can think of conflicts (like a fight between friends) happening in their lives right now.

A mural in New York City encourages peace.

Instructions

1. Have students work independently at first and then with a partner to discuss the two photographs.

2. Have them sort the words below the photographs into two categories based on the photos.

3. Explain that the two photographs and the words describing them are antonyms, or opposites, of each other.

4. Ask them to think of a word that would represent all the words in the first column, and one word that would represent all of the words in the second column. Have students write these headings above the two columns.

5. Ask if anyone has heard of the words *peace* and *conflict*. Where have they heard these words?

6. Ask students why they believe conflicts happen. Explain that conflicts happen for a variety of reasons: a lack of resources; a weak economy; a weak government; social divisions based on race, class, ethnicity, or religion; rapid population growth; or ready availability of lethal weapons. These are known as *root causes* of conflict.

7. Explain to students that, in Chapter 7, they will learn more about why conflict happens and ways in which people can work to prevent conflict and promote peace.

Activating Knowledge

Directions: The words in the box below can be divided into two categories, as depicted in the two photos. Decide which words belong with each picture.

hatred	acceptance	fighting	anger	love
harmony	violence	security	abuse	friendship

Answers

Left: acceptance, love, harmony, security, friendship

Right: hatred, fighting, anger, violence, abuse

A *conflict* is a fight, battle, or struggle.

Directions: Write about a time in your life when you had a conflict with another person. In your writing, answer the following questions:

How did the conflict start?

Who was involved?

Was the conflict resolved? If so, how?

What did you learn from this conflict?

Instructions

1. To prepare students for the writing warm-up, explain that they will be writing about a conflict they had with another person.

2. Ask students why people their age might have conflicts.

- **Differentiated Instruction:** If students need help generating ideas, share a conflict you have experienced with the class.

3. Give students time to write about their conflicts.

- **Differentiated Instruction:** If beginner students are more comfortable writing in their native language, allow them to do so.

- **Differentiated Instruction:** If beginner students want to draw diagrams to support their writing, allow them to do so.

4. Have students share their writing with a partner. Ask volunteers to share conflicts they have had in their lives with the class, if they feel comfortable doing so.

5. Ask students whether they think there are peaceful ways to resolve conflicts.

Instructions

1. Have students study the four photos independently.

2. Have students share what they think each word means either with a partner or the class.

3. Discuss possible definitions with them.

   • **Option:** Copy this page onto an overhead or display it with a document camera. As students are brainstorming ideas for each vocabulary word, list these in the box with the photo.

4. **Option:** Review the following derivatives:

   • *stability (n) – stable, stabilized*

   • *conflict (n) – conflicted, conflicting*

   • *tolerance (n) – tolerate, tolerant*

   • *violence (n) – violent, violate*

5. **Option:** Review the following suffixes:

   • *ity – the state of being (i.e., stability is the state of being stable)*

   • *ance – the state of being (i.e., tolerance is the state of being tolerant)*

Directions: Look at the following images and vocabulary words. Guess what you think the words mean based on the given images.

A

stability

B

conflict

C

tolerance

D

violence

Using Words in Context: Multiple Choice

Using Words in Context

Directions: For each of the four statements below, choose the answer that best completes each sentence.

1. A *conflict* between two sisters could be …

   a. a fight over who gets to use the car on Saturday night.
   b. a similarity in the way they look, act, and think.
   c. a friendship that lasts for years and years.
   d. a secret that is shared between the two of them.

2. In a country with *stability*, all people might …

   a. find it difficult to find work.
   b. have basic resources like food, water, and homes.
   c. only speak to people who look like they do.
   d. fight over land, food, and water.

3. To show *tolerance* toward a group of people who are from a different culture means that …

   a. you are willing to talk to them to understand them better.
   b. you would make fun of them.
   c. you avoid them and ignore them if they talk to you.
   d. you have knowledge about this group of people.

4. A video game that includes *violence* may involve …

   a. a person practicing karate with a teacher.
   b. a soldier shooting other soldiers in a war.
   c. two basketball teams playing against each other.
   d. a musician playing different types of instruments.

Instructions

1. Read the activity aloud to students.

2. As students listen, they can determine the appropriate multiple choice answers.

3. Have students read through the statements again and review their answers with a partner.

4. Ask volunteers to read the completed statements aloud to the class.

Answers

1. a

2. b

3. a

4. b

Instructions

1. Explain the directions. After reviewing the definitions, explain to students they will (1) answer the question, (2) create a sentence using the vocabulary word, and (3) choose the one word in the group that does not relate to the vocabulary word.

   • **Differentiated Instruction:** Demonstrate how the activity works by filling in one of the boxes.

   • **Differentiated Instruction:** Enlarge the four boxes to poster size and fill in one of the boxes. Work as a class to fill in answers within each box and write them on the poster. The poster can then remain hanging in the room throughout this unit of study.

2. This activity could be done independently, in pairs or small groups, or as an entire class.

3. **Option:** Have students search for and cut out magazine pictures that relate to each vocabulary word.

4. **Option:** As a homework assignment, have students write a single paragraph using the four vocabulary words.

Directions: Each box below includes one of the four vocabulary words from the previous page, as well as its definition. Below each definition:

1. Answer the question.

2. Write a sentence using the vocabulary word.

3. Choose the one word in the group that does not relate to the vocabulary word.

---

stability

Definition: *the condition of being dependable or not likely to fall apart*

1. Why might the stability of an old bridge be questionable?

2. Use *stability* in a sentence.

3. Which word does not belong?
   peaceful   balanced   safe   dangerous

---

conflict

Definition: *a fight or struggle*

1. What is one conflict you have seen recently?

2. Use *conflict* in a sentence.

3. Which word does not belong?
   war   unity   hatred   abuse

---

tolerance

Definition: *acceptance of differences*

1. What things could someone do to show tolerance to a group of people?

2. Use *tolerance* in a sentence.

3. Which word does not belong?
   acceptance   open-minded
   racist   harmony

---

violence

Definition: *physical force that causes damage or injury*

1. What type of violence have you seen on television?

2. Use *violence* in a sentence.

3. Which word does not belong?
   fighting   combat   weapons   friendly

Answers

stability

1. The bridge may have parts that are worn out and be unsafe to walk on.
2. The school has experienced stability ever since parents, teachers, and students became involved in making it a bully-free zone.
3. dangerous

conflict

1. Answers will vary. Example: I have seen two students fighting at school.
2. The conflict began when she decided to sit at a lunch table where she normally did not sit.
3. unity

tolerance

1. A person could show tolerance to a group of people by talking to them, accepting their differences, and inviting them to take part in meetings and activities.
2. Martin Luther King, Jr. was a leader who spoke about the importance of tolerance and accepting people who are different.
3. racist

violence

1. Answers will vary. Example: Last week, I watched a show in which a boyfriend hit his girlfriend.
2. The middle school students worked with younger students to teach them that violence is not a good way to deal with anger.
3. friendly

Dialogue: Funny, Isn't It?

In groups of four, you will work to understand the meaning of a poem titled *Funny, Isn't It?* Before you read the poem, you will be assigned one of the following roles: summarizer, questioner, predictor, or clarifier.

Directions: Find the section of the table below that explains your role. Read the explanation of your role. Using this information, work with your group to understand the meaning of the poem.

Summarizer

As the summarizer, you will read the poem and summarize the main idea of the poem. Remember that the main idea is the most important message and is supported by details.

Phrases you can use:

This main idea of this poem is…

This poem is about…

The author wrote this poem because…

Questioner

As the questioner, you will read the poem and come up with at least three questions about the meaning of the poem.

Phrases you can use:

I wonder why…

I'm not sure if…

Why did…

Who was…

Predictor

As the predictor, you will make predictions about the poem before, during, and after the poem is read.

Phrases you can use:

I predict…

I think…

I bet…

Clarifier

As the clarifier, you will write down any ideas, words, or phrases you find confusing. You will also try to help anyone who is confused about any part of the poem.

Phrases you can use:

What I would like to know from the author is…

I don't understand why…

I don't understand the following words or phrases…

Instructions

1. Explain to students that they will have a dialogue with each other about a poem they will read, using a strategy called *reciprocal reading.*[1] Through reciprocal reading, they will try to interpret the meaning of the poem by discussing it with each other.

2. Divide students into groups of four. Within each group, designate a specific reciprocal reading role for each person in the group: summarizer, predictor, clarifier, and questioner.

3. Review the roles with students. Make sure that all students understand their roles.

4. **Differentiated Instruction:** Model an example of reciprocal reading using another poem or short writing sample.

Instructions

1. Read the poem aloud to model proper pronunciation.

2. Have students reread the poem in their groups of four.

3. After reading the poem, give students 5-10 minutes to summarize, make predictions, question, or clarify, depending on their roles. Each person will be working to answer different questions.

   • Students can use the phrases from the previous page to analyze the poem or you can assign the following tasks: the summarizer writes a summary of the poem; the predictor comes up with three or four predictions about the poem; the clarifier asks the group three or four clarifying questions; and the questioner asks the group three or four questions about the meaning of the poem.

4. Conclude the activity by bringing the class back together and reflecting on any additional thoughts or comments about the meaning of the poem. Possible discussion questions:

   • What is the significance of the title, *Funny, Isn't It?*

   • What was the conflict in the poem?

   • Was it resolved?

Funny, Isn't It?

When I was younger,
I didn't care to know him.
He was new and I was not,
reaching out was something I forgot.

When I was younger,
I didn't want to see him.
He didn't have anything to offer me,
I thought friendships shouldn't be free!

When I was younger,
I didn't try to talk with him.
He spoke in a tongue I didn't understand,
I couldn't tolerate him or lend a hand.

I found him easy to ignore
because he was new and I was not.

I found him easy to avoid
because he had nothing and I did not.

I found him easy to dismiss
because he spoke strangely and I did not.

Now that I'm older,
I wish I had reached out to him.
I wish I had spent time with him.
I wish I had tolerated him.

I wish I knew why we sometimes choose
to do what's easy instead of what's right.

Funny, isn't it?

The **theme** of a reading is an important message about life that the author wants to express to the reader. While the *main idea* of a text focuses on what the reading is about, the *theme* focuses on a lesson.

Examples of themes include:

- Love and sacrifice
- Community
- Revenge
- The meaning of freedom
- The meaning of friendship
- Overcoming racism
- Fulfilling your dreams
- Good and evil in the world
- Saving the environment
- Treating others as you would want to be treated
- Stopping violence

Example: Read the poem on the following page. As you read, think about what lesson the poem is trying to teach. What is the theme of the poem? What details provide clues about the theme?

Instructions

1. Ask students to think about a book they read recently. Ask them what they think the message of this book was. Did the book have an overall message for the reader? Did it attempt to teach a lesson or reveal something about life?

2. Explain that when an author wants to share a message with his or her readers, this message is called a *theme*.

3. Explain that, as they read the upcoming poem, they will be practicing the skill of identifying theme.

4. Read the top of the page together as a class.

5. Have students brainstorm other themes they may be familiar with and write these in a place everyone can see. Alternatively, ask them to recall books they have read that have any of the themes listed on the page.

6. Explain that you will read a poem aloud to them. Tell them that as you read, they should be actively trying to identify the theme, or message, of the poem.

7. Read the poem aloud.

   - **Differentiated Instruction:** Have a student with strong decoding skills read the poem aloud.

Instructions

1. Option: Use the following *think aloud* to demonstrate how to identify a theme:

"I notice this poem was dedicated to an Asian American youth killed because of racial conflict. I wonder if this poem will be about youth violence.

The author writes that the sky is getting darker and that we are losing our stars one at a time. I don't think he actually means 'stars in the sky.' I think the stars are symbols for people.

Yes, the next line says, 'our sons are dying in the city scenes they call home.'

The author writes that a 'generation [is] disappearing before its light has a chance to shine through.' I think he's talking about how young people are disappearing before they can grow up and contribute to society.

He finally writes that another one of the stars has fallen to the ground. I believe he's saying another young person has lost his life.

If I were to look at all these details from the poem and reread the dedication, I would say the theme of this poem is that youth are losing their lives too early to violence."

2. Ask students if they have any questions or interpreted anything else from the poem.

This poem is dedicated to an Asian American teenager killed because of racial conflict.

The sky is getting darker.
We're losing our stars one at a time
to streets that don't hear prayers
and calls to stop the violence.

Our sons are dying in the city scenes they call home
as their mothers send breakfast-time chants in their direction,
keeping them safe until streetlights come clean
to serve as makeshift guardian angels.
A generation disappearing before its light has a chance
to shine through,
etch its shadow in our minds,
decorate our night sky with spirits
we can remember without having to try.

A generation disappearing, begging for blessings
from anyone who might have them to give.

It's harder to notice stars from the city
because lights from the ground
make them harder to see.
Another one of our stars has fallen to the ground,
and all we can do is keep our heads up,
eyes toward the heavens,
and wish there was an answer that
would keep our night sky from falling,
falling,
trying to lull us back to sleep.

But it's hard to find sleep tonight,
because looking into the sky,
we know another one of our stars was taken
before his time.

© Giles Li, 2004. Reprinted with permission from the author.

Identifying Theme

Based on evidence from the poem, what is the theme of the poem?

Detail #1: *"Our sons are dying in the city scenes they call home"*

Detail #2: *"A generation disappearing"*

Detail #3: *"we know another one of our stars was taken before his time"*

Theme: Youth are losing their lives too early due to violence.

In addition to poems, books, and other readings, visual art can also have themes. Just as an author might communicate an important message about life through a story, an artist may communicate an important message in a painting or drawing.

Directions: Look at the drawing below. Identify the theme of this drawing. Then, find three details from the drawing that support this theme.

Detail #1:

Detail #2:

Detail #3:

Theme:

Reading Skill Focus

Instructions

1. Explain that themes are found in all sorts of places, not just in readings. For example, movies, works of art, and dance performances can all have themes.

2. Have students look at the drawing and determine the theme of the drawing based on three details from the picture.

3. Have them write the theme in their own words, along with three or more details that support the theme.

4. Review answers together.

Instructions

1. Have students complete the exercise.

   • **Differentiated Instruction:** If students need support with the multiple choice quiz, read the questions aloud to them.

   • **Option:** Lead the class in a discussion about the answers they chose and why.

2. Ask them to identify possible reasons that conflicts happen. Are there certain conditions that foster conflict? Are there certain triggers that start conflicts? List student responses where all students can read them.

3. Remind students that causes of conflict include: a lack of resources; a weak economy; a weak government; social divisions based on race, class, ethnicity, or religion; rapid population growth; or ready availability of lethal weapons.

4. **Option:** Ask students if they can think of conflicts that are happening now throughout the world and what the causes of these conflicts might be.

5. **Option:** Bring newspapers to class and have students search for stories about different conflicts. Ask students to determine the causes of these conflicts and possible solutions for resolving them.

Directions: Read each of the following scenarios about conflict. Decide what you would do in each situation. Choose from the multiple choice answers below.

1. Class has just started and a new student walks in. You notice that she looks very different than the rest of the students in your class. As soon as she sits down, a few classmates begin making fun of her. What do you do?

   a. Remain silent; you don't know her, and at least they are not making fun of *you!*

   b. Join your classmates in making fun of her. She looks very different than you, so you know you'll never be friends with her.

   c. Stop your classmates from making fun of her. You point out that they haven't even learned her name and know nothing about her.

   d. Walk over and introduce yourself to her; she will meet someone in her new school, and your classmates will see an example of tolerance.

2. Imagine you live in a country with a population that includes different groups of people. You are part of the majority group (90% of the population), and your friend is part of the minority group (10% of the population). Lately, you have started seeing cartoons on the Internet and **graffiti** in your neighborhood that make fun of your friend's group. In addition, news reports on television speak negatively about the group. Your family tells you that you must stop spending time with your friend. What do you do?

   a. Do what your family says. You do not want to upset them.

   b. Talk to your family respectfully, and let them know you cannot end your friendship.

   c. Do what your family says. Talk to your friends from the majority group to let them know they should not be friends with anyone from the minority group either.

   d. Pretend to agree with your family and keep seeing your friend in secret.

---

graffiti (n) – drawings or writings on a wall that can be seen by the public

continued ▶

3. You are a world leader. Conflict has increased along the border of two countries because both places need freshwater for drinking. You, along with other world leaders, have been asked to help decide how this water should be shared between the two countries. What do you do?

   a. You allow the country with the stronger leader to take control of the water. That country will know how to divide the water fairly.

   b. Since both countries need the freshwater, you decide to help them write an agreement with each other in which they will share the water equally.

   c. The country with more money should decide how the freshwater is distributed.

   d. Since the two countries cannot agree, you decide for them how much freshwater each country will get.

4. You are president of a country and have been trying to deal with the issue of overpopulation. Within thirty years, the number of young people between thirteen and twenty-four years old will triple. What should you do now to prepare for this increase in youth population and avoid conflicts in the future?

   a. Put limits on the amount of resources each person will be allowed to consume. This group of young people could decrease the already limited food and water in your country.

   b. Increase money spent on education. Providing youth with an excellent education could make your country stronger in the future.

   c. Increase money given to the military. The youth are at the right age, and a large military could make your country stronger.

   d. Do nothing because you will no longer be the leader by the time the growing population becomes a real problem.

Two young refugees in the country of Kosovo carry bread for their family.

Instructions

1. Explain that this reading will be done as a jigsaw activity. The purpose of the jigsaw activity is for them to learn about different types of conflicts.

2. Explain that students will become experts on one specific conflict that they will read about.

3. Divide students into groups for the jigsaw reading activity.

   - **Differentiated Instruction:** For lower-level readers, break the class into small groups of 3-4 students. Have each group read one of the passages, taking turns reading the paragraphs aloud. Then, have each group report back to the whole class about their passage, using the *Identifying Theme* graphic organizer as a guide (see p. 164).

   - **Differentiated Instruction:** For higher-level readers, divide the class into groups of four and assign a reading passage to each group. Have the group read this passage together and work to complete their section of the Reading Skill Follow-up table (see p. 165). Assign a number to each student within a group. After the group reads a passage together, have all of the 1's in the class get together and share what they read, all of the 2's get together to share what they read, and so on.

   - **Differentiated Instruction:** Have higher-level readers read *The Dirt on Diamonds*.

Stories of Conflict

Reading 1: Choosing a Better Life

When Anderson Sa was only ten years old, he saw a man shot on the street. He lived in the city of Rio de Janeiro in the country of Brazil. The neighborhood he lived in is called Vigario Geral and, at the time, was one of the most violent **favelas** in Rio de Janeiro.[1]

By the age of thirteen, Anderson was already part of a drug army. At first, belonging to the drug army gave Anderson a sense of belonging and helped him to make more money than he could at any other job. However, while he was part of this drug army, he lost some of his friends and family to violence. He began to realize the lifestyle he was living was not the one he wanted to keep on living. How could he escape?

Favelas in Brazil

The city of Rio de Janeiro has a population of 10 million people. Around 30% of people live in favelas, where many people do not have basic resources like electricity and clean water. Conflicts and violence happen often in these areas because people are poor and struggling to survive.[2]

Why would anyone choose to live in a place with no clean water or electricity? Many people who live in favelas have no choice. In Brazil, large populations of poor people move to cities from **rural** areas in search of a better quality of life, better job opportunities, good health care, and education for their children. However, they are often unable to find the necessary work to help them survive.[3]

---

favela (n) – a run-down part of a city; a slum
rural (adj) – of or relating to the countryside or farming

Afro Reggae performs and spreads positive messages about the future.

A young child stands in front of his home in a slum.

Finding Peace in the Afro Reggae Cultural Group

During the same time Anderson wanted to leave the drug army, a DJ by the name of Jose Junior started the Afro Reggae Cultural Group. This group was created to give youth an **alternative** to being involved in the drug trade. At first, this group published a newspaper for young people to share news about popular music. Soon the group opened a community center in in Vigario Geral, where young people could learn about soccer, music, **capoeira**, and dance. The goal was to help youth to become positive leaders in the community who shaped their own futures instead of joining the drug armies.[4] Thanks to the Afro Reggae Cultural Group, young people in Vigario Geral finally had real choices to make in their lives.

Anderson joined the Afro Reggae Cultural Group and was soon an active member of a band. He played different instruments, wrote songs, and taught other young people in the favela about music. During this time, he left the drug army and became a positive role model for many young people. His songs were about both the struggles of living in a favela and how young people should say no to violence.

These days, Anderson Sa is the president of the Afro Reggae Cultural Group. In 2006, Afro Reggae **expanded**, offering programs to over 2,000 young people in favelas throughout Rio de Janeiro.[5] Anderson made a huge decision in his life by choosing the path of peace instead of the path of violence. Through this choice, he has taught thousands of others that they also have choices—that they can choose their own future.

---

alternative (n) – a choice between two or more things
capoeira (n) – a dance form that includes martial arts, started in Brazil as a system of physical discipline and movement
expanded (v) – increased in size

Reading 2:
Not Your Average Teenager

Anne Frank was thirteen years old when she received a **diary**. She wrote in this diary for two years and included her deepest thoughts about her life, her family, and falling in love. Many teenagers write in diaries or on blogs to reflect about their lives, but two facts separated Anne Frank from a typical teenager:

- She mostly wrote in her diary while she was living in a secret hiding place.

- She was a **Jew** living in Europe during **World War II**.

Anne Frank was born in Germany in 1929. World War I ended just ten years earlier. Germany was one of the countries that had lost World War I and had to pay other countries for the damages they caused. The country was not doing well. By 1932, unemployment had increased from 3 million people to 6 million people.[6] Anti-Semitism, or **discrimination** against Jews, also started to increase. Some people blamed Jews for the difficulties Germany was experiencing.

Beginning in 1933, Adolf Hitler became the leader of the Nazi political party that ruled Germany at that time. Hitler was clear about his hatred for Jewish people. His plan, called the *Final Solution*, was to rid Germany and other countries in Europe of all Jews as well as other

Jewish refugee girls, including Anne and Margot Frank, have a tea party with their dolls at a private home in Amsterdam.

groups of people.[7] Slowly but surely, the Nazi party was able to convince German **citizens** that Jewish people could not be trusted.

In Hiding

When Anne was young, her parents decided to move the family to the Netherlands because Germany was becoming less and less safe for Jews. Slowly, life became more difficult for Jewish families all over Europe. The Nazi party forced Jewish stores and businesses to close,

---

diary (n) – a private journal in which a person can record their personal thoughts, experiences, and feelings

Jew (n) – a person whose religion is Judaism

World War II (n) – the war between the Axis powers (including Germany, Italy, and Japan) and the Allies (including the UK, the USSR, and the United States), beginning on September 1, 1939, with the German invasion of Poland and ending with the surrender of Germany on May 8, 1945, and of Japan on August 14, 1945

discrimination (n) – different treatment of a group of people based on their membership in a group (such as social class, religion, or race)

citizens (n) – natives or naturalized members of a state or nation who owe allegiance to its government and are entitled to its protection

Jews had to start wearing the **Star of David** on their clothing, and children were no longer allowed to attend non-Jewish schools.

World War II started in 1939. Germany eventually invaded the Netherlands, where the Frank family was living. In 1942, Anne's father decided that the family needed to go into hiding. Along with another family, they moved into a secret hiding place above the office where Mr. Frank had worked. No one was allowed to leave the secret hiding place. Since there were people that worked in the office below and in the building next to the office, the families in hiding could not talk above a whisper during the day. There was a small attic that let in some sunlight; this attic was the only place that opened to the outside world.[8]

Life was not safe for Jews anywhere that the Nazi party had power. Anyone who was Jewish risked being sent to work in **concentration camps**.

Anne Frank: A Hero at a Young Age

While Anne lived in the secret hiding place, she kept herself busy by studying French, reading books, and writing in her diary. She wrote about fights she would get into with her mother and sister and how she really liked Peter, a boy from the other family that she and her family lived with. In addition, she wondered about what caused other people to hate Jews so much and when the war would end. In one of her diary entries, she wrote, "I still believe, in spite of everything, that people are still truly good at heart."[9]

In 1944, Nazi soldiers discovered the secret hiding place and forced both families to go to concentration camps. The women were separated from the men. In March of 1945, Anne Frank died in a concentration camp at the age of fifteen. The only member of Anne Frank's family to survive was her father, Otto Frank.

Ultimately, 6 million Jewish people died in concentration camps. This mass killing is known as the *Holocaust*. Many countries, shocked at this **genocide**, put Nazi leaders on trial for war crimes after the end of World War II in 1945.

Anne Frank lost her life at a young age, but she had hope that the world could be a better place and that unnecessary conflict would end. In 1999, *TIME* Magazine chose Anne Frank as one of the 100 most important people of the 20th Century.[10]

Star of David (n) – a symbol of the religion of Judaism

concentration camps (n) – camps created by the Nazi party to imprison Jews, gypsies, homosexuals, and other people considered racially inferior to the Nazis, or anyone who spoke out against the Nazis

genocide (n) – the planned destruction, in whole or in part, of an ethnic, racial, religious, or national group

7 Peace and Conflict

159

© FACING THE FUTURE www.facingthefuture.org

7 Peace and Conflict

159

© FACING THE FUTURE www.facingthefuture.org

Reading 3:
The Dirt on Diamonds

When you think of a diamond, what words come to mind? Perhaps you think of words like *sparkly*, *shiny*, or *expensive*. Would you ever connect a diamond with the words *conflict* or *war*? If not, it may surprise you to learn that during the 1990s, several countries in Africa, including the Democratic Republic of Congo (DRC), Sierra Leone, and Angola, all experienced conflicts involving diamonds.

Some of the African countries where diamonds are found are not stable. Think of going to class all year without having the same teacher every day. This type of classroom is not stable because one teacher may not know what the other teacher taught. You might be confused by the new teacher's classroom rules. It is difficult to know what to expect without stability. When a country is not stable, its people may not know what will happen from one day to the next.

More diamonds come from Africa than from any other continent. In countries like Sierra Leone and the Democratic Republic of Congo, groups have traded diamonds for **illegal** purposes.[11] *Conflict diamonds* are diamonds used in wars or conflicts. Armed **rebel forces** rule over war zones and trade these diamonds illegally for weapons and other war-related needs.[12] Why diamonds? Diamonds are extremely valuable and also extremely easy to **smuggle** since they are so small.[13]

Conflict in the Democratic Republic of Congo

The Democratic Republic of Congo (DRC) has 26% of the world's diamonds. Although the country is rich in resources like diamonds, copper, silver, and gold, 80% of its citizens do not have safe

illegal (adj) – forbidden by law
rebel forces (n) – groups that fight against the government
smuggle (v) – to import or export something secretly and against the law
life expectancy (n) – the number of years a person is expected to live

Refugees from the Democratic Republic of Congo cross the border to Uganda.

drinking water, 70% have little or no health care, and the average **life expectancy** is just forty-three years. Since the 1990s, over 4 million people in the DRC have died as a result of the effects of war.[14]

How can a country so rich in diamonds have so much suffering? Looking at the history of the DRC helps to understand why the country is the way it is today. The DRC is a former **colony** of Belgium, a European country. Under the rule of Belgium, it was known as the Congo. During the late 1800s, King Leopold II of Belgium changed the Congo from a place where people had freedom to a place where people were forced to harvest rubber for the king. People were forced to live under horrible conditions. Millions of **innocent** people were killed or worked to death during this time.[15]

The country slowly began to regain its independence, or freedom, over the next several decades. In 1960, the Congo became independent from Belgium. Independence was not easy, however. Belgium no longer controlled the DRC, but there was no clear idea of how to run the country. The country was unstable for many years to follow. Both **civil wars** within the country and conflicts in surrounding countries increased instability in the DRC.[16]

Throughout this time, rebel groups traded conflict diamonds with each other to buy guns and other weapons to support civil war. Diamond miners, including children, worked in dangerous conditions and were paid extremely low wages. Children were also forced to become soldiers and participate in the war.

Diamonds, a natural resource, were used as a way to trade weapons and support conflict instead of

Diamonds have been used in the DRC to support conflict, not peace.

helping to support the growth of the DRC in a positive way. People bought these diamonds in jewelry stores around the world, not realizing where they came from or the weapons they had helped to pay for. Unfortunately, several countries in Africa continue to trade conflict diamonds for weapons.

Decreasing Conflict

The good news is that people around the world are becoming aware of the true cost of diamonds. Buying conflict diamonds contributes to ongoing conflicts and violence in Africa and to a decreased quality of life for many people. In 2000, many countries came together to create the Kimberley Process. By establishing guidelines for certifying *conflict-free* diamonds, the Kimberley Process has helped to reduce the number of conflict diamonds sold around the world. During the 1990s, as much as 15% of internationally traded diamonds were believed to be conflict diamonds. Today, less than 1% of diamonds available for sale are conflict diamonds.[17]

colony (n) – a region or country controlled by another country
innocent (adj) – free from guilt; without fault
civil wars (n) – wars between different groups within a single country

7 Peace and Conflict — 161 — © FACING THE FUTURE www.facingthefuture.org

Reading 4:
Discrimination in America

Imagine you decide to meet your friends for dinner at a restaurant to celebrate your birthday. A sign in the front of the restaurant says to sit anywhere you would like. The four of you decide to sit at a booth. Suddenly, the manager of the restaurant comes over to your table and angrily tells you that you are not allowed to sit in the section you chose and that *your people* can only sit in one small area separate from everyone else.

This situation may seem highly unlikely to you, but not too long ago, African Americans and other people of color living in the United States were forced to eat in separate sections of restaurants, sit in separate parts of trains, attend separate schools, and even use separate public bathrooms from white people. Many people thought this type of treatment was unfair and started to work toward ensuring equal rights for all people, including African Americans, Native Americans, Asian Americans, and Latinos. The **Civil Rights Movement** began when people started to speak out against **racial inequality**.

Looking Back

In 1865, slavery—the practice of forcing people to work against their will—ended in the United States. During slavery, many African Americans were forced to work on **plantations** and for white owners without pay. They lived under horrible conditions and were treated **inhumanely**.

Civil Rights Movement (n) – the national effort made by black people and their supporters in the 1950s and 1960s to eliminate segregation and gain equal rights

racial inequality (n) – the lack of equality between people of different races

plantations (n) – large farms or estates on which cotton, tobacco, coffee, sugar cane, or other crop is cultivated, usually by resident laborers

inhumanely (adv) – without pity or compassion

Members of the Bourne Youth Center created this mural in Bourne, England, to speak out against racism.

Even though slavery ended in 1865, a number of laws and rules were put into place that kept black people from having the same rights as white people:

- In 1881, laws in Tennessee and other southern states separated white people from black people in public places like restaurants, trains, and schools.

- In 1890, the state of Mississippi required a poll tax for all voters. Most African American people in Mississippi could not afford to pay this tax and therefore could not vote in elections.

- In 1896, a Supreme Court case known as *Plessy* v. *Ferguson* ruled that segregated public places were allowed. Public places included schools.[18]

The Greensboro Four

Four young black men who were students at North Carolina A&T State University were tired of being treated differently because of their skin color. They made history on February 1, 1960, when they said no to racism. Ezell Blair Jr., David Richmond, Joseph McNeil, and Franklin McCain went to Woolworth's, a store and a restaurant that had a whites-only lunch counter. These four young men bought a few items at the store and then sat at the restaurant's lunch counter. When they were refused service, they continued to sit at the counter until the restaurant closed. Over the next several days, they continued to sit at this lunch counter and thousands of people joined them at Woolworth's to show their support of this act of **nonviolent protest**. People inspired by these men known as the Greensboro Four held **sit-ins** at restaurants in forty other cities across the country. Finally, on July 26, 1960, Woolworth's decided to **integrate** its lunch counter by allowing people of all races to eat there.[19]

Before the Civil Rights Movement, water fountains were segregated by race.

This victory was one of many in the Civil Rights Movement. Other famous victories include a successful bus **boycott** in Alabama in 1955, which began when Rosa Parks refused to give her seat to a white person on the bus, and the integration of a high school in Little Rock, Arkansas, in 1957. As a result of these victories, President Lyndon B. Johnson signed the Civil Rights Act on July 2, 1964. This act made it illegal, or against the law, for employers to **discriminate** against people based on their skin color, race, or religion.[20] The passage of this act was a significant moment in American history.

---

nonviolent protest (n) – an act of peaceful resistance; an expression of disagreement without violence

sit-ins (n) – organized protests in which people refuse to move from an area

integrate (v) – to combine into one system; the opposite of segregation, or separation

boycott (n) – a refusal to buy or to use something

discriminate (v) – to treat people differently based on their membership in a group (such as social class, religion, or race)

Instructions

1. Students may use the graphic organizer to record details and identify theme as they read their section.

2. Be sure that they make a note of which section they read.

Directions: As you read a specific section from the chapter reading with your group, write down at least three important details that provide clues to the theme of the reading. Use these details to identify the theme of the reading. Be prepared to share this information with the rest of the class.

Details ➝ **Theme**

1.

2.

3.

Reading Skill Follow-up: Identifying Theme

Directions: With your reading group, record information about the section you read. Your group will then share information about the section with the other reading groups. Other groups will also share information about the sections they read.

	What was the conflict?	Where did the conflict happen?	Why did the conflict happen?	When did the conflict happen?	Theme
1. Choosing a Better Life					
2. Not Your Average Teenager					
3. The Dirt on Diamonds					
4. Discrimination in America					

Answers

See p. 172J

Reading Skill Follow-up

Instructions

1. After students have completed their readings and shared information with the other groups, bring the groups together as a class.

2. Have a representative share their part of the jigsaw table from their reading with the class.

3. **Option:** As each representative shares information, write this information on an overhead for all students to see. Allow students to record this information in their notes.

4. **Additional Resources:** Allow students to explore resources related to the readings.

   • Anderson Sa's story is chronicled in the documentary *Favela Rising:* www.favelarising.com.

   • View a summary of Anne Frank's life, quotes from her diary, and pictures at www.annefrank.org.

   • Learn more about the diamond trade and conflict-free diamonds at www.conflict freediamonds.org and www. un.org/peace/africa/Diamond. html.

   • Read more about the Greensboro Four at www.sitins.com.

Instructions

1. Before students begin answering the comprehension questions, share with them the academic language they will see in many of the questions (see Appendix B).

2. Explain that the questions are divided into five sections according to how these questions are meant to support their comprehension of what they read. (See Appendix B for a detailed explanation of each section.)

3. Note that all students will answer five questions about the section they read. All students will answer the last three questions on p. 167.

4. **Differentiated Instruction:** Differentiate the questions students must answer based on their reading levels. Support comprehension by working with students who may need more guided instruction.

Directions: Answer the following questions about the section you read to support your comprehension of the chapter reading.

Reading 1: Choosing a Better Life

Understanding what you read

1. What group did Anderson join at the age of thirteen?

2. What percentage of people in Rio de Janeiro lives in favelas?

Thinking about what you read

3. Why did Anderson Sa join the drug army?

4. Identify the change Anderson Sa made in his life.

Questioning what you read

5. Analyze the author's purpose in writing about a 13-year-old.

Reading 2: Not Your Average Teenager

Understanding what you read

1. Where did Anne Frank write most of her diary entries?

2. When did Hitler become leader of Germany?

Thinking about what you read

3. Why did life become more difficult for Jewish people in Europe during the 1930s?

4. Why do you think Anne Frank was named one of the 100 most important people in the 20th century?

Questioning what you read

5. Determine the author's purpose in writing about a teenager.

continued ▶

Answers

Reading 1

1. a drug army
2. 30%
3. The army gave him a sense of belonging and he made money.
4. He left the army and decided to become a musician. He chose peace instead of violence.
5. The author wanted to show how young people can overcome significant conflicts in their lives.

Reading 2

1. in a secret hiding place above her father's business in the Netherlands
2. in 1933
3. Germany had lost World War I and Jewish people were blamed for the country's hardships.
4. Anne Frank wrote about anti-Semitism and World War II through a first-hand account while hiding from the Nazis. Throughout the conflict, she remained hopeful.
5. The author wanted to show how young people can have significant conflicts in their lives.

Reading 3

1. Africa
2. Belgium
3. Harvest rubber, hunt animals, and give all the money they earned to Belgium
4. Eighty percent of the country does not have safe drinking water, and there are many violent conflicts.
5. This shows how something usually connected with such positive imagery actually has a negative past.

Reading 3:
The Dirt on Diamonds

Understanding what you read

1. Which continent has more diamonds than any other?

2. What country once ruled over the country now known as the Democratic Republic of Congo?

Thinking about what you read

3. When Belgium ruled over Congo, what were people forced to do?

4. Why do you think life expectancy in the Democratic Republic of Congo is so low?

Questioning what you read

5. If the author is writing about how diamonds are related to war, why would he or she first want you to think of positive words related to diamonds?

Reading 4:
Discrimination in America

Understanding what you read

1. Who were the Greensboro Four?

2. What did the court case *Plessy* v. *Ferguson* rule?

Thinking about what you read

3. Why did the Greensboro Four decide to do a sit-in at Woolworth's?

4. What happened as a result of the sit-in at Woolworth's?

Questioning what you read

5. Evaluate why you think the author begins the reading by having you imagine the scenario in the restaurant.

All Readings

Making connections to what you read

6. Identify ways you could work to decrease conflict in your life.

Further Discussion Questions

7. How can resource scarcity lead to conflict?

8. Explain why a country with a high number of unemployed people would have more conflicts than a country with a high number of employed people.

Reading 4

1. four African-American men who attended North Carolina A&T State University: Ezell Blair Jr., David Richmond, Joseph McNeil, and Franklin McCain

2. In 1896, the U.S. Supreme Court ruled that segregated public places were allowed.

3. They did not think the lunch counter should be whites-only.

4. On July 26, 1960, people from all races were allowed to sit at the counter. This was part of the Civil Rights Movement that led to the Civil Rights Act.

5. The author wants you to sympathize with the people in the reading.

All Readings

6. e.g., treat people from all backgrounds fairly, mentor younger children who are having conflicts with each other

7. If people do not have enough resources (like access to food, water, and jobs), they may fight with others who also want to use these resources.

8. If many people do not have work, they do not have the ability to support themselves or their families. This could lead to increased conflict for resources, including money.

Instructions

1. Students will be writing an advice column for a student who needs help with a conflict in his/her personal life.

2. Read through the top portion of the page.

3. **Option:** Show real-life examples of advice columns (such as *Dear Abby*) so students can see what they look like.

4. Read the letter from *Confused Gal* together.

Has anyone ever asked you for advice about a problem? Have you ever asked someone to help you with a conflict you are having? Sometimes people write to an advice columnist to get help with their problems.

An **advice column** is a piece of writing in a magazine, newspaper, or online written by a person called a *columnist*. This person gives people advice on problems or conflicts they are facing in their lives.

Imagine you have your own student advice column and you give advice to young people about how to resolve conflicts peacefully. Your *pseudonym*, or assumed name, is Conflict Solver.

Example: Before you write an advice column for a student in need, you will analyze advice columns written by two students. When you analyze writing, read it carefully to see what the writer did well and how the writer could improve. Grade the advice columns on a scale of 1-3 (1 needs a lot of work, 2 is pretty good, and 3 is great). Use the following questions to help you grade:

- Did the columnist give advice on what the girl should and should not do?

- Did the columnist think of a positive solution to the conflict?

First, read the letter sent to the advice column:

Dear Conflict Solver,

I have become friends with a group of people I like spending time with. They go out almost every evening during the school week. Over the past month, I spent time with them during most weekdays. Yesterday I received two tests back from my math and social studies classes. I failed both tests. I'm not sure what to do. I want to keep spending time with these friends, but not at the expense of my grades. Help!

Sincerely,
Confused Gal

---

continued ▶

Now, read and evaluate two sample responses:

ADVICE COLUMN 1

Dear Confused Gal,

I know you must be confused—you have a great group of friends that you are spending time with and you are having fun with them, but of course you don't want your grades to suffer.

What you do *not* want to do is continue failing tests in your classes. If you follow this pattern, you could end up failing your classes. Think about the consequences of this. Ask yourself: is it worth having fun with your friends if you are not learning what you need to prepare you for your future, or if you have to repeat your classes in summer school?

Consider taking a balanced approach. You can spend time with your friends, but you can also spend time on your schoolwork and your classes. Try creating a schedule that allows you to complete all of your work and leaves time to see your friends. If you are still failing in class at this point, talk to your teachers and ask them for help. You might have to spend time with your friends on the weekends and leave the weekdays for schoolwork.

You're very smart to be thinking about your future. I know you'll come up with a great plan!

Conflict Solver

What grade would you give this advice column? Why?

ADVICE COLUMN 2

Dear Confused Gal,

It sounds like you are having such a fun time with your friends! Be sure to keep up with your schoolwork. You are allowed to have fun, but you don't want to let your grades suffer. If your friends are true friends, they will understand if you can't come out with them all the time. In fact, maybe some of them could use the extra study time, too!

Conflict Solver

What grade would you give this advice column? Why?

Instructions

1. Have students analyze the advice columns according to the criteria from the preceding page.
2. Share the Chapter 7 writing rubric with students, explaining that these categories will be used to assess their writing. You may want to add relevant spelling and grammar components to the rubric.

Chapter 7 Writing Rubric

Category	3	2	1
Development of Information	Writes a paragraph about what the student *should* do and a paragraph about what the student *should not* do	Attempts to write a paragraph that explains what the student should do and a paragraph about what the student should not do	Does not write a paragraph that explains what the student should or should not do
Positive Message	Provides advice that will resolve the conflict peacefully	Provides advice that attempts to resolve conflict peacefully	Does not provide advice that results in a peaceful solution; advice would increase conflict
Vocabulary	Uses at least two chapter vocabulary words correctly	Uses one chapter vocabulary word correctly	Does not attempt using vocabulary words

Total = _____ / 9

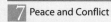

Writing about Peace and Conflict: Advice Column

Instructions

1. Have students read the two letters either independently or with a partner.

2. Ask students to choose one letter to respond to with an advice column.

Directions: Read the following two letters. Decide which one you will respond to in your advice column.

LETTER 1

Dear Conflict Solver,

My family recently had to move to a new place because my mom was transferred for her job. I am happy for my mom, but I had to say goodbye to all my friends, my basketball team, and my favorite teachers. I've been at my new school for two months, and I still don't have a single friend. I have tried sitting with different people at lunch, but nobody seems to be interested in talking to me. One group even laughed at me when I sat near them and moved from the table. Lately, they have been making fun of me more and more whenever they see me. I miss my old life! Can you please advise me on what I should do?

Looking for Real Friends

LETTER 2

Dear Conflict Solver,

Last week, I was in class when my phone accidentally rang. I know I am not supposed to have a phone in class, but I honestly forgot to turn off the ringer because I had so much to do before coming to school. My teacher took my cell phone from me, gave me a week of detention, and told me I could only get my phone back after I serve my detention. I need the phone to communicate with my family. My mom expects me to call her when I get home every day. My teacher is being so unfair about this situation. What should I do?

Need My Cell

Writing Steps : Advice Column

Step 1: Choose one of the letters from the previous page to respond to in your advice column. Your response will be in the form of a letter.

Step 2: Write a rough draft of your advice column using the Writing Organizer on the next page.

Step 3: Edit the advice column using the Edit Checklist below.

Step 4: Have a peer read and edit your advice column using the Edit Checklist.

Step 5: Revise your column based on the edits.

 Edit Checklist

	Author Check	Peer Editor Check
Did you include an introductory sentence?		
Did you include a paragraph about what the student *should* do and a paragraph about what the student should *not* do?		
Did you offer advice that will resolve the conflict peacefully?		
Did you use chapter vocabulary words correctly?		

Instructions

1. Review the writing steps with students.

2. **Grammar Suggestion:** Since students are writing an advice column, they will be advising a student on what he or she should do in the future. Teach them the future progressive verb tense to support them in their writing. (Example: Since you *will be spending* time with your friends during the weekend, you can study during the week.)

3. **Differentiated Instruction:** For beginning students who may need more guidance, work with them in a small group to assist them in writing their advice column. You can even write the column with them as a shared writing exercise.

Instructions

1. If students need a structured format, they can use the writing organizer to write a rough draft.

2. Once they finish writing their columns, they will exchange them with a classmate, edit them using the Edit Checklist, and then revise them.

3. **Option:** Have students type their columns into a blog so that everyone can read them online.

Writing Organizer: Advice Column

Dear _____,

Introductory sentence about what you think about this student's situation:

_____

_____

Advice on what you think she or he should *not* do:

_____

_____

_____

_____

_____

_____

_____

Advice on what you think she or he *should* do:

_____

_____

_____

_____

_____

_____

_____

_____

Closing statement:

_____

_____

Sincerely,

Conflict Solver

Culminating Activity: To Fight or Not to Fight? (1.5 hours)

Overview
Students examine several types of conflicts through a role-play activity. They learn to identify the roots of conflict, how to separate positions from interests in a conflict, and experience mediating a conflict.

Materials/Preparation
- *Conflict Resolution Instructions*, one per student
- *Conflict Resolution Worksheets*, two copies per student (copy the handout on both sides of a single sheet of paper), plus one copy displayed on an overhead or with a document camera
- *Conflict Scenarios*, three copies for each group of 6 students (these will be read in pairs)

Introduction
1. Ask students to reflect about the conflict they wrote about in the Chapter 7 Writing Warm-up.

2. Ask for a volunteer to share his or her conflict with the class.

3. While the student is explaining the conflict, write the following questions on the board:

   - Who were the parties involved in the conflict?

   - Why did the student think he/she was right? (This is their position. Explain how to identify a position by writing the following terms common to position statements on the board: *It's my right to …, I've always done it this way, It's my responsibility/job to…, My beliefs teach me that ….*)

   - What was the conflict about? (This is the student's interest. Did the student want something he/she could not have? Was it an argument based on different values or beliefs?)

   - Was the conflict resolved? If yes, how? If not, why not?

4. Ask students to answer these questions based on the information provided by the student volunteer.

5. Tell the class they are going to role-play different conflicts taking place around the world. Some of these conflicts arise from people competing for a scarce resource, and others from differences in culture, religion, or ethnic identity.

Steps
1. Pass out one *Conflict Resolution Instructions* page to each student.

2. Read aloud the sample conflict, *Who Owns the Forest?*, and have students follow along on the *Instructions* page.

3. Read through the directions with students. You will work through the *Who Owns the Forest?* example together to understand how to use the worksheet.

4. Walk students through the *Conflict Resolution Worksheet* you have displayed, having them identify the parties involved, each party's *position* (why they think they're right), and each party's *interests* (what they want).

5. Lead the class in brainstorming how the conflict might be resolved, focusing on the interests they identified for each party.

   - **Option:** Have a few students volunteer to be the Tribespeople, Government, and Mediators, and role-play how they would negotiate using the *Conflict Resolution Worksheet*.

6. Tell the class they are going to repeat this process in small groups. Explain that each group will work on three scenarios. Students will work alongside a partner for the entire activity. For each scenario, two student pairs will take opposing sides in the conflict, and one student pair will act as mediators. The mediators can suggest

resolutions to the conflict if the two sides are not able to resolve their conflict. The mediator's job is to objectively help both sides reach a resolution through compromise, but without giving up their interests.

7. Explain that for each scenario, the two student pairs taking opposing sides in the conflict will read their scenario and fill out their *Conflict Resolution Worksheet* with their partners. They will present their positions and interests to the other side and try to reach an agreement. Be sure to emphasize that students will not be graded based on reaching an agreement. Some scenarios may not have resolutions. Students should keep in mind that they are representing an entire group or country in this negotiation, and that it is the students' duty to represent their best interests. Therefore, they should think carefully before agreeing to a solution.

8. Arrange the class into groups of 6 and give each group three copies of the handout, *Conflict Scenarios*. Each pair of students will share one handout. Give each student two (or one double-sided copy) copies of the *Conflict Resolution Worksheet*.

9. Structure the class so that students:

   • Read the scenario aloud in their groups.

   • Divide into partners to complete the *Conflict Resolution Worksheet*. (Mediators can use the worksheet to determine how they think each side will respond.)

   • Begin role-playing the conflict scenario.

10. Have students begin role-playing their conflict scenario, starting with Scenario 1 and continuing until they finish Scenario 3. Circulate around the room, listening and helping as students work through their scenarios. Allow 10 minutes for each scenario. Each pair will mediate one conflict and take sides in two conflicts.

11. After each group has completed the three scenarios, bring the class back together to discuss the following reflection questions:

   • How many of you reached a solution to at least one of the scenarios you role-played? (If time permits, have students briefly summarize one of their scenarios.)

   • Did you have to give up something you wanted in order to reach a solution, or did you find a solution that gave both sides everything they wanted (met everyone's *interests*)?

   • Did you think the mediators in your group were fair, or did you feel the mediators were favoring the other side? Did you trust the mediators?

   • Do you think the solutions you reached are sustainable (i.e., meet the needs of people now without compromising the ability of future generations to meet these needs), or do you think there will be another conflict around the same issue in the future?

   • If you didn't reach a solution, what prevented you from doing so?

   • Which scenarios did you find more difficult to solve: conflicts over resources or conflicts over culture and identity?

Conflict Resolution Instructions

Conflict Resolution Vocabulary

position – a point of view

interest – support for a certain cause

scenario – a situation

mediate – to resolve or settle differences between two or more people or groups of people

negotiate – to discuss with another person or group in order to come to an agreement

resolution – a decision made based on agreement by two or more groups

---

Sample Scenario:
Who Owns the Forest?

Sides: Tribespeople and Government

The Tribespeople of Arborland have lived in the Big Forest for hundreds of years. Arborland is a poor country, and recently the Government decided that, in order to raise money, it would start heavy logging (cutting down trees) in the Big Forest and sell the wood to people in the North. The Tribespeople have refused to leave the Big Forest because it is their home and they do not believe the Government has the right to make them leave. The Government believes that selling wood from the Big Forest will bring in much-needed money for the country, which it will use to pay off debts and provide jobs to thousands of people in Arborland. The Government is willing to pay the Tribespeople some money to move out of the Big Forest.

Activity Directions:

1. In your group of six, count off pairs from one to three. Pair 1 will mediate, pair 2 will take one side, and pair 3 will take the opposing side.

2. The mediators will assign sides to the two remaining groups for each scenario.

3. The entire group will read the scenario together.

4. Each side will complete answer #1 on the *Conflict Resolution Worksheet* with their partner.

5. As a group, you will work on the rest of the worksheet together.

6. The mediators' job is to objectively help both sides reach a resolution.

7. For each scenario, assign a different pair to be mediators.

Scenario 1: Ethnicity and Power
Sides: Tralas and Zilis

The country of Izkara is populated by two ethnic groups: ***Tralas*** (the minority) and ***Zilis*** (the majority). Izkara has been ruled by its military for many years. Nearly all members of the military are from the minority Tralas group. Recently, the majority Zilis group has wanted the military government to step down, and asked for elections to be held. If fair elections are held, the Zilis will almost certainly come to power, since they are the majority. The Zilis have made it clear that if elections are not held soon, they will fight in a civil war against the military.

Scenario 2: Growing Pains
Sides: Burbists and Densers

More and more people have moved to Capital City looking for jobs, and soon there will not be enough housing for everyone to live there. ***Burbists*** want to build homes outside of Capital City, which they think is too noisy and dangerous. Many landowners are willing to sell their land to them so they can build homes. ***Densers*** want to build taller apartment buildings within Capital City, and keep the land outside the city in its natural state. They want to protect trees and the natural environment. The Burbists, who give large amounts of money to provide services to the people of Capital City, recently threatened to move to another state if they are not allowed to build their homes where they want.

Scenario 3: Water Rights
Sides: Farmers and Fisherfolk

Farmers in the country of Aguaville depend heavily on the Blue River for water for their crops, which they sell to support their families. ***Fisherfolk*** in Aguaville also depend on the Blue River for fish, which they sell to support *their* families. Due to a long period of dry weather, there is less and less water in the Blue River. With the Blue River running low, the Aguaville Fisherfolk worry there will be less fish if the farmers continue to use the same amount of water for their crops.

To Fight or Not to Fight?
Conflict Resolution Worksheet

1. With a partner, read your assigned scenario and write answers to the following questions:

   a. I am (the **side** you are representing):_____

   b. My **position** is (why you think you are right):

   _____

   c. My **interests** are (what you want/need to get out of this negotiation):

   _____

   d. The **interest(s)** I absolutely *can't* give up during negotiations are:

   _____

   e. I think the *other side's* **interests** are (what you think the other side wants/needs):

   _____

2. Discuss the conflict. Tell the other side what your positions and interests are. Write their position and interests here:

   a. Their **position** is (why they think they are right):

   _____

   b. Their **interests** are (what they want/need to get out of this negotiation):

   _____

3. Do you believe that your needs and the other groups' needs can be met at the same time? How could both sides get what they want? (Mediators should negotiate with both sides to try to come to an agreement.)

   _____

   _____

4. After your discussion and negotiation, briefly explain the resolution you reached (if any):

   _____

   _____

Chapter 7 Extension, Action Project, and Resources

Drama Extension

Have each group of six students choose one conflict from the scenarios they discussed. Ask them to prepare a skit in which they act out the different sides of the conflict and express the opposing positions and interests to the class. Afterward, have the class brainstorm ways to help solve the group's conflict.

Action Project

Have students find and join their nearest PeaceJam affiliate, an international organization that connects students with the inspiring stories and personalities of leading Nobel Peace Laureates. Through the program, students can join the Global Call to Action, a campaign to create and document 1 billion projects addressing ten of the most pressing global issues. Visit www.peacejam.org to learn more.

Additional Resources on Peace and Conflict

The Lost Boys of Sudan
www.lostboysfilm.com

Civil war in Sudan has killed millions of people. This documentary follows two boys who lost their families to the war and had to flee Sudan. The boys move to the United States and have to start their lives over again. (83 minutes, Actual Films/Principe Productions)

Favela Rising
www.favelarising.com

A man emerges from the slums of Rio de Janeiro to lead the nonviolent cultural movement known as Afro-reggae. (82 minutes, Sidetrack Films)

Anne Frank: The Diary of a Young Girl, by Anne Frank

This book documents two years of Anne Frank's life during the Holocaust while she is living in a secret annex in the Netherlands.

Nelson Mandela: No Easy Walk to Freedom, by Barry Denenberg

This book chronicles the life of Nelson Mandela from birth to his presidency of South Africa. The history of apartheid in South Africa is written in an accessible way for middle and high school students.

Peace Games
www.peacegames.org

Peace Games' mission is to support young people as peacemakers and to change the way our nation views young people in the context of violence. They do this by working with elementary schools, families, and young adult volunteers to create safe classrooms and communities.

Chapter 7 Student Assessment, page 1
Knowledge about Peace and Conflict

Vocabulary

Directions: Read each sentence and circle the letter next to the correct definition of the **bold-faced** word.

1. Thirty years after the war, the country finally had **stability** and people were able to live peacefully with each other.

   a. the condition of being dependable and not likely to fall apart
   b. a state that is not likely to last
   c. the condition of being important and noteworthy
   d. the condition of being wealthy and prosperous

2. The **conflict** between Suzanne and her mother was resolved when Suzanne agreed she would finish her homework before going to the movie.

   a. peace talks and negotiation
   b. violence between two people
   c. fight or struggle
   d. agreement after a fight

3. Even though students from all different races and religions attended New High School, fights never happened because the students treated each other with **tolerance**.

   a. hatred and anger
   b. acceptance of differences
   c. bullying children until they listen
   d. dressing in similar ways so as to not look different

4. Due to **violence** in the country of Sudan, many people have had to escape in search of more peaceful places to live.

   a. physical force that causes damage or abuse
   b. developing community within countries to make sure everyone gets along
   c. sickness that can easily spread from one person to another
   d. natural disasters like hurricanes, forest fires, or tornadoes

Chapter 7 Student Assessment, page 2

Content

Directions: For 5, read the sentence and circle the letter next to the correct answer.

5. Which one of these could be a solution to a conflict related to child abuse?

    a. volunteering with an organization that works to end violence in families

    b. writing letters to your local mayor about building a youth center near your school

    c. reading books to younger children to improve their reading level

    d. playing soccer three times per week in order to stay healthy and fit

6. Draw a line from each conflict on the left to its root cause on the right.

a. Drinking water has decreased in certain areas of the world, leading to fights between different groups of people.	divisions between groups of people
b. When World War I ended, many people in Germany did not have jobs. The number of people without jobs increased from 3 million to 6 million people in 1932.	lack of resources
c. Millions of people died during the 1990s in the country of Rwanda. Two different ethnic groups—the Hutus and the Tutsis—were in a conflict with each other.	weak economy

Reading Comprehension

Directions: Read the paragraph below. For 7 and 8, circle the letter next to the correct answer.

Hannah was very young when she arrived in the United States. Her parents had to bring her sister, brother, and Hannah over because they couldn't live in their country anymore. Life was too dangerous because of the war. Her parents sacrificed so much for their three children. Her mom and dad worked long hours to put food on the table, provide them an education, and make sure they could live a happy life.

7. Imagine this paragraph was part of a short story Hannah wrote about her life. What might be the theme of the story?

    a. the tragedy of war

    b. love can overcome hatred

    c. love and sacrifice for children

    d. conflict with cultural identity

8. What might the title of this short story be?

    a. A Tribute to My Parents

    b. The Problems of an American Teenager

    c. Running from War, Running from Myself

    d. Balancing Life, Balancing Identity

Chapter 7 Student Assessment, page 3
Outlook and Personal Beliefs

Answer the following questions based on your personal beliefs. There are no right or wrong answers.

Directions for 1 and 2: Place a check mark (√) in the box next to your response to each statement.

1. I think resolving conflicts in a peaceful way is important.
   ☐ True
   ☐ False

2. I know of ways to resolve some types of conflicts.
   ☐ True
   ☐ False

3. **Complete the following sentence:**
   One way I can personally work to promote peace and prevent conflict is by…

   _____

   _____

   _____

   _____

Directions for 4 and 5: Fill in the ovals below based on your level of agreement. 1 means you strongly agree, and 7 means you strongly disagree.

1 = yes, definitely!   7 = no way!
⟵──────────────────────────⟶

4. I believe my personal actions can have an impact on peace and conflict.

   1   2   3   4   5   6   7
   ⬭   ⬭   ⬭   ⬭   ⬭   ⬭   ⬭

5. I believe I have the ability to prevent conflict from happening.

   1   2   3   4   5   6   7
   ⬭   ⬭   ⬭   ⬭   ⬭   ⬭   ⬭

Reading Skill Follow-up, p. 165

	What was the conflict?	Where did the conflict happen?	Why did the conflict happen?	When did the conflict happen?	Theme
1. Choosing a Better Life	1. There was violence in the favela of Vigario Geral. 2. Anderson Sa was not sure how he should live his life.	Vigario Geral, a favela in Rio de Janeiro	The favela has a high number of people living in poverty. Youth did not have many opportunities and resorted to crime and violence.	The reading refers to Vigario Geral during the 1990s and Anderson Sa's struggle throughout the next several years.	choosing peace instead of violence
2. Not Your Average Teenager	1. Jews were discriminated against by the Nazi party. 2. World War II was a conflict among many nations.	Germany and the Netherlands	Adolf Hitler, the head of the Nazi party, created the Final Solution as a way to get rid of all the Jewish people in Nazi-controlled areas.	This conflict happened right before and during World War II.	injustice and discrimination
3. The Dirt on Diamonds	Civil war in the Democratic Republic of Congo (DRC)	Democratic Republic of Congo	The country has had a history of instability beginning with colonization. Multiple conflicts have taken place over the nation's history.	Conflict diamonds have been a part of the history of DRC for many years. They were traded during the civil war in the 1990s.	violence in unstable countries
4. Discrimination in America	1. Four young men were not allowed to sit at a whites-only lunch counter. 2. African Americans and other people were discriminated against on the basis of their race.	Greensboro, North Carolina	After slavery ended, there were many laws that denied African Americans equal rights.	The Greensboro Four sit-in happened in 1960. The Civil Rights Movement happened during the 1950s and 1960s.	nonviolent action to make changes

Chapter 7 Student Assessment, pp. 172 G, H

1. a
2. c
3. b
4. a
5. a
6. a – lack of resources; b – weak economy; c – divisions between groups of people
7. c
8. a

Community Development

Students reflect on what makes a community and what communities they belong to. In a dialogue activity, students learn about each others' personal identities. After learning vocabulary related to community, students read about different individuals and groups who worked together to improve an urban community. Students use context clues to assist them in understanding the reading passage. After reading, students write a speech to be delivered to a community leader. The chapter culminates with an activity in which students map their school neighborhood in order to evaluate its sustainability. Students then brainstorm possible improvements.

Possible Scope and Sequence
(based on one-hour class periods)

Day 1	Day 2	Day 3	Day 4	Day 5
Activating Knowledge Writing Warm-up Expanding Vocabulary	Vocabulary in Context: *Completing the Story* Breaking Down the Meaning	Dialogue: *Who Are You?* Reading Skill Focus: *Context Clues*	Pre-reading: *Anticipation Guide* Chapter Reading: *Building Sustainable Communities* Reading Skill Follow-up	Comprehension Questions

Day 6	Day 7	Day 8	Day 9
Writing about Community: *Preparing a Speech*	Writing about Community *(cont'd)*	Culminating Activity: *Putting Our Community on the Map*	Culminating Activity *(cont'd)*

Time
Eight to nine one-hour class periods

Essential Questions
- What is a community?
- What are different types of communities?
- How can global issues be solved through community?
- How can individuals work together to create sustainable communities?

Integrated Subject Areas
- Social Studies
- English Language Arts

Content Objectives
Students will:
- Explore personal and cultural identity
- Identify different kinds of communities
- Analyze how communities can create sustainable change

Language Objectives
Students will:
- Discuss characteristics of different communities by analyzing photos
- Write in response to a prompt about personal and cultural identity
- Discuss identity and culture during a dialogue
- Define and use new vocabulary words
- Read about real examples of community development
- Use context clues to define vocabulary words
- Write, prepare, and deliver a speech

Key Concepts
- Personal and cultural identity
- Sustainable communities
- Community development

Vocabulary
- Community
- Identity
- Culture
- Development

Standards Addressed
- TESOL standards
- NCTE standards
- NCSS standards
- NSES standards

* Please see Appendix A for a list of national standards addressed.

Assessment Option
Use the Chapter 8 assessments of student knowledge and outlook/personal beliefs as pre-tests for the chapter. Follow up with the same assessments at the end of the chapter to determine changes in knowledge and outlook/personal beliefs.

8 Community Development

What defines a community? How can members of a community work together to build a better future?

In Chapter 8, you will learn what different kinds of communities look like. You will also learn how people work together to create change where they live and in the world around them. Throughout the chapter, you will **speak** to your classmates about who and what defines your community. You will **listen** to your classmates speak about their personal identities and the communities they belong to. You will **read** about different types of communities that have worked well together in the face of challenges. Finally, you will **write** a speech to present your ideas for community improvement.

Instructions

1. Read the introduction with students.
2. Go over the picture with students. Based on the photo, what do students think *community* means?
3. Ask students if they have ever witnessed communities of people that have worked together. (For example, a community might work together on a neighborhood carnival, or they might work to build a new playground.)

A volunteer at the Neighborhood House reads to children. Neighborhood House is an organization that focuses on building strong families and strong communities.

Instructions

1. Have students look at the four photos.

2. Have students work with a partner to answer the questions at the bottom of the page.

3. Ask students if they can think of other examples of communities (for example, a school, a religious community, or a city).

4. Explain to students that, throughout this chapter, they will learn about different types of communities and how communities have the power to make significant changes, both locally and throughout the world.

Activating Knowledge

Directions: Each of the photos on this page shows a different community. Work with a partner to answer the questions below the photos.

What do these communities have in common?

Are you a member of any communities like these?

What are positive things that you see in each community?

What are other examples of communities not pictured here?

Writing Warm-up

Instructions

Directions: Write about a time in your life when you worked with another person or a group of people in a positive way to accomplish a goal. Describe exactly what you did as a group, and explain why working with other people helped you to accomplish this goal.

1. To prepare students for the writing warm-up, share with them a time you worked with a group of people to accomplish a goal. (For example, perhaps you worked with other teachers to organize a school event, or perhaps you worked with students to create a video or website.)

2. Read the writing directions with students.

   • **Differentiated Instruction:** If students need guidance, give them time to brainstorm different moments in their lives when they worked with others on a project and the result was more powerful than working alone. (This could be schoolwork, building or painting something, etc.)

3. Give students about 10 minutes to write independently.

   • **Differentiated Instruction:** If beginner students are more comfortable writing in their native language, allow them to do so.

   • **Differentiated Instruction:** If beginner students want to draw diagrams to support their writing, allow them to do so.

4. Have students share their writing with a partner or with the class.

Instructions

1. Have students study the four photos independently.

2. Have students collaborate with a partner to come up with possible definitions for each word.

3. Discuss students' ideas.

- **Differentiated Instruction:** Copy this page onto an overhead or display it with a document camera. As students are brainstorming ideas for each vocabulary word, list these next to the photo in each box.

4. **Option:** Review the following derivatives:

- *culture (n) – cultured, cultural, multicultural*
- *community (n) – commune, communal, unity*
- *development (n) – developed, developing, developer*
- *identity (n) – identify, identification*

5. **Option:** Review the following prefix:

- *com – together* (other examples: compare, compile)

Directions: Look at the following images and vocabulary words. Guess what you think each word means based on the given photos.

A	B

culture	community
C	D

development	identity

Using Words in Context

Directions: Read the story below and fill in the blank spaces with the following chapter vocabulary words.

culture	community	identity	development

Sophea had just stepped off the plane and couldn't believe her eyes. She was finally in Beijing to meet her family. When they picked her up, she saw many things that surprised her: different types of restaurants from around the world, a bunch of teenagers in a park blasting music, and at least five different Internet cafés. This was her first time visiting China. She had imagined the country would look very different than what she was seeing right now. She did not expect to see this type of _____ in the country.

"Uncle Tony, I had no idea Beijing was like this!"

"What do you mean?" her uncle asked.

"I thought society in Beijing would be completely Chinese and not have influences from other parts of the world," Sophea replied.

"Sophea, our world is connected. I am proud of my Chinese _____. It's who I am—it is part of my _____. At the same time, I love learning about people, music, and cultures from around the world. With help from technology like the Internet and the TV, we are able to share ideas and learn about other people and countries."

Sophea nodded in agreement. "I guess I always pictured Beijing like the photographs my mother showed me. Those photos are thirty years old. It looks like Beijing has changed a lot over the past thirty years!"

"The world is changing. Just like we have influences from different cultures, you do too. Think about it—in the United States, you can eat at restaurants from all over the world and you live next to people from all over the world."

Sophea sat quietly for a moment and then replied, "You're right, Uncle Tony. I guess we are all part of one big global _____!"

Instructions

1. Read the activity aloud.
   - **Option:** Have two speakers take turns reading the sections aloud.
2. As students listen, they can determine the appropriate placement of vocabulary terms.
3. Have students review their answers with a partner.
4. Ask a volunteer to read the completed story aloud to the class.
5. **Option:** Ask students to write about a place they have visited where there was a mix of cultures (this could also be where they live). Include all four vocabulary words in the writing.

Answers

1. development
2. culture
3. identity
4. community

Instructions

1. Explain the directions. After reviewing the definitions, explain to students they will (1) answer the question, (2) write a sentence using the vocabulary word, and (3) choose the one word in the group that does not relate to the vocabulary word.

   • **Differentiated Instruction:** Demonstrate how the activity works by filling in one of the boxes.

   • **Differentiated Instruction:** Enlarge the four boxes to poster size and fill in one of the boxes. Work as a class to fill in answers within each box and write them on the poster. The poster can then remain hanging in the room throughout this unit of study.

2. This activity could be done independently, in pairs or small groups, or as an entire class.

3. **Option:** Have students search for and cut out magazine pictures that relate to each vocabulary word.

4. **Option:** As a homework assignment, have students write a single paragraph using the four vocabulary words.

Directions: Each box below includes one of the four vocabulary words from the previous page, as well as its definition. Below each definition:

1. Answer the question.

2. Write a sentence using the vocabulary word.

3. Choose the one word in the group that does not relate to the vocabulary word.

---

culture

Definition: *the behavior, arts, beliefs, and traditions of a group of people*

1. What different cultures do you see where you live?
2. Use *culture* in a sentence.
3. Which word does not belong?
   American   jeans   French   youth

---

community

Definition: *a group of people who share common interests or live together*

1. What would a community leader care about?
2. Use *community* in a sentence.
3. Which word does not belong?
   neighborhood   citizens
   population   court

---

development

Definition: *the act of growing or expanding*

1. What kind of development might you see in a city?
2. Use *development* in a sentence.
3. Which word does not belong?
   grow   expand   decrease   increase

---

identity

Definition: *the set of characteristics that make a person who he or she is; each person has a unique identity*

1. What is one part of your identity someone would not know just by looking at you?
2. Use *identity* in a sentence.
3. Which word does not belong?
   personality   unique
   character   education

Answers

culture
1. Answers will vary.
2. In many cultures, elders are given the utmost respect.
3. jeans

community
1. Example: the well-being of community members and the environment, both now and in the future
2. The community painted a mural at the school to represent the students' different cultures.
3. court

development
1. Answers will vary. Example: The city might have more businesses or new apartment buildings.
2. The neighborhood wanted to continue its development by opening a youth center where teenagers could get help with their homework.
3. decrease

identity
1. Answers will vary. Example: I am an artist.
2. He always said being a member of the army was a strong part of his identity.
3. education

Dialogue

Example: Read information about Amelia and her life. After you read this example, use the graphic organizer on the next page to fill in information about yourself.

> My name, where I am from, and the languages I speak:
>
> *My name is Amelia. I am from Houston. I speak Spanish and English.*

> Who I am:
>
> *I am a girl, sister, granddaughter, basketball player, singer, dancer, community member, flute player, and Panamanian American.*

> Where I live:
>
> *I live in a two-bedroom apartment in a building with fifty apartments.*

> What I like about where I live:
>
> *I like seeing people from different cultures and learning about the different countries they come from. I like that people say hello to me in my apartment building.*

> Problems or issues where I live:
>
> *I notice some people from different cultures do not like to talk to each other.*

> Possible solutions to these problems:
>
> *We should have a community block party. We can offer games, prizes, and live music so people can meet each other and get to know each other better. I think this would make people feel safer and more like a part of the community.*

Instructions

1. Introduce students to the dialogue activity. Explain that they will be speaking to each other about their culture, their identity, and their community.

2. Review the example about Amelia and her life. You could read the entire example aloud to students, or just read the questions aloud and have students take turns reading Amelia's responses aloud.

Dialogue

Instructions

1. Have students write down information about their culture, identity, and community using the questions in the graphic organizer.

Directions: Complete the graphic organizer with information about your identity, culture, and community.

> My name, where I am from, and the languages I speak:

> Who I am:

> Where I live:

> What I like about where I live:

> Problems or issues where I live:

> Possible solutions to these problems:

Dialogue: Who Are You?

Directions: Ask your partner the following questions and write down the information you learn about your partner. Your partner will then ask you the same questions; use the information from the previous page to help you answer them. When you write your partner's response to each question, make sure to use complete sentences.

1. What is your name?

2. Where are you from?

3. What languages do you speak?

4. Who are you?

5. Where do you live?

6. What do you like about where you live?

7. What are some problems or issues in the place where you live?

8. What are possible solutions to these problems?

First Person versus Third Person

When your partner interviews you, respond by speaking in first person.

Example: **My** name is Tran Pham. **I speak** Vietnamese and English.

When you write your partner's responses to your questions, write in third person.

Example: **She** is Tran Pham. **She speaks** Vietnamese and English.

Dialogue

Instructions

1. Have students pair up with a partner and interview each other using the information they just wrote about themselves. The student who is interviewing should record the other student's answers.

2. Go over the information in the box at the bottom of the Dialogue page about first and third person. When students are speaking about their lives, they will speak in first person. When students are recording their partner's answers, they will write in third person.

3. Have partners introduce each other to the class using information they gathered in the interview.

- **Differentiated Instruction:** Demonstrate this by giving a mock introduction of a student.

Instructions

1. Explain that the reading skill for this chapter is using context clues to define vocabulary.

2. Review the definitions of *context* (context is the set of circumstances in a particular situation) and *clue* (a clue solves a mystery).

3. Based on these definitions, ask students what they think a context clue is.

4. Read the top portion of the page with students.

5. After you read the example, ask students what they think *incredulous* means. What clues support their definitions?

6. If no one guessed it, explain that incredulous means indicating or showing disbelief.

7. Review the four types of context clues with students. What type of context clue appeared in the example sentences? (Inference: *She had no idea.*)

Imagine you are reading a paragraph and you suddenly come across the word *incredulous*. What do you do?

    a. Keep reading; you have never seen that word before, and you have no idea what it means!

    b. Stop for a moment and guess the meaning.

    c. Stop and use clues from the reading to figure out exactly what the word means.

    d. Pull out your dictionary. There's no use in guessing what the word means!

As you read about different subjects, you will come across words you do not know. A dictionary is useful, but, before looking in a dictionary, you can use **context clues** to help you determine the meaning of a word. Context clues are clues within a sentence or paragraph that can help you understand the meaning of a word.

Example: There are different types of context clues that can help you to uncover the meaning of what you have read. Read the following sentences and determine what the word *incredulous* means.

> She had an **incredulous** look on her face when he told her that the city spent $3 million dollars to build the community center. She had no idea it would cost that much!

The following types of clues will help you figure out the meaning of unfamiliar vocabulary.

Clue	How the Clue Is Used	Example in a Sentence
synonym	This clue includes a synonym of the vocabulary word. A synonym is a word with a similar meaning.	She had an incredulous, **shocked** look on her face when he walked in.
explanation	This clue includes an explanation of the vocabulary word.	She had an incredulous look on her face, **meaning she was completely surprised**, when he walked in.
antonym	This clue includes an antonym of the vocabulary word. An antonym is a word with an opposite meaning.	She had an incredulous look on her face, unable to **believe** what she was seeing when he walked in.
inference	This clue includes words around the sentence that can help you uncover the meaning of the word.	She had an incredulous look on her face, and he could tell because **her mouth was wide open with shock**.

Reading Skill Focus: Context Clues

Directions: Read the following story. Define the **bold** words in the paragraph by using context clues. The first two have been done as an example.

Greening a School Community

In the United States, the average person throws away 4.6 pounds of garbage each day. Think about how many students and teachers are in your school. If each person produces over 4 pounds of garbage, imagine how much garbage your school produces in just one day!

Students at Prospect Sierra School weigh their garbage.

Prospect Sierra School in California did some investigating about how much trash they produce. Students began studying the idea of **reducing**, rather than increasing, waste in their schools. They completed a **trash audit** of the school's waste—a careful examination of the amount of garbage produced by students and teachers. They discovered that the school produced over 30,000 pounds of garbage each year. (To compare, the average car weighs about 2,000 pounds.)

Prospect Sierra formed a *Green Squad*—a group of students, parents, and teachers with the goal of cutting down waste. They were successful in **achieving** their goal through a number of efforts: reducing lunch waste, reducing the amount of paper thrown away, and using email to send the school newsletter instead of regular mail. The school actually saved money because less trash had to be **hauled**, or taken away, by garbage trucks.[1]

Bold Word	Definition	Type of Context Clue
reducing	*to make smaller*	*antonym*
trash audit	*an examination of the amount of waste created*	*explanation*
achieving		
hauled		

Reading Skill Focus

Instructions

1. Read the first two paragraphs together as a class.

2. Review the two bold-faced words in the second paragraph. Check to make sure students understand that the context clue for *reducing* is an antonym (*increasing*) and the context clue for *trash audit* is an explanation (a careful examination of the school's garbage).

3. Have students read the final paragraph on their own and work to define the two remaining bold-faced words.

- **Differentiated Instruction:** Have students think-pair-share with a partner about the meaning of the vocabulary words based on the context clues.

Answers

Bold Word	Definition	Type of Context Clue
achieving	accomplishing or fulfilling a goal	inference
hauled	to carry or transport	synonym

Instructions

1. Have students read and complete the Anticipation Guide. Explain that they should answer the questions based on their personal beliefs; there are no right or wrong answers.

2. **Option:** Have students participate in a sides debate on one or two of the statements. Label one wall of the room with an *Agree* sign and the opposite wall with a *Disagree* sign. Read aloud a statement from the Anticipation Guide and have students move to the *Agree* or *Disagree* side of the room based on their response to the statement. Give them the opportunity to verbally explain their thinking.

Directions: Read each statement below. Determine whether you agree or disagree with each statement. Write a sentence or two explaining why you agree or disagree with the statement.

Agree or Disagree?

1. Art can support the development of a community.

2. The environment is an important part of a community.

3. People can turn unsafe communities with crime and drugs into safe places.

4. Creating community can solve problems like homelessness and poverty.

5. People can do more together than individuals can do alone.

People in Chicago join together to make sure that everyone in the community has a home.

Building Sustainable Communities

Creating Community

Think of all the different problems happening around us in the world—poverty, climate change, crime, war, polluted air and water, overpopulation...the list could go on and on. You might be thinking, *What can I do? I'm only one person!* You are right; solving these problems alone would not be easy. Have you ever thought about how working with other people could be a powerful way to find solutions and create change?

Throughout history, communities have worked together to create **sustainable** solutions to the problems we face. There are many different types of communities. Just a few examples include:

- a *local* community—people who live together in a neighborhood or city

- a *global* community—people from around the world who work together on a common cause

- a *religious* community—people who attend a temple, mosque, or church together

- a *cultural* community—people who come from the same cultural background

- an *online* community—people connected by the Internet

- a *school* community—people who attend the same school

---

sustainable (adj) – able to meet people's needs now and in the future

Festivals like this one can bring members of a local community together.

The following examples from the city of Philadelphia show the power of what can happen when people in a community work together to create change.

Instructions

1. Give students a minute to preview the reading, noting photos, titles, and subheadings.

2. Ask students the following questions:
   - What do you think this reading will be about?
   - What is this reading *not* going to be about?
   - What do the photos and illustrations in this reading have in common?

3. Remind students to search for context clues as they come across words in bold green letters. After reading, they will be asked to define these words without using a dictionary.

4. Pair students with a partner to read the passage.

   - **Differentiated Instruction:** Have students read one section at a time. After each section, stop to ask them what they read and how they would define the bold-faced green words.

Painting a Brighter Community

The state of the environment where you live can say a lot about what is happening in your town, neighborhood, or city. For example, what would you think if you saw a city with broken bottles all around, garbage on the streets, empty buildings, and no parks?

Several years ago, the city of Philadelphia made a decision. In order to clean up negative **graffiti** written on buildings around the city, develop after-school activities to help youth stay out of trouble, and make neighborhoods safer, they decided to put aside money to paint thousands of beautiful **murals** on buildings in the city. Creating these murals would help to give people pride in where they lived.

The city of Philadelphia began a mural arts program which replaced this type of negative graffiti with positive murals throughout the city.

Philadelphia's mural arts program has worked with 100 different communities, like schools, neighborhood organizations, and churches. They have painted the city with over 2,500 murals about peace, unity, music, history, culture, and education. Community members from youth to the elderly decided on themes and designs for the murals, and they were also involved with the painting. This project has turned churches, museums, schools, libraries, and playgrounds into places with positive messages for everyone to see.[2]

Norris Square: Planting New Seeds

If you were to walk through Norris Square, a neighborhood in Philadelphia, you would see many gardens, parks, murals, and trees. That wasn't always the case. Years ago, Norris Square was known for its drug problem and crime.[3] Community members didn't feel safe in their own neighborhood. They were **frustrated** and unhappy with what was happening, so they came together to share their concerns and figure out how to improve it. Iris Brown was one of these people. She had lived in Norris Square for a while and had seen her community change. She wanted to speak out against the crime she saw, but she was scared at first.

Then, she and other community members realized the more time they spent on the streets at night, the less **illegal** and criminal activity there was. Instead of sitting at home at night, they **patrolled** the streets. When they saw any sign of drug dealing, they called the police. Thanks to this teamwork, drug dealers had more and more trouble controlling the neighborhood. After working for some time to make Norris Square a safe place, Iris took action in a part of the neighborhood known for drug deals. She and a few

Community members from Norris Square transformed the neighborhood into a safe place.

volunteers went to a **vacant**, empty parking lot. They painted a mural, planted fruit trees, and even built a small swimming pool. No one bothered them as they did this work. Finally, Iris had gained the courage to reclaim her community.[4]

Today in Norris Square, children have safe places to play, people are planting vegetables and fruits in gardens, and murals give people a sense of pride about their identity and culture. The Norris Square Neighborhood Project is a community center with many different services to support neighborhood development: women empowerment projects, community gardening, afterschool child care, and youth leadership programs. Norris Square **transformed** from a neighborhood full of crime into a safe and healthy place. More and more people want to move into this community instead of leave it. As community leader Iris Brown stated, "We want our youth to be proud of who they are and of where they come from."[5]

Up and Running

Anne Mahlum would get up early in the morning to run through the neighborhoods of Philadelphia. She loved running and had even been in a few **marathons**, 26-mile races. On her route in the city, she would always pass by a homeless men's shelter and they would cheer her on. At one point, she realized she was always running past them, but they never moved. These were people who lived in her community, but were not able to fulfill their personal goals. Anne wanted to help the men at the shelter accomplish their goals just like she accomplished her goals each time she completed a marathon. Anne talked to the director of the shelter and started a running club called *Back on My Feet*. Members of this group run three mornings a week to improve their health. Additionally, the organization helps those who are homeless to improve their lives by providing them with opportunities to go to school and gain computer and job skills.[6]

Back on My Feet has **expanded** and grown. There are now Back on My Feet groups in three different shelters in Philadelphia. Anne was able to create a community of people from very different backgrounds who could support each other to achieve their personal goals.[7]

Anne Mahlum and members of Back on My Feet

Through community support and teamwork...

- thirty-three members have been able to complete a half-marathon.
- forty-six members have found jobs.
- thirty-three members have found housing.
- thirty-five members have decided to go back to school or get job training.[8]

Communities that Last

Throughout the city of Philadelphia, people have come together in different ways to build strong communities. What type of world do you want to be a part of in the future? What are ways you could work with the people around you to create this kind of world? There are many problems in the world, but when communities, both local and global, join together to think of positive solutions, they have the ability to make an **impact**, or change. There are many ways you can work to improve the communities where you live and around the world. Here are a few ways to get involved:

- Join a youth volunteer group.
- Become part of a community theater.
- Work with younger students as a mentor or tutor.
- Volunteer with an organization supporting communities around the world.
- Take an inventory of your community's resources, like grocery stores and libraries. If any important resources are missing, write a letter to your mayor or city council.

Reading Skill Follow-up: Using Context Clues

Directions: Look at the bold-faced green words in the reading and determine the meaning of these words by using context clues. Also, identify the type of context clue used for each word.

Bold Word	Definition	Type of Context Clue
graffiti		
murals		
frustrated		
illegal		
patrolled		
vacant		
transformed		
marathons		
expanded		
impact		

Reading Skill Follow-up

Instructions

1. After they finish reading, have students determine the meaning of the bold-faced words based on context clues. Use the graphic organizer to record answers.

2. **Option:** Have students consult a dictionary to see if their definitions are correct.

3. Review definitions with students.

Answers

See p. 195H

Comprehension Questions

Instructions

1. Before students begin answering the comprehension questions, share with them the academic language they will see in many of the questions (see Appendix B).

2. Explain that the questions are divided into five sections according to the different ways they support comprehension. (See Appendix B for a detailed explanation of each section.)

3. **Differentiated Instruction:** Differentiate the questions students must answer based on their reading levels. Support comprehension by working with students who may need more guided instruction.

Comprehension Questions

Directions: Answer the following questions to support your comprehension of the chapter reading.

Understanding what you read

1. How many murals have been created in Philadelphia?

2. Identify what kinds of services Norris Square Neighborhood Project provides the community.

Thinking about what you read

3. Evaluate how Norris Square is different today than in the past.

4. Explain how Back on My Feet helps build community.

Questioning what you read

5. Do you think the author believes communities are a positive or negative thing? Why?

6. What three problems did the author discuss in the reading?

Making connections to what you read

7. What is a challenge or problem you could work on together with a community of people, either in your school or where you live?

8. Identify possible challenges to creating a community.

Further discussion questions

9. What is a way a community could work together to solve environmental issues?

10. How might people around the world connect as a community to solve global issues?

Answers

1. over 2,500

2. women empowerment projects, community gardening, afterschool child care, and youth leadership programs

3. Norris Square was known for its drug dealers and crime in the past. Now, the neighborhood is safe and full of gardens, parks, and trees.

4. People who are part of the organization support each other by running three times a week and working to achieve their personal goals.

5. The author believes communities are positive. The author says that communities can work together to solve problems.

6. graffiti, crime, and homelessness

7. Answers will vary.

8. e.g., the community may be spread out and it may be difficult for people to come together frequently; there may be tensions between different groups of people in the community; people may not have much free time

9. e.g., start a recycling program, work to reduce ecological footprint, create more gardens, plant trees in the area, lobby the city to build sidewalks

10. e.g., by speaking with each other over the Internet, by keeping up on current events, by volunteering with organizations working to support people around the world

How can you start to make change in your community and the world? One way is to identify problems that you think are important to solve. Once you find key leaders in your community you can talk to about these problems, you can reach out to these leaders and ask them for support.

Identify a problem you see within your community. This could be a problem in your neighborhood, around your school, or in your wider community. Problems could range from not having curbside recycling service to needing sidewalks and wheelchair ramps along public streets.

> You will write a speech to deliver to a leader in your community. A **speech** is a formal way of speaking to an audience. In your speech, you will tell a leader in your community why this problem is an important concern for you and what you think should be done to solve the problem.

Your speech should include:

- An introduction—thank the audience for taking time to listen to you, and introduce yourself

- An explanation of the problem and why it concerns you

- A solution that would solve the problem and ways to achieve this solution

- A conclusion—finish with a powerful statement

Tips to Keep in Mind

Before giving the speech:

1. Read the speech out loud to yourself several times.
2. Practice reading it to a classmate.
3. Work to memorize key ideas from the speech.

During the speech:

1. Make eye contact.
2. Do not read directly from your paper. You can use cards to remind you of the key ideas.
3. Sound excited and passionate about what you are talking about!
4. Speak loudly and clearly so everyone can hear you.

Instructions

1. Students will choose an issue they believe is a problem in their community and write a speech to a community leader (or group) to express their concern.

2. Read the information about writing a speech with students.

3. The tips in the call-out box are for the delivery of the written address. Explain to students that they will use these tips *after* they finish writing and editing their speech.

4. **Additional Resource:** Detailed suggestions and ideas for speechwriting are available at Scholastic's *Writing with Writers* website: http://teacher. scholastic.com/writewit/ speech/index.htm.

5. **Grammar Suggestion:** Since students are writing a formal speech, teach them how to form the present perfect when expressing their concerns. For example, *I **have noticed** more and more litter on the sidewalks in the past several months.*

Instructions

1. Read the sample speech aloud to students, speaking as if you were delivering the speech publicly.

Sample Speech

Example: The following example is a speech written by student Timothy Lee to address his school principal and school board members about a problem in his school community.

Hello, Principal Scott and esteemed School Board members!

My name is Timothy Lee, and I am a sophomore at West High School in the Cedar Grove neighborhood. I want to express a concern I have about my school. During the past year, I have noticed that students are not taking as much pride in the school as they could be. I can tell when I see graffiti all over the school, when I attend assemblies and no one cheers, and when I see friends who are embarrassed to tell people they attend West.

I came to West High School so excited be a Cougar. I was ready to join the basketball team and take part in the international club. I soon realized there were only six people on the basketball team, and no one came to watch our games. I also learned our international club hasn't existed for five years. I believe a lack of school pride doesn't help our school to have a sustainable future. If students don't believe in our own school, who will? I don't want to leave in two years and think of high school as a sad memory. Being a Cougar is part of my identity, and I want it to be something I can be proud of.

I think the problem could be resolved if we were to have more opportunities to create school spirit. I know other schools have a spirit week and sports mascots. I have also heard of student councils at other schools where student representatives have a voice in how to make their schools better. I think we should bring these things to West High School. They would help build community at our school. School culture must change if we want a high school that people are proud to attend. Once we give West students something to be proud of, you'll see a great change in our attitude. I'm betting our grades will improve, too!

If you seriously consider these solutions, West could be the school everyone wants to attend.

Thank you very much for your time.

Writing Steps: Preparing a Speech

Step 1: Brainstorm problems you see in your community using the Writing Brainstorm Page (see next page).

Step 2: Choose one problem you care about most, and choose a leader in your community who you can talk to about this problem.

Step 3: Use the Speech Organizer to help you write your speech.

Step 4: Edit your speech using the Edit Checklist below.

Step 5: Have a classmate read and edit your speech using the Edit Checklist.

Step 6: Rewrite the speech on a fresh sheet of paper.

After Writing: Use the tips provided on page 191 to help you practice and deliver your speech. Give your speech at a community meeting.

 Edit Checklist

	Author Check	Peer Editor Check
Did you begin by thanking your audience and introducing yourself?		
Did you explain your concern?		
Did you offer a possible solution to this problem?		
Did you conclude by thanking your audience and giving a powerful closing statement?		
Did you include at least two vocabulary words from the chapter?		

Writing Steps

Instructions

1. Review the writing steps with students.
2. Share the Chapter 8 writing rubric with students. You may want to add relevant spelling and grammar components to the rubric.

Chapter 8 Writing Rubric

Category	3	2	1
Organization	Includes information about a community problem, why the problem is a concern, and a possible solution to the problem	Attempts to include information about the problem, why the problem is a concern, and a possible solution to the problem	Does not include information about the problem, why the problem is a concern, or a possible solution to the problem
Development	Uses all elements of a formal speech, including an introductory greeting and a convincing closing statement	Attempts to use all elements of a formal speech	Hardly uses any elements of a formal speech
Vocabulary	Uses two or more chapter vocabulary words correctly	Uses only one chapter vocabulary word correctly	Does not use any of the chapter vocabulary words correctly

Total = _____ / 9

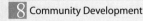

Instructions

1. Students can use this page to brainstorm ideas and collect their thoughts.

   • **Differentiated Instruction:** If students need extra help, work through this page as a class. Together, brainstorm different challenges that various communities (such as schools, neighborhoods, and cities) might face.

Writing Brainstorm Page: Preparing a Speech

1. What are problems you see in your community, or what could be improved?

2. Which problem is most important to you? Why do you care about this problem?

3. What are possible solutions to this problem? What needs to happen to achieve these solutions?

4. Who is a community leader you should speak to about this problem?

Writing Organizer: Preparing a Speech

Hello, _____. I want to thank you for taking
the time to listen to me today.

My name is _____, and I am here because
I have a concern.

(State your concern): _____
_____

(State two to three reasons you have this concern):
_____
_____
_____
_____

I think there are solutions to this problem. (State your solution):
_____
_____

(Explain why your solution is important and how it can be achieved):
_____
_____
_____
_____

Closing statement (sound convincing!):
_____
_____

Thank you again for your time.

Writing Organizer

Instructions

1. Students can use the template to write a rough draft of their speeches.

2. Once they have written their speeches, they will exchange them with a classmate, edit them using the Edit Checklist, and then revise them.

3. Return to the suggestions for practicing and delivering a speech.

4. Give students ample time to practice their speeches to each other. Help them to focus on key ideas from their speeches so that they do not have to read the speeches word for word. They might write these key ideas on note cards they can refer to during the speech.

5. **Option:** Develop a speech rubric with students. Use this rubric to evaluate student speeches.

6. Have each student present his/her speech to the class.

7. **Option:** Show students televised speeches from a national or local network. Better yet, take students to a local community meeting, such as a school board or a city council meeting. Ask them to note what makes some speeches more effective than others.

8. **Option:** Invite a community leader, such as the mayor or a state senator, to your classroom. Have students deliver their speeches to this leader.

Culminating Activity: Putting Our School Community on the Map (2 hours)

Overview

Students create representational maps of their school and the surrounding community to conceptualize and understand the relationships between resources, the environment, community, and sustainability. Students then brainstorm specific ways to make the school community more sustainable through improvements to the physical environment, and revise their maps to reflect these enhancements. In an extension activity, students present their ideas to the principal or other community stakeholders.

Materials/Preparation

- Assortment of maps (maps of the world from different perspectives, city maps, park maps, a Google map, etc.)

- Butcher paper, one sheet for each group of 3-4 students

- Pencils

- Marking pens

- (Optional) Additional drawing supplies, such as erasers and rulers

- (Optional) Internet access

Part 1: Mapping Community Resources

Introduction

1. Show students a number of different maps. Give them a few moments to review all the different maps.

2. Ask students, *What is the purpose of a map?* (In general, maps show how things are related.)

3. Tell the class they are going to create a representational map of their school and the surrounding community.

4. Review the word *community* with students.

Steps

1. Divide the class into groups of 3-4 students. Provide each group with a sheet of butcher paper, pencils, and other drawing supplies (rulers, erasers, etc.).

   - **Option:** If time permits, lead the class on a walk around the school grounds and surrounding neighborhood (2-3 block radius) to identify physical features of the community, such as streets, buildings, and green spaces like parks.

2. Their task is to draw their school and the neighborhood that surrounds it. Tell students that a representational map does not need to be accurate (in fact, a two-dimensional map of Earth's curved surface will never be accurate). Their maps should show **relative** spatial relationships rather than exact distances. For example, a post office that is three blocks away from the school should be farther away from the school on the map than a park that is two blocks away.

3. On the map, students should clearly label things that are important to them and/or that they think are important to the school community. Note that different groups will draw maps that include (or omit) different attributes of the neighborhood. The maps may be of varying scales and may be drawn from an aerial or other viewpoint.

   - **Note:** Do not use marking pens at this point. Draw the map in pencil first.

4. Ask each group to briefly present their map to the class.

5. Discuss the following questions with your students:

   • Are there places, resources, or streets that every group included in their maps? What are they? Why do you think that every group included them?

   • Are there things that some groups included in their map that others did not? Why do you think this happened?

   • How do you think this school community compares to other schools you have attended in the past?

Part 2: Sustainable Development

Introduction

1. Explain to students that a sustainable community is one that includes resources and physical spaces that meet the current needs of the community and will also meet the needs of people who live in the community in the future.

2. In a think-pair-share activity with a partner, have students create a list of five things they would include in a sustainable community (e.g., parks where children can play, a community garden, a mural that represents the people in the community, a health clinic).

4. Have each pair share their list with the entire class. Write all suggestions on the board.

Steps

1. Have students reconvene in their groups with their pencil-drawn maps.

2. Ask them to discuss specific ways of enhancing the sustainability of their school and surrounding community. Challenge them to think of specific ways that the environmental health, social well-being, and economy of their school's neighborhood could be enhanced through improvements to the physical environment. They will need to identify specific things that would promote environmental, social, and/or economic sustainability within the community. They can refer back to the components of a sustainable community that they identified in the introductory activity.

3. Pass out pencils, erasers, and colored marking pens. Now ask student groups to make changes to their original maps that would show how they want their school community to look. Completed maps should be in full color. Allow approximately 30 minutes for this part of the activity.

4. Display the completed color drawings around the room, and allow students to do a short art walk around the room to see each group's sustainable community map.

5. Reconvene the class and ask them the following questions:

   • What are your greatest concerns related to the sustainability of the environment surrounding your school?

   • How could those concerns be addressed? (e.g., school policies, government policies, neighborhood-organizing, changes in physical infrastructure)

   • How can you, as students, be the driving force for those improvements?

   • What are possible negative consequences of the changes you proposed?

Chapter 8 Extensions, Action Project, and Resources

Communications Extension

Invite the school principal or one or more community stakeholders, such as a city planner, an environmental engineer, a member of city council, a developer, an owner of a local business, or a resident, to visit your classroom. Ask what sustainability means to them. Have students present their ideas for making their community more sustainable. Ask the invited guests to give feedback on students' ideas. Are the proposed changes feasible? Have any of these ideas been suggested before? Are these issues already being addressed?

Math Extension

Using Google Maps (www.maps.google.com), calculate the distance between your home and the nearest locations of the following community resources: public library, a place for recreation (e.g., movie theater, bowling alley, basketball court), grocery store, and the school you attend. Would you consider your neighborhood a model for sustainable community development? Would you prefer that any of these resources were closer? Why or why not?

Social Studies Extension

Have students research a community that worked together to address a problem. They can create timelines to document this community's work, including facts about what they accomplished at different points in time. Students can then present this information via PowerPoint or through a poster presentation.

Action Project

As a class, choose one local community issue of interest, such as health care. Using Google Maps (www.maps.google.com), identify and map resources related to this issue in your community (for example, health care resources might include pharmacies, hospitals, and medical clinics). Then, explore the implications of where these resources are located. For example, how are people in an area affected by the location or absence of important resources? Generate ideas for enhancing existing resources, indicating on a community map where these enhancements should be located. Work with a neighborhood association or the city planner's office to bring the class's vision to life.

Additional Resources

America Street, by Anne Mazur

This multicultural anthology written for adolescents includes fourteen short stories about young people from different cultural backgrounds and communities living in America. The backgrounds of the characters are diverse, but all are trying to find a place for themselves.

TakingITGlobal

www.tigweb.org

TakingITGlobal (TIG) helps young people around the world create online communities to keep them informed and inspired about changing the world. The website educates users about various global issues and gives students opportunities to network with other students around the world who are working on the same issues they care about.

Walk Score

www.walkscore.com

Walk Score provides users with a measure of how many amenities are located within walking distance of a given address. Type in any address and find nearby grocery stores, movie theaters, schools, parks, libraries, fitness facilities, and more.

Whale Rider

This movie tells the story of a young girl, Paikea, who belongs to the Maori tribe in New Zealand. She questions certain traditions in her community and struggles to find her place, while still valuing the culture and values she has been taught. The movie brings up discussion questions about community, culture, traditions, and globalization. (101 minutes, directed by Niki Caro)

Edens Lost and Found

www.edenslostandfound.org

This PBS television series chronicles revitalization projects in four American cities, showcasing community activists and forward-thinking professionals who have worked to transform their urban environments. Practical solutions for improving the environment and quality of life in cities, both for ourselves and future generations, are a central part of the program.

Chapter 8 Student Assessment, page 1
Knowledge about Community Development

Vocabulary

Directions: Read each sentence and circle the letter next to the correct definition of the **bold-faced** word.

1. Tracy wanted to learn more about her **culture** after learning about different groups that immigrated to the United States. She decided to start by interviewing her grandmother.

   a. the history of a person's birthplace
   b. the reasons why a group of people speak a certain language
   c. a family tree that defines all the different family members that belong to the family
   d. the behaviors, traditions, art, and lifestyle that define a group of people

2. The **community** came together to raise money for the families whose homes were destroyed by the hurricane.

   a. a group of schools that work together in a local area cleaning up neighborhoods
   b. government leaders that make decisions about how to spend money without asking citizens
   c. a group of people with common interests, who may or may not live close to one another
   d. young people who are interested in making a difference

3. The **development** of the town was exciting to watch. New parks were built, and the number of businesses increased. People were excited about making their town safer, cleaner, and better.

   a. a decrease in size
   b. a population increase
   c. a growth or expansion
   d. a cutback in jobs

4. She always explained that she had many parts to her **identity**—she was a singer, a student, a sister, a daughter, and a Jamaican.

   a. daily activities of a person
   b. characteristics of a person
   c. career choice of a person
   d. educational background of a person

Chapter 8 Student Assessment, page 2

Content

Directions: Read each sentence and circle the letter that correctly completes the sentence.

5. An example of a community positively working together on a global issue is _____.

   a. a neighborhood that pressures the mayor to increase the number of fast food restaurants in the local area
   b. a group of young people who perform as a band in music competitions
   c. a youth center that raises money once a month to send books to schools in developing countries
   d. a basketball league that has competitions throughout the year

6. A challenge to creating a healthy and sustainable community could be _____.

   a. unsafe neighborhoods full of violence
   b. people from different cultures who do not understand one another
   c. factories that pollute the air with toxic chemicals
   d. all of the above

Reading Comprehension

Directions: Read the paragraphs below. For 7 and 8, circle the letter next to the correct answer.

Neighborhood House is an organization in Seattle, Washington, that has been around for over 100 years. Neighborhood House serves immigrants and refugees who come to Seattle from all over the world. The organization focuses on building strong families and strong communities. Neighborhood House has different centers throughout Seattle where families and individuals can receive education, employment, and health services.

When Hailu Gago, an immigrant from Ethiopia, moved to Seattle, a job **specialist** from Neighborhood House helped him to get job training. These services provided him with a hopeful future. As Gago stated, "Here you can earn at least a basic living if you work hard. Dreaming is allowed."

7. Using context clues, define the word **specialist**:

   a. a person who knows about a specific subject
   b. a person trained in teaching people how to drive
   c. a person who volunteers at a school to help others
   d. a person who teaches people how to use their time wisely

8. How does Neighborhood House support immigrants and refugees from around the world?

   a. by educating their children
   b. by providing education, employment, and health services they might need
   c. by giving them driver's licenses and teaching them the importance of money
   d. by driving them to work and school

Chapter 8 Student Assessment, page 3
Outlook and Personal Beliefs

Answer the following questions based on your personal beliefs. There are no right or wrong answers.

Directions for 1 and 2: Place a check mark (√) in the box next to your response to each statement.

1. I am not part of any community.
   ☐ True
   ☐ False

2. People my age have the ability to make a difference in our communities.
   ☐ True
   ☐ False

3. **Complete the following sentence:**
   One way I can personally help my community is by…

   _____

   _____

   _____

   _____

Directions for 4 and 5: Fill in the ovals below based on your level of agreement. 1 means you strongly agree, and 7 means you strongly disagree.

1 = yes, definitely!   7 = no way!

←——————————————————→

4. I believe my daily actions have an impact on both local and global communities.

   1   2   3   4   5   6   7
   ⬭   ⬭   ⬭   ⬭   ⬭   ⬭   ⬭

5. I believe I have the ability to help solve community issues.

   1   2   3   4   5   6   7
   ⬭   ⬭   ⬭   ⬭   ⬭   ⬭   ⬭

Reading Skill Follow-up, pp. 189

Bold Word	Definition	Type of Context Clue
graffiti	a drawing or writing on a wall or other surface usually meant to be seen by the public	inference
murals	very large images, often paintings, written or drawn on a wall or ceiling	inference
frustrated	disappointed	synonym
illegal	not permitted, against the law	synonym
patrolled	moved about an area, especially by an authorized and trained person or group	antonym
vacant	empty	synonym
transformed	noticeably changed the appearance or form of	inference
marathons	races of 26 miles	explanation
expanded	grown or enlarged	synonym
impact	an influence or effect	synonym

Chapter 8 Student Assessment,
pp. 195 D, E

1. d
2. c
3. c
4. b
5. c
6. d
7. a
8. b

Creating Our Future

9

Students consider what they want the world to be like in the future, and how they can help to make their vision of the future a reality. They begin by learning vocabulary related to personal and structural solutions to sustainability challenges. Students then practice identifying character traits as they read about people and organizations who are working toward making our world more sustainable. They will write a letter to themselves about their personal visions of the future and how they can make those visions become reality. The chapter culminates with a collaborative activity in which students set specific goals for alleviating a problem and then develop a plan to take action.

Possible Scope and Sequence
(based on one-hour class periods)

Day 1	Day 2	Day 3	Day 4	Day 5
Activating Knowledge Writing Warm-up Expanding Vocabulary	Using Words in Context: *Completing Sentences* Breaking Down the Meaning	Dialogue: *What are problems you see in the world?*	Reading Skill Focus: *Character Traits* Pre-reading: *Sustainable Solutions*	Chapter Reading: *What Can We Do?* Reading Skill Follow-up

Day 6	Day 7	Day 8	Day 9
Comprehension Questions	Writing about Sustainable Solutions: *A Letter*	Culminating Activity: *Creating Our Future*	Culminating Activity *(cont'd)* Vocabulary Challenge *(bonus)*

Time
Eight to nine one-hour class periods

Essential Questions
- Which global challenges are most pressing?
- What are personal and structural solutions to those challenges?
- How can people work together to develop and implement a plan for action?

Integrated Subject Areas
- Social Studies
- English Language Arts
- Science

Content Objectives
Students will:
- Visualize the future they desire
- Identify global issues they want to address
- Identify personal and structural solutions to these issues

Language Objectives
Students will:
- Discuss global solutions by matching photos with captions
- Write a free write in response to a prompt
- Discuss global issues and solutions through a dialogue
- Define and use new vocabulary words
- Read about people who have found personal and structural solutions
- Use character traits to describe a person's personality
- Write a letter

Key Concepts
- Personal solutions
- Structural solutions
- Sustainability

Vocabulary
- Citizen
- Government
- Personal solution
- Structural solution

Standards Addressed
- TESOL standards
- NCTE standards
- NCSS standards
- NSES standards

* Please see Appendix A for a list of national standards addressed.

Assessment Option
Use the Chapter 9 assessments of student knowledge and outlook/personal beliefs as pre-tests for the chapter. Follow up with the same assessments at the end of the chapter to determine changes in knowledge and outlook/personal beliefs.

Instructions

1. Read the introduction with students.

2. Ask students to name some issues that affect our world. How do these issues relate to sustainability?

3. Ask students to review the three photos. Can they recall from Chapter 1 how these photos relate to sustainability?

Creating Our Future

Throughout this book, you have learned about sustainability. Sustainability involves living your life today with the future in mind. Now, you will be challenged to think about ways that you can be part of a sustainable future.

In Chapter 9, you will identify sustainable solutions to issues that affect our world. You will **speak** to a classmate about important issues in the world and how you think they can be solved. You will **listen** to your classmates as they talk about which issues are most important to them. You will **read** about individuals and organizations who are working to find personal and structural solutions to economic, environmental, and social challenges, and make our world more sustainable. At the end of the chapter, you will **write** a letter about how you would like the world to be thirty years from now.

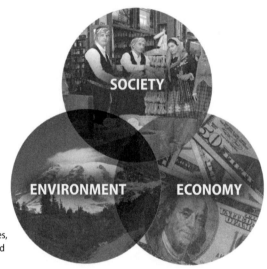

A sustainable future includes healthy economies, environments, and societies.

Directions: Match each photo to one of the statements on the right. Then, answer the questions that follow.

A.

B.

C.

D.

E.

F.

1. Volunteers combat homelessness by building houses for low-income neighbors.

2. Education and attending school is one way to prevent poverty.

3. Removing tires and other trash helps to keep rivers clean.

4. Students can voice their opinions by attending public rallies and protests.

5. Health education teaches mothers how to keep themselves and their children healthy.

6. Students can create peace and understanding by meeting people from different cultures.

Instructions

1. Instruct students to match the six photos with the six statements. These photos and statements represent real solutions to global sustainability challenges.

2. Have students work with a partner to discuss answers to the three questions.

3. Ask volunteers to share examples of activities they have participated in that are similar to the ones in the photos.

Have you ever participated in activities like the ones in the photos?

Which of the activities in the photos would you like to participate in someday?

How do these activities promote **sustainability**?

Answers

1. B
2. F
3. D
4. A
5. E
6. C

Instructions

1. Read through the writing warm-up directions and Gandhi's statement with students. Ensure that all students understand Gandhi's words.

2. Give students about 10 minutes to write a response to the quote. The bulleted questions are intended to help generate ideas. These do not necessarily need to be answered in the free write.

   • **Differentiated Instruction:** If beginner students are more comfortable writing in their native language, allow them to do so.

   • **Differentiated Instruction:** If beginner students want to draw diagrams to support their writing, allow them to do so.

3. **Option:** Have students research Gandhi. Who was he? What motivated him to become a spiritual and political leader? How have Gandhi's philosophies outlived him?

Mahatma Gandhi was a very famous political and spiritual leader in the country of India. He once said,

"It's not too late at all. You just don't yet know what you are capable of."

Directions: Reflect on Gandhi's quote in a free write. You may want to think about your answers to the following questions as you write.

• What do you think Gandhi meant?

• Do you agree with what Gandhi said?

• What are you capable of doing now?

• What would you like to become capable of in the future?

Directions: Look at the following images and vocabulary words. Guess what you think each word means based on the given photo.

A	B

citizen	**government**
C	D

personal solution	**structural solution**

Instructions

1. Have students study the four photos on the page independently.

2. Have students collaborate with a partner to come up with possible definitions for each word.

3. Discuss possible definitions with them.

   • **Differentiated Instruction:** Copy this page onto an overhead or display it with a document camera. As students are brainstorming ideas for each vocabulary word, list these next to the photo in each box.

4. Ask students if they have heard of these words before. If so, where? Can anyone share other examples of the vocabulary words? (For example, they may have learned in a civics class that democracy is a kind of government or that a governor is the state's political leader.)

5. **Option:** Review the following derivatives and root words:

   • *civic (adj) – relating to a citizen*

   • *govern (v) – to control, direct, or rule*

   • *person (n) – a human*

   • *structure (n) – the arrangement of parts into a whole*

   • *solution (n) – the process of solving a problem*

Instructions

1. Read the activity aloud.

2. As students listen, they can determine the appropriate placement of the vocabulary terms. Terms from Chapters 1 and 9 are included in the word bank.

3. Have students review their answers with a partner.

4. Ask volunteers to read the completed sentences aloud to the class.

Directions: For each of the sentences below, choose a word from the Word Bank to complete the sentence. One word will not be used.

Word Bank

personal solutions	economy	structural solutions
society	citizen	sustainability
government	environment	

1. There are many _____ to conflict. For example, instead of using your fists to fight, you could talk to the person you are having a problem with.

2. She had just become a _____ of the country and was excited that she could vote in the next presidential election.

3. Leaders from the _____ were open to hearing different people's ideas on how to improve the _____. One person mentioned that teaching our children how to take action against climate change was a possible solution.

4. As city leaders thought about _____ to end poverty, they decided to do a few things: increase the number of jobs, increase the minimum wage, and increase the number of young people who enroll in college. These three things would support the _____ and help to reduce poverty.

5. The community decided to make _____ a priority. This meant it would take whatever action necessary to make sure people's needs were met now and in the future.

A man puts his vote in the ballot box for national elections in the country of East Timor.

Answers

1. personal solutions
2. citizen
3. government; environment
4. structural solutions; economy
5. sustainability

Directions: Each box below includes one of the four vocabulary words from the previous page, as well as its definition. Below each definition:

1. Answer the question.

2. Write a sentence using the vocabulary word.

3. Choose the one word in the group that does not relate to the vocabulary word.

---

citizen

Definition: *a person who is a member of a community, state, or nation*

1. Which nation are you a citizen of?

2. Use *citizen* in a sentence.

3. Which word does not belong?
person   group   individual   voter

---

government

Definition: *an official organization that makes and enforces laws for a community, state, or region*

1. The United States government is a democracy. What is another kind of government?

2. Use *government* in a sentence.

3. Which word does not belong?
laws   president   election   hospital

---

personal solution

Definition: *a solution to a problem whereby an individual attempts to solve the problem*

1. What is a personal solution to climate change?

2. Use *personal solution* in a sentence.

3. Which word does not belong?
disposing   recycling
helping   volunteering

---

structural solution

Definition: *a solution to a problem that involves changing a system or an established structure*

1. What is a structural solution to poor health?

2. Use *structural solution* in a sentence.

3. Which word does not belong?
law   event   government   education

Instructions

1. **Explain the directions.** After reviewing the definitions, explain to students they will (1) answer the question, (2) write a sentence using the vocabulary word, and (3) choose the one word in the group that does not relate to the vocabulary word.

   • **Differentiated Instruction:** Demonstrate how the activity works by filling in one of the boxes.

   • **Differentiated Instruction:** Enlarge the four boxes to poster size and fill in one of the boxes. Work as a class to fill in answers within each box and write them on the poster. The poster can then remain hanging in the room throughout this unit of study.

2. This activity could be done independently, in pairs or small groups, or as an entire class.

3. **Option:** Have students search for and cut out magazine pictures that relate to each vocabulary word.

4. **Option:** As a homework assignment, have students write a single paragraph using the four vocabulary words.

Answers

citizen

1. Answers will vary. Example: I am a citizen of Chad.
2. As a citizen of Spain, Miguel has to follow Spanish laws.
3. group

government

1. e.g., monarchy, autocracy (dictatorship)
2. In the United States, the three branches of government are the Executive, the Judicial, and the Legislative.
3. hospital

personal solution

1. e.g., riding a bike instead of driving to reduce greenhouse gas emissions
2. A personal solution to conflict is to avoid buying conflict diamonds.
3. disposing

structural solution

1. e.g., educating women to reduce infant deaths and diseases
2. A structural solution to diseases like AIDS is educating people about how to prevent the disease, rather than just giving medicine to those who already have it.
3. event

Dialogue

Instructions

1. Read the dialogue directions and sample interview with students.

2. Have students listen as you read the dialogue aloud so they can hear proper pronunciation.

3. Give students time to read through the sample dialogue with a partner. If they need extra practice, tell them to read through the dialogue a second time, reversing roles.

Dialogue: What are problems you see in the world?

Example: With a partner, read the sample interview below to find out Matt's and Ji Sun's thoughts on important world issues.

Matt: Hi, Ji Sun. How are you today?

Ji Sun: Hi, Matt. I am great! What's on your mind?

Matt: This morning our teacher asked us what we think is the most important issue affecting the world today. What do you think is the most important issue in the world?

Ji Sun: Oh, that's a tough question! If I had to choose just one, I would say health.

Matt: Why do you think health is the most important issue affecting the world today?

Ji Sun: I know that many people are sick from diseases like AIDS and malaria, and many of them do not have money to pay for medicine.

Matt: Ji Sun, do you think there is a solution to this problem?

Ji Sun: Yes, Matt, I think there is. We need to learn more about how diseases spread and to tell people what they can do to prevent getting diseases.

Matt: Good idea!

Ji Sun: Thanks. What do you think is the most important issue affecting the world today?

Matt: I think conflict is the most important issue affecting the world.

Ji Sun: Why do you think conflict is such an important issue?

Matt: There are violent conflicts happening all around the world. For example, did you know that thousands of people have died in Sudan, a country in Africa, because of a conflict between different groups of people?

Ji Sun: No, I didn't know that. Do you think there is a solution to that kind of conflict?

Matt: Yes, I think there are many possible solutions. I think if we could start at a very young age treating each other better, people would have fewer conflicts when they are older.

Ji Sun: Interesting thought! Thanks for sharing your ideas with me.

Directions: Now it's your turn. Using the sentences below, have the following conversation with your partner. Fill in the blanks with your partner as you go. When you are finished, reread your completed dialogue.

A: Hi, _____ (partner B). How are you today?

B: Hi, _____ (partner A). I am great! What's on your mind?

A: This morning our teacher asked us what we think is the most important issue affecting the world today. What do you think is the most important issue in the world?

B: Oh, that's a tough question! If I had to choose just one, I would say _____.

A. Why do you think that is the most important issue affecting the world today?

B. I think it is important because _____.

A. _____ (partner B), do you think there is a solution to this problem?

B. Yes, _____ (partner A), I think there is. One solution is _____.

A. Good idea!

B. Thanks. What do you think is the most important issue affecting the world today?

A. I think _____ is the most important issue affecting the world.

B. Why do you think it is such an important issue?

A. I think it is important because _____.

B. Do you think there is a solution to this problem?

A. Yes, I think one solution is _____.

B. Interesting thought! Thanks for sharing your ideas with me.

Instructions

1. Divide the class into pairs. Assign one student in each pair to role A and the other student to role B.

2. Before reading the dialogue aloud together, student A will need to fill in information for his/her part, and student B will need to fill in information for his/her part. They can refer back to the sample dialogue for guidance.

3. When they have filled in the necessary information, ask pairs to read through the dialogue together.

- **Differentiated Instruction:** Challenge students to listen carefully to their partners and fill in their partner's responses as they read through the dialogue.

Instructions

1. Ask students to think of a close friend or family member.

2. Ask them to think of words that would describe this person's personality. Tell them that the words that they would use to describe this person are sometimes called *character traits*.

3. Ask students to define the word character. (In literature, a character is a person in a story. *Character* can also refer to a person's features and qualities.) What do they think a *character trait* is?

4. Together as a class, read through the definition of character traits and the sample sentences about Jack.

 • **Differentiated Instruction:** Ask students to think of other words that could be used to describe Jack. Point out that simple words like *hilarious* can be exchanged with synonyms like *funny* or *humorous*. Challenge them to think of some great character trait words that would be more descriptive than their simpler counterparts. (For example, *My sister is mad/furious.*) They can use a thesaurus to support their thinking.

Fiction and nonfiction stories of people taking positive action in the world often inspire us. These stories are really powerful if we learn details about the people in the story. The author of a story might tell you about a person's personality by using descriptive words, or the author might hint at the person's personality through his or her actions. These descriptors of a person in a story are called **character traits**.

Consider the following two sentences. They reveal character traits in different ways.

Jack is the funniest person I know.
Jack is always telling stories and jokes that make people laugh.

Jack's character trait is being funny. In the first example, the author tells you that Jack is funny. In the second example, the author does not actually say that Jack is funny. Instead, the author told you about Jack by describing his actions (telling stories and jokes that make people laugh).

Sample Character Traits

confident	courageous	determined	disinterested
enthusiastic	funny	generous	hard-working
intelligent	interesting	kind	lazy
mean	motivated	optimistic	outgoing
pessimistic	serious	shy	unfocused

Reading Skill Focus: Character Traits

Example: Read the following paragraphs. As you read, try to identify some of John Muir's character traits. Do any of the character traits you identified match those in the table below the reading?

John Muir was born in 1838 in Scotland. He and his family moved to the United States when he was a boy. As a young man, he became very curious about the environment. He enjoyed learning about plants and geology and formed theories about how valleys are formed. As an adult he traveled all around the country, exploring wild areas. He once walked all the way from Indiana to Florida to enjoy the beauty of nature!

Muir was very concerned about protecting the environment, and urged Congress and the President to protect wilderness areas. He argued strongly that natural areas should be protected from human development. He was even able to persuade President Teddy Roosevelt to create Yosemite National Park. Muir wrote many books and essays describing his feelings about nature and encouraging the protection of natural lands. Many environmentalists are still inspired by Muir's writings about nature.

Character Traits	Evidence from Reading
1. curious	enjoyed learning about plants and geology
2. passionate	argued strongly for protection of natural areas
3. persuasive	persuaded President Roosevelt to create national parks
4. inspirational	many environmentalists are inspired by his writings

The Muir Woods National Monument in California is named after John Muir.

Instructions

1. Have students read the passage about John Muir.

2. Review John Muir's character traits and evidence from the reading. Ask students to come up with other words that could be used to describe him.

Instructions

1. Have students read the passage about the Boston Youth Organizing Project (BYOP), either in pairs or small groups.

2. Ask them to identify character traits of BYOP members as they read.

3. Ask volunteers to share and explain the character traits they identified. There are quite a few possible answers. Students can use the character traits provided on page 204, or they could think of additional traits that apply to BYOP members.

Reading Skill Focus: Character Traits

Directions: Now it's your turn. Read the following selection. Then, choose words from the box of character traits that apply to BYOP members. Use evidence from the reading to support your choices.

In the 1990s, youth violence caused many deaths of young people living in Boston, Massachusetts. In response to the violence, a group of pastors from different religions began the Boston Area Youth Organizing Project, or BYOP. This group gave youth the chance to speak out against problems they saw in their schools and neighborhoods. BYOP works for social change and justice by helping young people to identify problems in the Boston community and to develop their own solutions to those problems. BYOP members have become leaders who work to create a strong and diverse Boston community.[1]

The youth-led group has chapters in over twenty-two high schools throughout the Boston area. High school students in these different chapters work to improve relationships between students and teachers, extend the service hours for public transportation, clean up schools, and speak to the local community about opening youth centers so that young people have safe places to spend time with each other. In 1999, because of the BYOP, schools in Boston made a promise to keep the bathrooms in high schools clean. Two years later, teenagers involved with BYOP organized an effort to win $2 million toward purchasing new textbooks.[2]

Character Traits of BYOP Members	Evidence from Reading

Members of the Boston Youth Organizing Project

Answers

Character Traits of BYOP Members	Evidence from Reading
1. confident	BYOP members are leaders in the Boston community
2. hard-working	worked to improve relationships between students and teachers, extend hours of public transportation, clean up schools, and raise money for textbooks

Instructions

1. Read the math problem at the top of the page aloud.
2. Work through the two solutions with students to show that both indicate the news coverage was not representative of actual youth violence.
3. Ask students to think of other examples of problems that have multiple solutions.
4. Read through the remainder of the page with students.

Did you know there are usually multiple solutions to every problem?

Consider this math problem:

Seven out of ten local TV stories on violence involve youth. 14% of local violent arrests involve youth. Is the TV coverage of youth violence representative of the problem of youth violence?

You could solve this problem in two different ways:

1. You could turn $\frac{7}{10}$ into a percent. Does it equal 14%? If not, the TV coverage is not representative. ($\frac{7}{10} = 70\%$)
2. You could see if the two fractions form a proportion. If the fractions are not proportional, the TV coverage is not representative. ($\frac{7}{10} \neq \frac{14}{100}$)

Just like the math problem, global issues like poverty and climate change have multiple solutions.

In this chapter, you will read about a variety of sustainable solutions—ones that take into consideration the well-being of people, economies, and environments, now and long into the future.

You will also be learning about two different kinds of sustainable solutions: personal solutions and structural solutions.

- A **personal solution** is an action that one person can take.
- A **structural solution** is a broader approach to solving a problem that involves changing a system, such as education or agriculture.

Before you read, you will practice identifying personal and structural solutions.

Instructions

1. Review the first two answers with students. Ask them to explain why the first solution is a personal solution and why the second is a structural solution.

2. Have students work with a partner to complete the table.

   • **Differentiated Instruction:** For beginning readers, work through the table together as a class, asking students to discuss why they think each statement represents a personal or structural solution.

   • **Differentiated Instruction:** For advanced students, challenge them to think of the solution not listed. If they identified recycling as a personal solution to resource scarcity, what might be a structural solution to the same problem?

3. **Option:** Return to the iceberg model from Chapter 2 to further explore the concepts of personal and structural solutions. Ask students to develop ideas for how to address the tip of the iceberg—the event that is visible. An example is shown to the right.

   Challenge students to come up with personal solutions (e.g., staying inside on days that are very smoggy) and structural solutions (e.g., creating a law that limits the amount of pollution that cars can emit) to reduce asthma rates.

Directions: Determine whether the following solutions are personal or structural solutions. The first two have been completed for you.

Global Issue	Solution	Personal or Structural?
1. poverty	Volunteer weekly to serve food to people who are homeless.	*personal*
2. poverty	Create a job training program to help people who are homeless find jobs.	*structural*
3. resource scarcity	Recycle your aluminum, glass, plastic, and paper items instead of throwing them in the trash.	
4. hunger	Teach farmers how to produce food when resources like water and fertilizer are limited.	
5. climate change	Create an international agreement for all nations to reduce their greenhouse gas emissions.	
6. conflict	Encourage your friends to treat other people respectfully.	
7. population	Make reproductive health care available to all women.	
8. air pollution	Carpool to school with friends instead of driving alone.	
9. human migration	Send food and other supplies to refugee camps.	
10. consumption	Create laws that require manufacturers of electronic items (televisions, computers, and cell phones) to repair items when they break.	

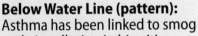

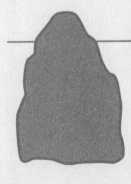

Tip of Iceberg (single event):
The number of people with asthma and respiratory diseases is higher than ever before.

Below Water Line (pattern):
Asthma has been linked to smog and air pollution in big cities.

At Base (underlying structures/ root causes):
Air pollution results from manufacturing items we buy and from travelling in cars, trucks, and airplanes.

Answers

3. personal
4. structural
5. structural
6. personal
7. structural
8. personal
9. personal
10. structural

What Can We Do?

"Whether you believe you can, or whether you believe you can't, you're absolutely right."
—**Henry Ford**, founder of the Ford Motor Company

Personal Solutions

Have you ever seen a problem and decided to do something about it? Maybe you have stopped a fight between two friends. Or, perhaps you have found a lost wallet and returned it to its owner.

These are examples of *personal solutions*. Personal solutions are ways in which individuals, or people acting on their own, can help solve problems. Anyone can be part of a personal solution. For example, to help prevent deforestation, you could write on both sides of your notebook paper. Or, you could help save water by educating people about how washing their cars at home wastes more water than going to a carwash.

As you read the following stories, see if you can identify the problem the individuals were trying to solve. What personal solutions did they come up with?

Wild Ambitions

Jarid Manos grew up in rural Ohio, where he first fell in love with the prairie **ecosystem**. Prairies, also known as grasslands or plains, are landscapes with tall grasses and few trees. They are home to many plants and animals.

The prairie served as a **refuge** where Jarid could go when life got difficult. Jarid's childhood was not easy. As a teenager, he ran away from home.

Jarid Manos founded the Great Plains Restoration Council.

He spent years moving from one city to another, making money any way he could. As a young man he struggled with depression and drinking. Eventually he resorted to selling drugs. During those **turbulent** times, Jarid yearned to return to the prairies he loved.

Now, Jarid's refuge is an ecosystem under attack. In the past, prairies were found all over the United States. Today, prairies in North America are disappearing because people are building homes and farms where prairies used to be.

---

ecosystem (n) – a community of organisms (plants, animals, and other living things) together with their environment, functioning as a unit
refuge (n) – a safe place
turbulent (adj) – characterized by much movement or instability

Instructions

1. Give students a few minutes to preview the reading, noting photos, titles, and subheadings.

2. Ask students what they think the reading will be about.

3. Explain to students that, as they read, they will be learning about real examples of people who have developed personal or structural solutions to sustainability challenges.

4. Remind students to pay close attention to the character traits demonstrated by each person as they read.

5. Start by reading the quote from Henry Ford.

   • **Option:** Use the following *think aloud* to model active reading.

   "I like that quote! My mom is always telling me that you can do anything you think you can. But if you don't think you'll succeed, you probably won't.

   I guess since that's the first line, this reading will deal with the idea that you can do something if you believe you can. People like Mr. Ford who are really successful are usually hard-working and determined."

6. Have students read the rest of the chapter reading with a partner.

Members of the Great Plains Restoration Council

Although Jarid had to live through difficult times, he grew from a troubled young man into a leader and role model. After spending years learning about efforts to save America's disappearing prairies, becoming healthy, and learning how to lead a **movement** for change, Jarid founded the Great Plains Restoration Council (GPRC).

The Great Plains Restoration Council **restores** prairie ecosystems in Texas and South Dakota with the help of people from different cultures, backgrounds, and communities. The Council works to protect natural prairie areas and the wildlife that live there. GPRC also helps young people to improve their lives by teaching them leadership skills. The Council strives to build healthy spaces and healthy people. Says Jarid, "This is Ecological Heath—healing ourselves through healing the Earth."[3]

Clean Sweep

Kelydra Welcker may be young, but she has already made a huge difference in the world. Kelydra grew up in Parkersburg, West Virginia, near the Ohio River. Parkersburg is home to a chemical plant that produces Teflon®. Teflon is a material used in nonstick pots and pans, among other things.

One of the ingredients used to make Teflon is a chemical called ammonium perfluorooctanoate, or APFO for short. Traces of the chemical have been found in the nearby Ohio River, which supplies drinking water to Parkersburg. When Kelydra was sixteen, people were **debating** the safety of APFO. As it turns out, APFO is a suspected carcinogen, meaning it may cause cancer. At the time, Kelydra feared that it was **toxic**, and started working on a way to remove APFO from water.

After two years of work, Kelydra developed a simple test to detect the presence of APFO in water (it creates foam when you shake it!).

---

movement (n) – an organized effort to accomplish a goal
restores (v) – returns something to its original state
debating (v) – considering or thinking about something
toxic (adj) – able to cause harm or death

She also created a **filtration** device that removes APFO from tap water. You can put water in the filtration device, let it sit overnight, and it will be APFO-free in the morning.

When Kelydra discovered that a potentially toxic substance was in her community's drinking water, she didn't wait for other people to figure out a solution. Instead, she took action and created a solution. Kelydra's filtration device has the potential to improve both the environment and human health. According to Kelydra, "Science isn't just white lab coats and big words, it's taking the brand new discoveries and helping your community, state, and even your country in a way that can be simple, and yet life changing."[4]

Structural Solutions

Jarid and Kelydra made a difference in their personal lives and in the communities around them. Another kind of solution, called a *structural solution,* involves more people and addresses the root cause of a problem. Structural solutions often involve organizations or governments, and they can have a lasting impact on people and places around the world. While a personal solution to hunger might be to give food to people who cannot afford to buy food, a structural solution might be to give people the tools and education they need to grow their own food.

Structural solutions can help solve complex global issues, including poverty. The following story shows how structural solutions can help solve problems in a big way. As you read, try to identify what structural problem is addressed. What are other structural solutions that might also help to solve that problem?

Kelydra Welcker at work in the laboratory

Small Loans, Big Impact

In 1976, an economics professor named Muhammad Yunus was visiting very poor households in Bangladesh, a country in South Asia, when he realized that very small loans could lift people out of poverty. In 1983, Yunus helped found the Grameen Bank to provide loans to poor Bangladeshis. This system of providing very small loans to poor people is now called *microcredit.*[5]

Microcredit is a tool used to break the cycle of poverty. As with any form of credit, borrowers pay back the loaned money, with **interest**. A microcredit borrower might buy materials to open a small store that sells basic household supplies or buy cooking materials to sell snack foods.

Successful microcredit programs improve the economic well-being of whole communities. Women, who receive the majority of these loans, often use their earnings to support their families and community projects such as schools.

---

filtration (n) – the act of moving through a filter, which separates things with a barrier
interest (n) – a fee paid to borrow money

Jill Paull, owner of Island Green Clean

A Green Business

Washington Community Alliance for Self-Help, or CASH, is an organization in the state of Washington. The organization was founded to help people find a way out of poverty through microcredit and job training. To date, they have helped improve the lives of 2,500 people with low incomes. One person who used a small loan from Washington CASH to get her business established is Jill Paull.

A few years ago, Jill was working as a house-keeper at a hotel. The cleaning products that she was using were making her sick, and she wasn't earning enough money to take care of her children. In January 2006, Jill joined the Washington CASH program.

She began making and selling her own *eco-friendly* cleaning products. Her products are made with natural ingredients like baking soda, lavender, and tea tree oil. "It actually is the

coolest thing I have ever done," she exclaimed, "and it sells! I make up my own organic cleaner and people call because of that."

Said Jill, "I remember starting out with $5 in my business bank account. Now I make a **deposit** every day. Washington CASH has been a big help in getting my business started." She has paid back her first $500 loan. "I plan on growing and going for another loan. And I'll be hiring two people in January. Right now I am figuring out my taxes!"[6]

The Solution Is You

All solutions, whether personal or structural, involve citizens like you. You can take part in both personal and structural solutions. Is there a problem you'd like to solve? How can you help?

---

deposit (n) – money placed in a bank

> **What are *green* or *eco-friendly* products?**
>
> The word *green* is often used to describe products that have a lower environmental impact than other products. For example, green tissue paper might be made from recycled, non-bleached paper.
>
> *Eco-friendly* is another term used to describe products that have a reduced environmental impact.
>
> **Buyer Beware:** Not all products that claim to be green or eco-friendly really are! Some companies use those terms just to persuade you to buy their products.

Reading Skill Follow-up: Character Traits

Directions: Identify at least one character trait for the following people. Identify evidence from the reading that supports this character trait.

Person	Character Trait	Evidence from Reading (at least two examples for each person)
Jarid Manos		
Kelydra Welcker		
Jill Paull		

Instructions

1. After students have finished reading, have them identify character traits for each person featured in the reading.

2. **Additional Resources:** Allow students to learn more about the people and solutions featured in the chapter reading.

   - See what students and other community members are doing with the Great Plains Restoration Council: www.gprc.org

   - View a 2-minute documentary about Kelydra Welcker's work, which received a 2007 Popular Mechanics Breakthrough Award: www.popularmechanics.com/breakthrough07/

   - See the products that Jill Paull has created: http://islandgreenclean.com

   - Learn more about micro-credit through Washington CASH: www.washingtoncash.org

Answers

Person	Character Trait	Evidence from Reading (at least two examples for each person)
Jarid Manos	courageous	• He spent years learning how to take care of the prairie and himself. • He did not let past troubles prevent him from creating a better future.
Kelydra Welcker	hard-working	• While others were talking about the problem, she was working to solve it. • She kept working on the solution for two years.
Jill Paull	enthusiastic	• She is very excited about making money by owning a business. • She thinks that the work she does is cool.

Comprehension Questions

Instructions

1. Before students begin answering the comprehension questions, share with them the academic language they will see in many of the questions (see Appendix B).

2. Explain that the questions are divided into five sections according to the different ways they support comprehension. (See Appendix B for a detailed explanation of each section.)

3. **Differentiated Instruction:** Differentiate the questions students must answer based on their reading levels. Support comprehension by working with students who may need more guided instruction.

Directions: Answer the following questions to support your comprehension of the chapter reading.

Understanding what you read

1. Why did Kelydra create a filtration device?

2. When Jill Paull was working as a housekeeper in a hotel, what did she realize about the cleaning products she used?

Thinking about what you read

3. Explain how the Great Plains Restoration Council is working to develop healthy spaces and healthy people.

4. Kelydra Welcker said that a simple solution could be life-changing. How can her water filtration device be considered simple yet life-changing?

5. How is microcredit different than giving people food so they won't be hungry?

Questioning what you read

6. Identify the author's purpose in writing this chapter reading.

Making connections to what you read

7. Do you relate to any of these stories? Why or why not?

8. What character traits do you have now that can help you start making a difference in your life and creating a sustainable future?

Further discussion questions

9. In previous chapters, you read about issues that affect people all over the world, including poverty, population growth, environmental damage, and conflict. Which of these problems do you think is most urgent, and why?

10. What is a personal solution to the problem you identified? What is a structural solution to that problem? How could you be part of one of those solutions?

Answers

1. There were possible toxic substances in her community's drinking water.

2. The cleaning products were making her sick.

3. The Council develops healthy spaces by restoring prairie ecosystems. The Council develops healthy people by providing people with opportunities to work together and develop leadership skills.

4. The solution is simple because anyone can use her filtration device to purify water overnight. It is life-changing because people can reduce their chances of developing serious illnesses like cancer.

5. With microcredit, people can start businesses and learn to take care of themselves instead of depending on others to give them what they need.

6. The author wrote this chapter reading to explain how personal and structural solutions can make a difference in the world.

7. Answers will vary.

8. e.g., motivation, patience, determination, compassion

9. Answers will vary.

10. Example: A personal solution to poverty is donating food to a local food bank. A structural solution is a city providing more job training for people so they can find employment.

Writing about Sustainable Solutions: A Letter

Think about the world you want to live in thirty years from now. What would your ideal world look like?

- What do you want your community (your family, neighborhood, or city) to be like?
- What do you want the environment to be like?
- What kind of job do you want to have?

Now, think of the things you need to do to create the vision of the future you just imagined.

Directions: In a letter to yourself, you will describe what you want your community, environment, and job to be like. You will also explain the things you need to do to make sure your vision of the future becomes a reality. This letter will help guide you toward your vision of the future.

Instructions

1. Students will write a letter to themselves describing an ideal future for themselves and the world around them. Students can use this letter to support their work toward the future they envision and to measure progress toward their goals.

2. Read through the questions and the assignment with students.

Citizens work to improve a school community by building benches using recycled wood from old desks.

Instructions

1. Read the sample letter aloud to the class or ask a volunteer to read it aloud.

2. Ask students the following questions: How does the letter begin? What information is included in the body of the letter? How does the letter end?

3. Let them know that their letter will be written in a similar format.

March 9, 2010

Dear Juana,

After reading about sustainability, I started to think about the world I want to live in thirty years from now. I understand that my vision is going to take some work, but it will pay off in the end. I'm writing this letter to tell you about my vision and the ways I'm going to turn my vision into a reality.

First, I want my community to be built for people rather than cars. Right now I have to drive to see my friends because my neighborhood does not have sidewalks for walking. I can ask my neighbors to sign a petition for the city to build sidewalks in our neighborhood. Also, I would like there to be more places for me and my friends to play sports and spend time outdoors. I need to contact our city council to convince them to build more parks. I could also organize more outdoor community events, like picnics and basketball tournaments.

Second, I want the environment to be like it is now, but a little cleaner. I am concerned about the litter I see. People in my community sometimes throw their trash in the street instead of putting it in a garbage can. I think the area where I live is beautiful, but I wish there was less litter. I can join the Adopt-A-Street program to help clean up our neighborhood. I can also work with local environmental organizations to help educate people about the importance of keeping our environment clean. I learned in school that birds try to eat trash and plastic bags, which kills them. Maybe I can convince people not to litter by sharing this information.

Finally, I want to be a restaurant owner in thirty years. In order for this to happen, I need to make sure that I learn how to run a business. I like to cook, but I would like to learn how to cook more things. I want to own a Mexican restaurant that serves food like my family ate in Mexico. Most Mexican restaurants in my town don't serve food like we ate in Mexico. I want to share my culture with people. I think they would love my delicious family recipes! I need to write down my favorite family recipes so that I will always have them. Maybe someday I will even write a cookbook. I also need to start saving money so that I can go to cooking school and take some business classes.

As you can see, I have many hopes and dreams for the future. I know I will need to be determined to fulfill these dreams. Thinking about how I want the world and my life to look in the future will help me to make it happen!

Sincerely,

Juana Cortes Ramirez

Writing Steps: A Letter

Step 1: Brainstorm ideas on the Writing Brainstorm Page (see next page).

Step 2: Write a letter to yourself about what you hope the world will look like in thirty years. Use the Writing Organizer to write the rough draft of this letter.

Step 3: Edit your letter using the Edit Checklist below.

Step 4: Have a classmate read and edit your letter using the Edit Checklist.

Step 5: Rewrite the letter based on the edits. Then, sign it and put it in a safe place!

You may want to keep the letter somewhere that you can see it every day, or you may want to tuck it away somewhere safe and reread it in a few years. Either way, make sure you reread the letter in the future to check your progress on creating the future you want.

 Edit Checklist

	Author Check	Peer Editor Check
Did you write a paragraph about what you want your community to be like in thirty years?		
Did you write a paragraph about what you want the environment to be like in thirty years?		
Did you write a paragraph about what you want your job to be like in thirty years?		
Did you write in a letter format?		
Did you include at least two vocabulary words from the chapter?		

Instructions

1. Read through the writing steps with students.

2. **Grammar Suggestion:** Since students will write a friendly letter to themselves, teach them how to use transitions and coordinating conjunctions (i.e., however, on the other hand, but, yet) to contrast things. This skill can help them to contrast things between the present and the future. (Example: *The environment is not as clean as it should be;* **however,** *I can convince people that a clean environment will be good for our community.*)

3. Share the Chapter 9 writing rubric with students. You may want to add relevant spelling and grammar components to the rubric.

Chapter 9 Writing Rubric

Category	3	2	1
Content	Letter informs the reader about how the author wants his/her community, environment, and job to be like in thirty years	Letter partially informs the reader about how the author wants his/her community, environment, and/or job to be like in thirty years	Letter does not inform the reader about how the author wants his/her community, environment, and/or job to be like in thirty years
Vocabulary	Uses two or more chapter vocabulary words correctly	Uses one chapter vocabulary word correctly	Does not attempt to use chapter vocabulary
Organization	Uses letter format correctly	Attempts to use letter format	Does not write a complete letter

Total = _____ / 9

Writing Brainstorm Page: A Letter

Instructions

1. Students can use this page to brainstorm ideas and collect their thoughts.

   • **Differentiated Instruction:** If students need extra help, work through this page as a class. Together, brainstorm different possibilities for community, environment, and career.

In thirty years, what do you want your community, environment, and job to be like?

A. Your community:

How will you make sure this happens?

a.

b.

c.

B. The environment:

How will you make sure this happens?

a.

b.

c.

C. Your job:

How will you make sure this happens?

a.

b.

c.

_____ (date)

Dear _____ (your name),

After reading about sustainability, I started to think about the world I want to live in thirty years from now. I understand that my vision is going to take some work, but it will pay off in the end. I'm writing this letter to tell you about my vision and the ways I'm going to turn my vision into a reality.

First, I want my community to... _____
_____

In order for this to happen, I need to... _____
_____
_____

Second, I want the environment... _____
_____

Therefore, I need to..._____
_____
_____

Finally, I want to be a _____ (occupation)
in thirty years. In order for this to happen, I need to make sure that I...
_____
_____

As you can see, I have many hopes and dreams for the future. I know I will need to be _____ (character trait) in order to fulfill these dreams. Thinking about how I want the world and my life to look in the future will help me to make it happen!

Sincerely,

_____ (your name)

Instructions

1. Students can use the template provided to write their letters.

   • **Differentiated Instruction:** For beginning students who may need more guidance, work with them in a small group and assist them in writing their letters. Provide a number of ideas for them to choose from to write each paragraph.

2. **Option:** Have each student create a collage or drawing that represents how he/she wants his/her life and the world to be thirty years from now. Students can use this representation to generate ideas for writing their letters.

3. **Option:** Use letters to create a time capsule that students can reopen at their high school graduation or a reunion.

Instructions

1. The crossword includes all the words from Chapter 9, plus one to two words from each of the other chapters in this book. Students may need to review different chapters to remind them what the words mean.

2. Allow them time to work on the crossword either independently or in pairs.

3. Review answers with students.

Vocabulary Challenge

Directions: You have read about many different topics in this textbook, and you've learned a lot of new vocabulary words. Read the clues below and fill in the answers in the crossword. Some of the words are chapter vocabulary words. Others are words you have seen throughout this textbook.

ACROSS

1. A group of people who have shared interests
4. The state of being poor and living without necessary resources
5. The ability of people to take care of needs now and for future generations
6. A person who is a member of a community, state, or nation
13. Substances that contaminate the air, water and soil
14. The area of land and water required to support a certain lifestyle
16. An organization that makes and enforces laws for a community, state, or nation

DOWN

2. The movement of people from one place to another
3. An attempt to solve the root cause of a problem, usually with the help of many people
7. An individual person's attempt to solve a problem
8. The well-being of an individual
9. The use of resources and products
10. The variety of plants, animals, and other living things in an ecosystem
11. The behaviors, traditions, art, and lifestyle that define a group of people
12. The total number of people who live in an area
15. A fight or struggle

Answers

Across

1. community
4. poverty
5. sustainability
6. citizen
13. pollution
14. ecological/footprint (no space)
16. government

Down

2. migration
3. structural/solution (no space)
7. personal/solution (no space)
8. quality/of/life (no spaces)
9. consumption
10. biodiversity
11. culture
12. population
15. conflict

Culminating Activity: Creating Our Future
(1.5 hours, plus additional class time for implementing an action plan)

Overview

Using an action-planning model, students visualize their desired future, identify objectives, develop a plan to address local and global issues, and implement their vision through action and service learning.

Materials/Preparation

- *Action Planning Worksheet*, one per group of 3-4 students, and make an overhead to display
- Butcher paper, one sheet per group
- Colored marking pens, one set per group

Introduction

1. Ask students how old they will be thirty years from now.

2. Ask students what they **think** the world will look like thirty years from now, based on trends they see now. Have a couple of volunteers briefly describe the future as if it were a picture (they may paint a picture of environmental, social, and economic destruction).

3. Now ask them what they **want** the world to look like in thirty years for themselves and for future generations. (Note: You may need to define the difference between *think* and *want* for this part of the activity.) Ask them to describe what they will see, hear, smell, taste, and touch.

4. Ask, *If this is the future we want, how do we make it happen?* Explain that in order to create a world we want for ourselves and for future generations, we need to first envision what we want and then create a plan of action. This activity provides a model for doing just that.

Steps

1. Explain that, in order to help them focus their vision of the future, they could think about specific quality of life issues that are important to them. Brainstorm and list quality of life issues.

   - Quality of life issues may include: food, water, housing, energy, employment, transportation, education, environment, security, health care, elder care, child care, recreation, spirituality/religion, arts/entertainment

2. Explain that they will develop an action plan to address one of the quality of life issues in the list (such as food, water, health care, the environment, etc.) using a model called an *Action Planning Sequence.* Through this process, they will assess how the issue affects both local and global communities, and develop a plan to address the **structural** causes of the issue.

3. Give each student an *Action Planning Worksheet*, and display an overhead of the same worksheet.

4. Explain each step of the action planning process to the students, using the overhead as a guide.

5. Divide the class into groups of 3-4 students each. Assign or have each group choose a topic from the list of quality of life issues. Give each group a piece of butcher paper and pens.

6. Give them about 30 minutes to complete the steps outlined in the handout. They should begin by discussing and agreeing upon a shared vision. Circulate through the room and assist students as they are working.

7. After they complete the handout, have each group transfer the information to a piece of butcher paper. Encourage them to include pictures, graphs, quotes, etc. They do not need to rewrite everything from their handout; they can just write or illustrate the main ideas.

8. Have each group present their displays to the class.

9. Bring the class back together for the following reflection questions:

   - Why is describing what you want your future to look like an important step in creating the future you want?
   - Did the action planning sequence process work? How could the process be improved?
   - What will you do next to implement your plan?

Creating Our Future
Action Planning Worksheet, page 1

Group members: _____
_____

Issue we are focusing on: _____

Scope of the Issue

Who or what is currently being affected by this issue?

_____

How does this issue affect our local community?

_____

How does this issue affect our global community?

_____

Visualize Your Ideal Outcome

What is your ideal outcome for this issue? Brainstorm, discuss, and write a
summary (short statement) of the outcome you want.

Hint: *Think of your ideal outcome as something positive (what you want) instead of
something negative (what you don't want). For example, instead of saying you do
not want people to use fossil fuels like gasoline, you could say you **want** people to use
renewable fuels like wind and solar energy.*

_____

_____

_____

_____

_____

Creating Our Future
Action Planning Worksheet, page 2

Work Together

What is already being done about this issue? Brainstorm, discuss, and list at least three people or organizations that are working on solutions to this issue.

1. _____
2. _____
3. _____

Identify Objectives

What are some specific ways that your vision can become reality? For example, if your vision is *full access to health care for all people,* then the objectives might be more doctors per person, more clinics in poor neighborhoods, or more health education in schools. List and discuss three objectives that will help to make your vision a reality.

1. _____
2. _____
3. _____

Identify Resources

What resources will you need to get your vision going? Do you need information, money, time, or something else? How will you use these resources? Discuss and list information, resources, and other help you will need to realize your vision.

1. _____
2. _____
3. _____

Get to Work

What steps will you take to start working on your vision? Who will be responsible for beginning each step? List the steps you will take to begin working toward your vision.

_____

_____

_____

Art Extension

Have students create a mural that depicts their collective vision of the future, either at the school or as part of a local community development project.

Action Projects

- Have the class choose one topic, refine the action plan for that topic, and complete a service learning project that addresses the issue.

- Have the class develop an action project database of local opportunities for youth by researching issues, identifying and contacting organizations, and publishing the information on a website or as a "yellow pages" resource.

Additional Resources on Sustainable Solutions

Pay It Forward

In this film, a young boy attempts to make the world a better place after his teacher gives him the opportunity. (123 minutes, directed by Mimi Leder)

The Complete Guide to Service Learning,
by Cathryn Berger Kaye

This guide provides a wealth of activities, ideas, and resources to encourage service learning in K-12 and higher education.

The Kid's Guide to Social Action,
by Barbara A. Lewis

This book includes everything kids need to make a difference in the world: step-by-step directions for writing letters, conducting interviews, raising funds, getting media coverage, and more.

Facing the Future
www.facingthefuture.org

Facing the Future's website includes a variety of service learning resources, such as an action project database, loads of *Fast Facts & Quick Action* ideas, and examples of students taking action. The website also includes information and research on service learning, and a framework for developing service learning projects in your classroom.

The National Youth Leadership Council
www.nylc.org

The National Youth Leadership Council seeks to create a more just, sustainable, and peaceful world with young people, their schools, and their communities through service learning. They have a service-learning resource library and host an annual service-learning conference.

Chapter 9 Student Assessment, page 1
Knowledge about Creating Our Future

Vocabulary

Directions: Read each sentence and circle the letter next to the correct definition of the **bold-faced** word.

1. A **citizen** of the United States of America has the right to practice any religion.

   a. a person who is a member of a community, state, or nation

   b. an individual member of a religious organization

   c. a group of people who live by shared laws

   d. a religious or spiritual leader

2. In a democratic **government**, ordinary citizens take part in governing a country, often through voting.

   a. a type of organization that makes money through the sale of goods and services

   b. a group of citizens that enforce a city's rules and laws

   c. an official organization that makes and enforces laws for a community, state, or region

   d. a group of businesses that rely on input from individuals

3. Julie's **personal solution** to help end hunger is to donate food to a local homeless shelter.

   a. a solution to a problem that requires everyone to agree

   b. a solution to a problem that takes a very long time to complete

   c. a solution to a problem that involves changing a large system

   d. a solution to a problem whereby an individual attempts to solve the problem

4. A **structural solution** to help end hunger is to help people who are unemployed find jobs.

   a. a solution to a problem that requires everyone to agree

   b. a solution to a problem that takes a very long time to complete

   c. a solution to a problem that involves changing a system

   d. a solution to a problem whereby an individual attempts to solve the problem

Chapter 9 Student Assessment, page 2

Content

Directions: Read each sentence and circle the letter next to the correct answer.

5. A law that would make elementary education available to all citizens would be considered a(n) _____ to poverty.
   a. personal solution
   b. structural solution
   c. individual solution
   d. unusual solution

6. Microcredit is the practice of _____.
   a. making short movies
   b. loaning people small amounts of money
   c. building houses for homeless people
   d. giving people the benefit of the doubt

Reading Comprehension

Directions: Read the examples below and determine the character traits of these two people.

7. Steve always wants to help others. He helps younger kids in his neighborhood with their homework and volunteers every month to clean up the local playground. Last year he gave $25 to his favorite charity. Steve's friends all say that he is _____.
   a. stingy
   b. smart
   c. strong
   d. generous

8. Nicole grew up knowing she wanted to be a doctor. She saw many people where she lived develop major health issues, and she wanted to help them. She studied hard in school, went to college, and worked two jobs to pay her way through medical school. Nicole's mother always says she is _____.
   a. lazy
   b. motivated
   c. cynical
   d. cheerful

Chapter 9 Student Assessment, page 3
Outlook and Personal Beliefs

Answer the following questions based on your personal beliefs. There are no right or wrong answers.

Directions for 1-3: Circle the answer(s) you believe to be true for you.

1. When you think about problems in the world, how do you feel?

   a. I don't care.
   b. I feel like there's nothing I can do.
   c. I want to help solve those problems.
   d. none of the above

2. Which of the following personal solutions describe your everyday actions? (**Circle all that apply.**)

   a. I reuse items if possible and eventually recycle them.
   b. I use less energy by unplugging appliances, turning off lights, or using less heat and air conditioning.
   c. I participate in environmental clean-ups.
   d. I work to understand different points of view from different cultures.
   e. I consider how things I buy might impact other people.
   f. I spend time with people in my community, including my family and neighbors.
   g. I eat locally grown food whenever possible.
   h. I call or write to a government leader when I want him or her to vote for a law that is important to me.
   i. I think about my life in the future—how many kids I want, how I want to live, or what type of job I want.
   j. I volunteer with a group trying to improve the community.
   k. I learn about what is happening around the world.

3. *True or False:* Structural solutions are too big for me to be part of them.

   a. True
   b. False

4. **Complete the following sentence:**
   One way I can personally work on the issue of sustainability is by…

   _____

   _____

   _____

   _____

Directions for 5 and 6: For each statement, fill in the oval based on your level of agreement. 1 means you strongly agree, and 7 means you strongly disagree.

1 = yes, definitely!   7 = no way!
⟵——————————————————⟶

5. I believe my daily actions have an impact on people and places in other parts of the world.

6. I believe I have the ability to help solve community and global issues.

A Select National Education Standards Addressed in the Text

The chapters in this text have been aligned with the following national learning standards.

In addition, the chapters have been aligned with a number of state English Language Arts and English Language Development standards. To view these alignments, visit www.facingthefuture.org.

National Council for the Social Studies (NCSS) Standards

Strand 1—Culture
Strand 2—Time, Continuity, and Change
Strand 3—People, Places, and Environments
Strand 4—Individual Development and Identity
Strand 5—Individuals, Groups, and Institutions
Strand 6—Power, Authority, and Governance
Strand 7—Production, Distribution, and Consumption
Strand 8—Science, Technology, and Society
Strand 9—Global Connections
Strand 10—Civic Ideals and Practices

National Science Education Standards (NSES)

Content Standard A—Science as Inquiry
Content Standard B—Physical Science
Content Standard C—Life Science
Content Standard D—Earth and Space Science
Content Standard E—Science and Technology
Content Standard F—Science in Personal and Social Perspectives

International Reading Association (IRA)/ National Council of Teachers of English (NCTE) Standards for the English Language Arts

1. Students read a wide range of print and nonprint texts to build an understanding of texts, of themselves, and of the cultures of the United States and the world; to acquire new information; to respond to the needs and demands of society and the workplace; and for personal fulfillment. Among these texts are fiction and nonfiction, classic and contemporary works.

3. Students apply a wide range of strategies to comprehend, interpret, evaluate, and appreciate texts. They draw on their prior experience, their interactions with other readers and writers, their knowledge of word meaning and of other texts, their word identification strategies, and their understanding of textual features (e.g., sound-letter correspondence, sentence structure, context, graphics).

4. Students adjust their use of spoken, written, and visual language (e.g., conventions, style, vocabulary) to communicate effectively with a variety of audiences and for different purposes.

5. Students employ a wide range of strategies as they write and use different writing process elements appropriately to communicate with different audiences for a variety of purposes.

11. Students participate as knowledgeable, reflective, creative, and critical members of a variety of literacy communities.

12. Students use spoken, written, and visual language to accomplish their own purposes (e.g., for learning, enjoyment, persuasion, and the exchange of information).

Teachers of English to Speakers of Other Languages (TESOL) Standards, grades 4-8

Goal 2, Standard 1: To use English to achieve academically in all content areas: Students will use English to interact in the classroom

Goal 2, Standard 2: To use English to achieve academically in all content areas: Students will use English to obtain, process, construct, and provide subject matter information in spoken and written form

Goal 2, Standard 3: To use English to achieve academically in all content areas: Students will use appropriate learning strategies to construct and apply academic knowledge

Select National Standards Addressed by Chapter

	NCSS	NSES	NCTE/IRA	TESOL
Chapter 1	1, 3, 4, 7, 8, 9, 10	A, C, E, F	1, 3, 4, 5, 11, 12	Goal 2, Standards 1 - 3
Chapter 2	3, 8, 9	C, D, F	1, 3, 4, 5, 11, 12	Goal 2, Standards 1 - 3
Chapter 3	2, 3, 7, 8, 9	A, B, C, D, F	1, 3, 4, 5, 11, 12	Goal 2, Standards 1 - 3
Chapter 4	1, 4, 7, 8, 9	C, F	1, 3, 4, 5, 11, 12	Goal 2, Standards 1 - 3
Chapter 5	2, 3, 7, 9	C, F	1, 3, 4, 5, 11, 12	Goal 2, Standards 1 - 3
Chapter 6	1, 2, 3, 4, 9, 10	C, F	1, 3, 4, 5, 11, 12	Goal 2, Standards 1 - 3
Chapter 7	1, 2, 3, 5, 6, 7, 9, 10	F	1, 3, 4, 5, 11, 12	Goal 2, Standards 1 - 3
Chapter 8	1, 3, 4, 5, 10	F	1, 3, 4, 5, 11, 12	Goal 2, Standards 1 - 3
Chapter 9	1, 3, 4, 5, 10	A, F	1, 3, 4, 5, 11, 12	Goal 2, Standards 1 - 3

Reading Comprehension Support Materials

Academic Vocabulary

In an effort to support student increase in knowledge of academic words, a variety of words from the Academic Word List [1] have been used in the comprehension questions and in directions throughout the text. You can review these words with students to support student learning. You can also create an academic word wall to further enhance comprehension.

---

analyze (v) – to examine critically, so as to bring out the essential elements or give the essence of

compare (v) – to examine in order to note the similarities or differences of

consider (v) – to think carefully about

context (n) – part of a text or statement that surrounds a particular word or passage and determines its meaning

create (v) – to cause to exist; to produce

define (v) – to state the meaning of

determine (v) – to conclude or ascertain, as after reasoning and observation

evaluate (v) – to examine and judge carefully

evidence (n) – ground for belief; proof

identify (v) – to recognize or establish as being a particular person or thing

respond (v) – to reply or answer

Comprehension Questions: Sections

Understanding what you read – answers can be found directly in the text

Thinking about what you read – reader has to think about the meaning and use evidence from the text to support his or her answer

Questioning what you read – reader has to question the intentions of the author and his or her reasons for choosing to write about a certain topic, use a certain style, or include a certain story

Making connections about what you read – reader has to make connections to his or her own life

Further discussion questions – reader has to use higher-level thinking skills to analyze answers

---

1 Averil Coxhead, "A New Academic Word List," *TESOL Quarterly*, 34(2), 213-238.

Endnotes

Chapter 1

Student Pages

1 Global Campaign for Education, "Why Education for All?" www.campaignforeducation.org.

2 Global Youth Action Network, "Active Programs," www.youthlink.org/gyanv5/programs.htm and Global Youth Service Day, "About Global Youth Service Day," http://gysd.org/about (accessed January 11, 2010).

Teacher Instructions

1 Echevarría, Jana, MaryEllen Vogt, and Deborah J. Short. 2008. *Making Content Comprehensible for English Learners: The SIOP® Model*. 3rd ed. Boston: Pearson Education.

Chapter 2

Student Pages

1 Mark Lester R. Brown, Plan B 3.0: *Mobilizing to Save Civilization* (New York: W. W. Norton & Co., 2008), 102.

2 Janet Larsen, "The Sixth Great Extinction: A Status Report," *Earth Policy Institute*, March 2, 2004, http://www.earth-policy.org/Updates/Update35.htm.

3 E. O. Wilson, *The Diversity of Life* (New York: W. W. Norton & Co., 1999), 280.

4 Lester R. Brown, Plan B 3.0: *Mobilizing to Save Civilization* (New York: W. W. Norton & Co., 2008), 101.

5 NOAA (National Oceanic and Atmospheric Administration), "Ocean," http://www.noaa.gov/ocean.html (accessed January 10, 2010).

6 Monterey Bay Aquarium, "Wild Seafood: Plenty of Fish in the Sea?" http://www.monterey bayaquarium.org/cr/cr_seafoodwatch/issues/wildseafood.aspx (accessed January 10, 2010).

Teacher Instructions

Chapter 2 Student Assessment

National Coffee Association of U.S.A., Inc., "National Coffee Drinking Trends 2009," http://www.ncausa.org/custom/headlines/headlinedetails.cfm?id=667&returnto=171 (accessed January 12, 2010).

Grounds for Change, "Shade Grown Coffee," http://www.groundsforchange.com/learn/shadegrown.php (accessed January 12, 2010).

Chapter 3

Student Pages

1 World Wildlife Fund, "Climate Witness: Ben Namakin, Kiribati and Micronesia," May 7, 2007, http://www.panda.org/about_our_earth/aboutcc/problems/people_at_risk/personal_stories/witness_stories/?uNewsID=100800 (accessed January 10, 2010).

2 Intergovernmental Panel on Climate Change (IPCC), "Summary for Policymakers," in *Climate Change 2007: The Physical Science Basis*, S. Solomon, D. Qin, M. Manning, Z. Chen, M. Marquis, K.B. Averyt, M.Tignor, and H.L. Miller, eds. (Cambridge, UK: Cambridge University Press, 2007).

3 World Wildlife Fund, "Climate Witness: Nelly Damaris Chepkoskei, Kenya," November 16, 2006, http://www.panda.org/about_our_earth/aboutcc/problems/people_at_risk/personal_stories/witness_stories/?uNewsID=86060 (accessed January 10, 2010).

4 Center for International Forestry Research, "Forests and Biodiversity," http://www.cifor.cgiar.org/Publications/Corporate/FactSheet/forests_biodiversity.htm (accessed January 10, 2010).

5 FAO, "Global Forest Resources Assessment 2005," www.fao.org/forestry/fra/fra2005/en (accessed January 10, 2010).

6   Joe Pouliot, "Reducing Deforestation is Key to Addressing Climate Change, WWF Official Tells Congress," WWF Press Release, April 22, 2008, http://www.worldwildlife.org/who/media/press/2008/WWFPresitem8733.html.

7   World Wildlife Fund, "Climate Witness: Gung Qiu Lai Jia, China," July 6, 2008, http://panda.org/about_our_earth/aboutcc/problems/people_at_risk/personal_stories/witness_stories/?uNewsID=139801 (accessed January 10, 2010).

8   M. Boko, I. Niang, A. Nyong, C. Vogel, A. Githeko, M. Medany, B. Osman-Elasha, R. Tabo, and P. Yanda, "Africa," in *Climate Change 2007: Impacts, Adaptation and Vulnerability*, eds. M.L. Parry, O.F. Canziani, J.P. Palutikof, P.J. van der Linden and C.E. Hanson, 433-467 (Cambridge, UK: Cambridge University Press, 2007).

9   B.C. Bates, Z.W. Kundzewicz, S. Wu, and J.P. Palutikof, eds. "Technical Paper on Climate Change and Water," 16 (Geneva: IPCC Secretariat, 2008).

10 World Wildlife Fund, "Climate Witness: Gung Qiu Lai Jia, China," July 6, 2008, http://panda.org/about_our_earth/aboutcc/problems/people_at_risk/personal_stories/witness_stories/?uNewsID=139801.

11 Bates et al, 2008, 8.

12 WorldWatch Institute, *State of the World 2004* (New York: W. W. Norton & Co., 2004), 54.

13 United States Environmental Protection Agency (EPA), "Municipal Solid Waste Generation, Recycling, and Disposal in the United States: Facts and Figures for 2008."

14 Brian Halweil, "Plastic Bags," in *Good Stuff? A Behind-the-Scenes Guide to the Things We Buy* (Washington, DC: Worldwatch Institute, 2004), http://www.worldwatch.org/node/1499 (accessed January 11, 2010).

15 Elizabeth Royte, *Garbage Land: On the Secret Trail of Trash* (New York: Back Bay Books, 2005), 75.

16 Environmental Literacy Council, "Paper or Plastic?" http://www.enviroliteracy.org/article.php/1268.html (accessed January 11, 2010).

Teacher Instructions

1   John C. Ryan and Alan Thein Durning, *Stuff: The Secret Lives of Everyday Things* (Seattle: Sightline Institute, 1997), 55.

2   Sightline Institute, "Carbon Dioxide Emissions Per Mile Traveled," http://www.sightline.org/maps/charts/pollu_co2transp_ooh (accessed January 10, 2010).

3   Water Footprint Network, "Product Gallery: Cotton," http://www.waterfootprint.org/?page=files/productgallery&product=cotton (accessed January 10, 2010).

Chapter 3 Student Assessment

Michael Renner, "Vehicle Production Continues to Expand," in *Vital Signs* (New York: W. W. Norton & Co., 2006), 64-65.

International Development Research Center, "Taking Control of Air Pollution in Mexico City," http://www.idrc.ca/in_focus_health/ev-29135-201-1-DO_TOPIC.html (accessed January 12, 2010).

Chapter 4

Student Pages

1   Mark Brower Youth Awards, "Jessica Assaf," http://broweryouthawards.org/userdata_display.php?modin=50&uid=101 (accessed November 2, 2009).

2   Anup Shah, "Children as Consumers," http://www.globalissues.org/article/237/children-as-consumers/ (accessed November 15, 2009).

3   United Nations Development Programme (UNDP), *Human Development Report 1998* (New York: Oxford University Press, 1998). Also available online at http://hdr.undp.org/en/reports/global/hdr1998/ (accessed December 22, 2009).

Endnotes, *continued*

4 Nike, "ReUSE A SHOE," http://www.nikereuseashoe.com (accessed September 1, 2009).

Consumption Match-up Cards

Jeans:
- Levi Strauss & Co., "History of the Levi's® 501® Jeans," http://www.levistrauss.com/Downloads/history_of_levis_501_jeans.pdf (accessed March 27, 2009).
- *China Blue*, DVD, directed by Micha Peled (San Francisco, CA: Teddy Bear Films and the Independent Television Service, 2005). http://www.pbs.org/independentlens/chinablue/ (accessed March 29, 2007).

Hamburger:
- Sean Alfano, "Big Mac Hits the Big 4-0," CBS News, August 24, 2007, http://www.cbsnews.com/stories/2007/08/24/business/main3200598.shtml?source=RSSattr=Business_3200598 (accessed December 22, 2009).
- John C. Ryan and Alan Thein Durning, *Stuff: The Secret Lives of Everyday Things* (Seattle: Northwest Environment Watch, 1997), 55.

Cola:
- The Coca-Cola Company, "The Chronicle of Coca-Cola: A Global Business," http://www.thecocacolacompany.com/heritage/chronicle_global_business.html (accessed March 27, 2009).

Chocolate:
- Chris Bright, "Chocolate," in *Good Stuff?: A Behind-the-Scenes Guide to the Things We Buy* (Washington, DC: Worldwatch Institute, 2004), http://www.worldwatch.org/node/1483 (accessed December 22, 2009).

Car:
- Library of Congress, "Everyday Mysteries," http://www.loc.gov/rr/scitech/mysteries/auto.html (accessed August 31, 2009).
- U.S. Department of Energy and U.S. Environmental Protection Agency, "How can a gallon of gasoline produce 20 pounds of carbon dioxide?" http://www.fueleconomy.gov/Feg/co2.shtml (accessed August 31, 2009).

Gold:
- Brook Larmer, "The Real Price of Gold," *National Geographic*, January 2009, 34-61.

CDs:
- Agence France-Presse, "More Americans buy music online, fewer buy CDs," The Age, March 18, 2009, http://news.theage.com.au/breaking-news-technology/more-americans-buy-music-online-fewer-buy-cds-20090318-9162.html (accessed December 22, 2009).
- U.S. Environmental Protection Agency Office of Solid Waste and Emergency Response, 2003. "The Life Cycle of a CD or DVD." Educational poster. http://www.epa.gov/osw/education/pdfs/finalposter.pdf (accessed March 29, 2009).

Cell phone:
- Alon Avdi, "1.1 Billion Cell Phones Sold Worldwide In 2007, Says Study," *Switched*, January 25, 2008, http://www.switched.com/2008/01/25/1-1-billion-cell-phones-sold-worldwide-in-2007-says-study/ (accessed December 22, 2009).
- Chris Carroll, "High-Tech Trash," *National Geographic*, January 2008, 64-81.

Cardboard box:
- Dave Tilford, "Paper," in *Good Stuff?: A Behind-the-Scenes Guide to the Things We Buy* (Washington, DC: Worldwatch Institute, 2004), http://www.worldwatch.org/node/1497 (accessed December 22, 2009).

Teacher's Guide

1 Worldwatch Institute, "Richer, Fatter, and Not Much Happier," in *State of the World 2004* (Washington, DC: Worldwatch Institute, 2004). Also available online at http://www.worldwatch.org/node/1785.

2 TNS Media Intelligence, "TNS Media Intelligence Reports U.S. Advertising Expenditures Grew 0.2 Percent in 2007," March 25, 2008, http://www.tns-mi.com/news/03252008.htm.

3 American Academy of Pediatrics Committee on Communications, "Children, Adolescents, and Advertising," *Pediatrics* 118 (2006), http://aappolicy.aappublications.org/cgi/content/full/pediatrics;118/6/2563.

Are You Buying This?! Consequence Cards

Mega Burger:

- John C. Ryan and Alan Thein Durning, *Stuff: The Secret Lives of Everyday Things* (Seattle: Northwest Environment Watch, 1997), 55.

- National Center for Health Statistics, "Prevalence of Overweight Among Children and Adolescents: United States, 2003-2004," April 2006, http://www.cdc.gov/nchs/data/hestat/overweight/overwght_child_03.htm (accessed January 10, 2010).

- American Diabetes Association, "Diabetes Statistics," http://www.diabetes.org/diabetes-basics/diabetes-statistics/ (accessed January 11, 2010).

Pine Valley Estates:

- American Farmland Trust, "Farming on the Edge Report," http://www.farmland.org/resources/fote/default.asp (accessed January 10, 2010).

Super Clean Car Wash Foam:

- Maryland Department of the Environment, "Water Conservation and Washing Vehicles," http://www.mde.state.md.us/Programs/WaterPrograms/Water_Conservation/Household_Tips/carwashing.asp (accessed January 11, 2010).

Handi-Lunches:

- U.S. Environmental Protection Agency, "Municipal Solid Waste Generation, Recycling, and Disposal in the United States: Facts and Figures for 2006."

Way Cool Jeans:

- Water Footprint Network, "Product Gallery: Cotton," http://www.waterfootprint.org/?page=files/productgallery&product=cotton (accessed January 11, 2010).

Chapter 5

Student Pages

1 United Nations Population Fund (UNFPA), *State of World Population 2008 – Reaching Common Ground: Culture, Gender, and Human Rights* (New York: UNFPA, 2008). Also available online at https://www.unfpa.org/public/publications/pid/1382 (accessed October 13, 2009).

2 Water Partners International, "Water Facts," http://www.water.org/learn-about-the-water-crisis/facts/ (accessed May 7, 2009).

3 United Nations Foundation, "Bombay Population Projected to Hit 27M by 2015," *U.N. Wire*, July 13, 2000, http://www.unwire.org/unwire/20000713/9773_story.asp (accessed December 31, 2009).

4 Matthew Bloch and Robert Gebeloff, "Immigration Explorer," *The New York Times*, March 10, 2009, http://www.nytimes.com/interactive/2009/03/10/us/20090310-immigration-explorer.html?hp (accessed December 31, 2009).

5 Population Reference Bureau, *2007 World Population Data Sheet* (Washington, DC: Population Reference Bureau, 2007). Also available online at http://www.prb.org/pdf07/07WPDS_Eng.pdf (accessed December 31, 2009).

Endnotes, *continued*

6 United Nations Population Fund (UNFPA), *State of World Population 2003 – Making 1 Billion Count: Investing in Adolescents' Health and Rights* (New York: UNFPA, 2003). Also available online at https://www.unfpa.org/public/publications/pid/2519 (accessed December 31, 2009).

7 United Nations Department of Economic and Social Affairs, *World Population Prospects: The 2004 Revision* (New York: United Nations, 2005). Also available online at http://www.un.org/esa/population/publications/WPP2004/wpp2004.htm (accessed December 31, 2009).

8 Arthur Lubow, "The Road to Curitiba," *The New York Times,* May 20, 2007, http://www.nytimes.com/2007/05/20/magazine/20Curitiba-t.html (accessed December 31, 2009).

9 Jonas Rabinovitch, "Curitiba: Toward Sustainable Urban Development," *Environment and Urbanization,* 4(2) (1992): 62-73.

10 Bill McKibben, "Curitiba: A Global Model for Development," CommonDreams.org, November 8, 2005, http://www.commondreams.org/views05/1108-33.htm (accessed December 31, 2009).

11 Ruth Limmer and Andrew S. Dolkart, "The Tenement as History and Housing," *Thirteen Online,* http://www.thirteen.org/tenement/eagle.html (accessed December 18, 2009).

12 PBS, "Destination America," http://www.pbs.org/destinationamerica/usim_wn_ flash.html (accessed December 18, 2009).

13 Population Reference Bureau, *2007 World Population Data Sheet* (Washington, DC: Population Reference Bureau, 2007). Also available online at http://www.prb.org/pdf07/07WPDS_Eng.pdf (accessed December 31, 2009).

14 Farzaneh Roudi-Fahimi, "Iran's Family Planning Program: Responding to a Nation's Need" (Washington, DC: Population Reference Bureau, 2002). Also available online at http://www.prb.org/pdf/IransFamPlanProg_Eng.pdf.

15 World Education, "Girls' and Women's Education Initiative," http://www.worlded.org/WEIInternet/gwe/index.cfm (accessed May 5, 2009).

16 Central Intelligence Agency (CIA), *The World Factbook,* https://www.cia.gov/library/publications/the-world-factbook/index.html (accessed May 6, 2009).

17 Batonga Foundation, "Batonga in Action," http://www.batongafoundation.org/see/batonga-in-action.html and "Vision," http://www.batongafoundation.org/discover/vision/ (accessed January 11, 2010).

18 Adapted from Jane Braxton Little, "The Lake and the 'hood," *Yes! Magazine,* May 20, 2004, http://www.yesmagazine.org/issues/whose-water/the-lake-and-the-hood (accessed December 31, 2009).

19 Los Angeles Almanac, "General Population by City Estimated Populations, 1990-1994, Los Angeles County," http://www.laalmanac.com/population/po24b.htm (accessed November 24, 2009).

Teacher Instructions
Chapter 5 Student Assessment

NOVA, "Human Numbers through Time," http://www.pbs.org/wgbh/nova/worldbalance/numbers.html (accessed January 11, 2010).

Chapter 6

Student Pages

1 John de Graaf, ed. *Take Back Your Time: Fighting Overwork and Time Poverty in America* (San Francisco: Berrett-Koehler Publishers, Inc., 2003), 209.

2 Calculations based on WWF, Zoological Society of London, and Global Footprint Network, *Living Planet Report 2008* (Gland, Switzerland: WWF, 2008).

3 New Economics Foundation, *The Happy Planet Index 2.0* (London: New Economics Foundation, 2009). Available online at http://www.happyplanetindex.org/public-data/files/happy-planet-index-2-0.pdf (accessed January 11, 2010).

4 UNICEF, "Education for All," http://www.unicef.org/girlseducation/index_44870.html (accessed November 30, 2009).

5 Hyon B. Shin with Rosalind Bruno, U.S. Census Bureau, "Language Use and English-Speaking Ability: 2000," *Census 2000 Brief,* October 2003, http://www.census.gov/prod/2003pubs/c2kbr-29.pdf.

6 Estimate based on information available from CIA, *The World Factbook,* https://www.cia.gov/library/publications/the-world-factbook/index.html (accessed January 2, 2010).

7 Earth Island Institute's New Leaders Initiative, "2008 Award Winners: Marisol Becerra," http://broweryouthawards.org/userdata_display.php?modin=50&uid= 3678 (accessed January 2, 2010).

8 Karin Shankar, "Three Voices: Monologues for radio or stage" (adapted with permission), UNICEF, http://www.unicef.org/voy/media/radiodrama-en.pdf (accessed January 2, 2010).

Teacher Instructions
Chapter 6 Student Assessment

Story based on interviews with Devin Hibbard, Kenya, 2000.

Chapter 7

Student Pages

1 Reebok Human Rights Awards, "Anderson Sa," http://www.reebok.com/Static/global/initiatives/rights/pdf/sa.pdf (accessed January 4, 2010).

2 Joseph Carter, "Residents of Rio's Favelas Face Diverse Risks," November 28, 2006, http://www.worldwatch.org/node/4756 (accessed January 3, 2010).

3 Geography of World Urbanization Seminar, Macalester College, "Rio de Janeiro, Many Cities in One," Macalester College, http://www.macalester.edu/courses/geog61/chad/titlepag.htm (accessed January 4, 2010).

4 Reebok Human Rights Awards, "Anderson Sa," http://www.reebok.com/Static/global/initiatives/rights/pdf/sa.pdf (accessed January 4, 2010).

5 Reebok Human Rights Awards, "Anderson Sa," http://www.reebok.com/Static/global/initiatives/rights/pdf/sa.pdf (accessed January 4, 2010).

6 Florida Center for Instructional Technology, "The Rise of the Nazi Party," *A Teacher's Guide to the Holocaust,* http://fcit.usf.edu/HOLOCAUST/TIMELINE/nazirise.HTM (accessed December 1, 2009).

7 United States Holocaust Memorial Museum, "The Holocaust," *Holocaust Encyclopedia,* http://www.ushmm.org/wlc/article.php?lang=en&ModuleId=10005143 (accessed January 7, 2010).

8 Anne Frank Trust UK, "Guide for Anne Frank and Second World War," *Anne Frank Guide,* http://www.annefrankguide.net/en-GB/default.asp?resetculture=1 (accessed January 4, 2010).

9 Anne Frank, *Anne Frank: The Diary of a Young Girl* (Geneva: Bantam, 1993).

10 Roger Rosenblatt, "Anne Frank," *Time 100: The Most Important People of the Century,* June 14, 1999, *Time,* http://www.yachtingnet.com/time/time100/heroes/profile/frank01.html (accessed January 4, 2010).

11 Louis Goreux, "Conflict Diamonds" (working paper series no.13, Africa Region, World Bank, March 2001), http://www.worldbank.org/afr/wps/wp13.pdf (accessed January 4, 2010).

12 World Diamond Council, "Conflict Diamonds," Diamondfacts.org, http://www.diamondfacts.org/conflict/index.html (accessed January 4, 2010).

13 Louis Goreux, "Conflict Diamonds" (working paper series no.13, Africa Region, World Bank, March 2001), http://www.worldbank.org/afr/wps/wp13.pdf (accessed January 4, 2010).

14 Jens Glüsing, Alexander Jung, Uwe Klussmann and Thilo Thielke, "The Curse of Natural Resources," August 30, 2006, http://www.spiegel.de/international/spiegel/0,1518,426730,00.html (accessed January 7, 2010).

Endnotes, *continued*

15 Mark Dummett, "King Leopold's Legacy of DR Congo Violence," February 24, 2004, http://news. bbc.co.uk/2/hi/africa/3516965.stm (accessed January 11, 2010).

16 Amnesty International USA Human Rights Education Program, "Companion Curriculum to Blood Diamond," http://www.amnestyusa.org/education/pdf/bd_curriculumguide.pdf (accessed January 11, 2010).

17 Kimberley Process, "Background," http://www.kimberleyprocess.com/background/index_en.html (accessed December 23, 2009).

18 Thirteen Online, "Timeline: Building Democracy (1866-1953)," African American World, PBS, http://www.pbs.org/wnet/aaworld/timeline/building_01.html (accessed January 4, 2010).

19 Independent Lens, "February One: The Story of the Greensboro Four," PBS, http://www.pbs.org/ independentlens/februaryone/sitin.html (accessed January 4, 2010).

20 Elexis Silverman, "Marking a Civil Rights Milestone," *Time for Kids*, July 2, 2004, http://www. timeforkids.com/TFK/kids/news/story/0,28277,660464,00.html (accessed January 4, 2010).

Teacher Instructions

1 Mark A.L. Brown and A.S. Palinscar, "Reciprocal Teaching of Comprehension Strategies: A Natural History of One Program for Enhancing Learning," (technical report no. 334, Center for the Study of Reading, University of Illinois at Urbana-Champaign, 1985).

Chapter 8

Student Pages

1 Green Schools Initiative, "Prospect Sierra School," http://greenschools.live.radicaldesigns.org/ display.php?modin=52&uid=40 (accessed July 21, 2009).

2 City of Philadelphia Mural Arts Project, "Community Murals," http://www.muralarts.org/ whatwedo/community (accessed January 6, 2010).

3 Harry Wiland and Dale Bell with Joseph D'Agnese, *Edens Lost & Found: How Ordinary Citizens are Restoring Our Great American Cities* (White River Junction, VT: Chelsea Green Publishing Company, 2006), 75.

4 Ibid., 121-126.

5 Pennsylvania Horticultural Society, "Norris Square," http://www.pennsylvaniahorticulturalsociety. org/phlgreen/pp_norrisquare.html (accessed January 6, 2010).

6 Ricki Ptakowski, "Back on my Feet," *Philadelphia 76ers*, http://www.nba.com/sixers/community/ back_on_my_feet.html (accessed November 20, 2009).

7 CNN.com, "Runner gets homeless on right track," http://www.cnn.com/2008/LIVING/04/02/heroes. mahlum/index.html (accessed November 20, 2009).

8 Back on My Feet, "Program Statistics," http://philadelphia.backonmyfeet.org/Program-Statistics. html (accessed January 11, 2010).

Teacher Instructions

Chapter 8 Student Assessment

Neighborhood House, "Agency History," http://www.nhwa.org/lookinside/agency-history.php, and "Job training helps refugee find his way," http://www.nhwa.org/lookinside/success_story.php?story=Job+ training+helps+refugee+find+his+way (accessed January 6, 2010).

Chapter 9

Student Pages

1 Boston Youth Organizing Project, http://www.byop.org.

2 Daniel Hosang, "Youth and Community Organizing Today" (occasional papers series no. 2, Funders' Collaborative on Youth Organizing, February 2003), http://www.whatkidscando.org/archives/whatslearned/PapersNo2.pdf (accessed January 6, 2010), 8-9.

3 Jarid Manos, personal communication, July 18, 2009, and "Mission," Great Plains Restoration Council, http://gprc.org/mission.html.

4 Kelydra Welcker, personal communication, July 28, 2009.

5 Grameen Bank, "A Short History of Grameen Bank" and "Microcredit," http://www.grameen-info.org.

6 Washington CASH, personal communication, August 26, 2009, and http://www.washingtoncash.org.

Photo and Image Credits

Thank you to the generous and talented photographers and artists who contributed their photos and art.

Front Cover

Fresh vegetables by **Christine Zilka**
Sayulita beach by **Kim Rakow Bernier**
Earthcorps volunteers by **Mark Howard, Earthcorps**
Seattle by **Laura Skelton**
Gung Qui Lai Jia's wife courtesy of **WWF International, Climate Witness**

Chapter 1

p. 2 Students in China by **Sherry Deckman**
p. 3 DRC, Internally displaced peoples/Hundreds of IDPs-roughly 500 families (approximately 2,500 people) all of whom have arrived since the Sept 07 fighting. Shelter on the school grounds, they have to be outside during school hours with some belongings stacked inside classrooms, by **UNHCR/S. Schulman**/February 2008
p. 4 Peace rally by **Lee Ekstrom**
p. 4 Deforestation by **Laura Skelton**
p. 4 Slums in India by **Sherry Deckman**
p. 4 Pollution at harbor by **Mandar Sengupta**
p. 6 (society) Greek people from the peninsula of Eritrea in a bazaar by **John Elians**
p. 6 (environment) Mount Rainier by **Kim Rakow Bernier**
p. 6 (economy) U.S. currency by **Damien Lee Benoit**
p. 6 (sustainability) Venn diagram by **DECODE, Inc.**
p. 13 Photo courtesy of **Young Soldiers**
p. 14 Raul and his family by **Sharla Halvorson**
p. 15 Photo courtesy of **Maria Sebastian**
p. 16 Weaving process in Chinchero by **Jessica McDougall**

Making Global Connections cards

p. 21B Education by **Facing the Future**
p. 21B Conflict by **Lee Ekstrom**
p. 21B Population by **Sherry Deckman**
p. 21B Environment by **Kim Rakow Bernier**
p. 21B Health courtesy of **Suubi Trust,** www.suubitrust.org.uk/
p. 21B Food by **Laura Skelton**
p. 21B Discrimination © **iStockphoto/kickstand**
p. 21B Economy by **Damien Lee Benoit**
p. 21D Sustainability by **DECODE, Inc.**
p. 21D Poverty - DRC, Internally displaced peoples/Hundreds of IDPs-roughly 500 families (approximately 2,500 people) all of whom have arrived since the Sept 07 fighting. Shelter on the school grounds, they have to be outside during school hours with some belongings stacked inside classrooms, by **UNHCR/S. Schulman**/February 2008
p. 21D Society - Greek people from the peninsula of Eritrea in a bazaar by **John Elians**
p. 21D Government by **Jesse Stanley**
p. 21D Migration – DRC/Thousands flee IDP site in Kibati, North Kivu, DRC on Friday, November 7th, 2008. Gunfire was heard near the IDP site causing a panic leaving a steady stream of IDPs heading south toward the provincial capital Goma by **UNHCR/P. Taggart**/November 2008

Photo Credits, *continued*

The views or opinions expressed in this book, and the context in which the images are used, do not necessarily reflect the views or policy of, nor imply approval or endorsement by, the United States Holocaust Memorial Museum.

Photo Credits, *continued*

p. 160 Uganda/Congolese refugees from DRC crossing into Kisoro District in South-West Uganda/**UNHCR/R. Russo**/29 October 2008

p. 161 Diamond ring by **Jack Wallace**

p. 162 Stop Racism mural by **riot68** (riot68.com)

p. 163 Segregated water fountains © **iStockphoto/kickstand**

Chapter 8

p. 173 Volunteer with students by **Neighborhood House**

p. 174 Volunteers by **Jesse Stanley**

p. 174 Bad Taste Cru by **Madli-Liis Parts**

p. 174 Dominoes players by **Sheeba Jacob**

p. 174 Diverse young adults © **iStockphoto/CEFutcher**

p. 176 (culture and identity) All along the clock tower by **David Pham**

p. 176 (community) People at Seattle Center by **Jessica C Levine**

p. 176 (development) Under development © **iStockphoto/SweetCapture**

p. 183 The Green Squad by **Prospect Sierra School**

p. 184 Housing is a Human Right by **David Marques**

p. 185 Man on unicycle by **Jesse Stanley**

p. 186 Graffiti © **iStockphoto/andipantz**

p. 187 Norris Square garden by **Norris Square Neighborhood Project**

p. 188 Anne Mahlum and members of Back on My Feet courtesy of **Back on My Feet**

Chapter 9

p. 196 Sustainability diagram by **DECODE, Inc.**

p. 197 Climate change rally by **Dave Wilton**

p. 197 Habitat for Humanity volunteers courtesy of **Maria Sebastian**

p. 197 Girls in Peru by **Jessica McDougall**

p. 197 River clean up by **Virginia State Parks**

p. 197 Health education courtesy of **Suubi Trust,** www.suubitrust.org.uk/

p. 197 Students with teacher by **Facing the Future**

p. 199 (citizen) Person gathering Washington voters by **Jessica C Levine**

p. 199 (government) Washington State Capitol by **Jesse Stanley**

p. 199 (personal solution) Boy recycling by **Gilda Wheeler**

p. 199 (structural solution) Secretary General Addresses Security Council by **UN/Eskinder Debebe**

p. 200 Timor-Leste Holds Second National Village Elections Under UNMIT Supervision by **UN/Martine Perrett**

p. 205 Muir Woods by **Richard Reynolds**

p. 206 Photo courtesy **Boston Youth Organizing Project**

p. 209 Photo courtesy **Jarid Manos**

p. 210 Photo courtesy **Great Plains Restoration Council**

p. 211 Photo courtesy **Kelydra Welcker**

p. 212 Jill Paull by **Brad Camp, courtesy of Washington CASH**

p. 215 Community members creating benches by **Prospect Sierra School**

Assorted Clip Art Images

Brainworks © iStockphoto/Brainworks
Blankpage © iStockphoto/stdemi
Books © iStockphoto/geopaul
Speech bubbles © iStockphoto/anzlydrm
Book © iStockphoto/geopaul

*All other clip art images are from **Art Explosion, Nova Development Corp., Calabasas, CA.**

Teacher Notes

Teacher Notes

Teacher Notes